BRIEF REVIEW IN

EARTH
SCIENCE

NEW EDITION

BRIEF REVIEW IN
EARTH SCIENCE

NEW EDITION

JEFFREY C. CALLISTER
Newburgh Free Academy
Newburgh, New York

Prentice Hall
Needham, Massachusetts   Englewood Cliffs, New Jersey

Staff Credits:

Editorial Development: Lois B. Arnold
Production and Manufacturing: Roger Powers
Art Direction: L. Christopher Valente

Outside Credits:

Design Coordination: Denise D. Wallace, Michael C. Burggren
Editorial Services: Elizabeth A. Jordan
Illustration: ANCO/Boston, Michael C. Burggren
Cover Design: Richard Hannus

 A Simon & Schuster Company

CONTENTS

ABOUT THIS BOOK

BRIEF REVIEW IN EARTH SCIENCE is a concise text and review aid for the current New York State Syllabus in Earth Science and a means of preparing for the Regents Examination in this subject. The following features will be of special interest to teachers and students.

1. Brief, simple explanations of all concepts and major understandings included in the syllabus.

2. Organization by *Topics* closely following the syllabus.

3. Particular emphasis on essential vocabulary. Each important term is printed in **bold type** where it is defined and discussed in the text. These terms are also presented for review at the end of each Topic and are defined in the *Glossary*.

4. An abundance of illustrations. There are more than 100 drawings in the text alone, each designed to help students visualize and understand the concepts and vocabulary of the subject. They also familiarize students with the types of diagrams they will be required to interpret in Regents Examination questions.

5. Hundreds of practice questions covering all the major understandings of the syllabus. There are over 350 questions reproduced from past Regents Examinations, plus nearly 350 original questions of Regents type.

6. Four complete Regents Examinations. The four most recent examinations are included in their entirety. For convenience in using these exams as an additional source of questions for each Topic, a question number key is provided at the beginning of the Questions section of each Topic.

7. An exceptionally complete index. The index has been carefully planned and compiled to make it easy for the student to locate the portion of the text where any specific term is defined and any specific subject matter is treated.

I believe this book will be highly effective in helping every student achieve mastery of the course content and objectives of the New York State Syllabus in Earth Science.

The author would like to acknowledge the invaluable contributions of Vernon G. Abel, Bertram Coren, and my wife Angie to earlier editions of this book. I would also like to thank Tim Denman, Andrew J. Verdon, Jr., Tom McGuire, and hundreds of students for their suggestions regarding this newest edition.

Jeffrey C. Callister

TOPIC 1 Observation and Measurement

OBSERVATION. An **observation** occurs through the intèraction of one or more of the **senses**—sight, hearing, touch, taste, or smell—with a part of the environment. The ability of the senses to make observations is limited in range and precision. **Instruments** are devices invented by people to extend the senses beyond their normal limits and thus enable them to make observations that would otherwise be impossible or highly inaccurate. For example, a microscope makes it possible to see objects and details that are too small for the unaided eye to detect; a magnet allows one to observe something that the senses do not respond to at all.

INFERENCE. An **inference** is an interpretation of observations. It is a mental process that proposes causes or explanations for what has actually been observed. For example, the observation of an impression in mud, shaped like a dog's foot, leads to the inference that a dog has been present. This inference may or may not be correct. Additional observations, such as a series of similar impressions in the mud, may make the inference more likely to be true.

CLASSIFICATION. Scientists group similar things together in order to make the study of objects and events in the environment more meaningful. This grouping is called **classification,** and it is based on the observed properties of the objects or events.

MEASUREMENT. A **measurement** is a means of expressing an observation with greater precision. It provides a numerical value for some aspect of the object or event being observed. Every measurement includes at least one of the three basic *dimensional quantities*—length, mass, and time.

Length may be defined as the distance between two points.

Mass is the quantity of matter in an object. It is often determined by weighing the object, but mass should not be confused with *weight,* which is the pull (force) of the earth's gravitation on an object. The weight of an object may vary with its location, but its mass remains the same.

Time may be described as our sense of things happening one after another.

Some types of measurements require mathematical combination of basic dimensional quantities. For example, a unit of volume is actually a unit of length cubed, as in 25 cm³ (25 cubic centimeters). Other examples are density (mass per unit volume, as in 4 g/cm³); pressure (force per unit area—15 lb/ft²); speed (distance per unit time—9.8 km/sec).

All measurements of the basic quantities (length, mass, and time) are made by a direct comparison with certain accepted *standard units* of measurement. For example, length is measured by comparing it with a standard unit such as the centimeter, mass with a unit such as the gram, and time with a unit such as the second. A measurement must always state the units used; for example, 27.9 *grams.*

ERROR.   No measurement is perfect, because it is limited by the imperfection of the senses and of instruments. Human error may also result from carelessness or from improper use of an instrument. Any measurement is therefore an approximation of a true, or absolute, value and must be considered to contain some error.

PERCENTAGE ERROR.   Often in science there is an accepted value for a given quantity (for example, the density of water). It is then possible to determine the accuracy, or amount of **error,** of a given measurement by comparing it with the accepted value. When the amount of error is expressed as a percentage, it is called **percentage error** (or **percent deviation.**) The percentage error is obtained by dividing the difference between the measured and accepted values by the accepted value, and multiplying the result by 100%.

$$\text{percentage error} = \frac{\text{difference between measured value and accepted value}}{\text{accepted value}} \times 100\%$$

For example, suppose a student measures the mass of an object as 127.5 grams and the accepted value is 125.0 grams. Then,

$$\text{amount of error} = \text{difference between measured value and accepted value}$$
$$= 127.5 \text{ grams} - 125.0 \text{ grams}$$
$$= 2.5 \text{ grams}$$
$$\text{percentage error} = \frac{\text{amount of error}}{\text{accepted value}} \times 100\%$$
$$= \frac{2.5 \text{ grams}}{125.0 \text{ grams}} \times 100\%$$
$$= 2.0\%$$

DENSITY.   The concentration of matter in an object is known as its **density.** The density of an object is the ratio of its mass (quantity of matter) to its volume; that is, density is the mass in each unit of volume. (**Volume** is the amount of space an object occupies.) To determine the density of an object, its mass is divided by its volume:

$$\text{density} = \frac{\text{mass}}{\text{volume}}$$

The density of a material does not depend on the size or shape of the sample, as long as the temperature and pressure remain the same. For example, a cube of aluminum with a volume of 20 cm³ has a mass of 54 grams. Its density is 54 g/20 cm³ = 2.7 g/cm³. An aluminum ball with a volume of 40 cm³ (twice the volume of the cube) will have a mass of 108 g (twice the mass of the cube), but its density will be the same: 108 g/40 cm³ = 2.7 g/cm³.

FLOTATION.   An object immersed in a liquid is buoyed up by a force equal to the weight of liquid it displaces (Archimedes' Principle). If the density of the object is less than the density of the liquid, the weight of displaced liquid will be greater than the weight of the object. Therefore, the upward force will be enough to support the object, and it will float in the liquid. Flotation of objects in liquids (and in gases) is one method of determining their relative densities. The lower the density of a floating object, the higher it floats in the liquid, that is, the greater the percentage of its volume that is above the surface. As the density of a floating object increases, it sinks relatively deeper into the liquid. If its density is greater than that of the liquid, it will sink to the bottom. If an object and a liquid have exactly the same density (for example, a fish in water), the object can remain stationary anywhere in the liquid.

FACTORS THAT AFFECT DENSITY.   Changes in temperature and pressure affect the density of substances, especially of gases. If the temperature of a gas increases, and its pressure remains the same, its molecules move farther apart (that is, the gas expands). The temperature rise thus results in less mass per unit volume, so that the density of the gas decreases. This explains why hot air rises when surrounded by cooler air.

If the pressure on a gas increases, the molecules come closer together (the gas contracts). The pressure rise thus results in more mass per unit volume, and the density increases.

The expansion and contraction caused by temperature and pressure variations occur also in solids and liquids, but to a much smaller extent. Therefore the density of solids and liquids is less affected by such environmental changes.

PHASES OF MATTER.   Matter on earth exists in three main forms: solid, liquid, and gaseous. Each form is known as a **phase,** or **state,** of matter. The density of a substance changes with changes in its phase. Most substances increase in density as they change from a gas to a liquid, and from a liquid to a solid. They have their highest density as a solid because the atoms are closest together in that phase. Water is an exception, having its highest density in the liquid state at a temperature of 4° C. Therefore, solid water (ice) floats on liquid water, while in most substances the solid sinks in the liquid. Water at 4° C will also lie below layers of water at any other temperature.

VOCABULARY

observation	measurement	density
senses	mass	volume
instrument	error	phase (state)
inference	percentage error or	
classification	percent deviation	

QUESTIONS ON TOPIC I—
OBSERVATION AND MEASUREMENT

Questions in Recent Regents Exams (end of book)

June 1984: 1, 3, 56, 57, 58, 60, 78
June 1985: 1, 2, 4
June 1986: 1, 2, 3, 56–60, 65
June 1987: 1–3, 56–60

Questions from Earlier Regents Exams

1. Which is the best definition for the mass of an object?   (1) the amount of space the object occupies   (2) its ratio of weight to volume   (3) the quantity of matter the object contains   (4) the force of gravity acting on the object

2. Which characteristic of an object will always change as the object travels from the earth to the moon?   (1) mass   (2) volume   (3) density   (4) weight

3. Which graph represents the behavior of water as it is warmed from 0° C to 16° C?

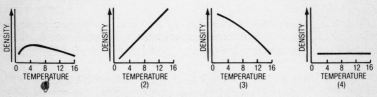

4. Which descriptive term illustrates an inference?   (1) transparent   (2) bitter   (3) younger   (4) smooth

5. Using the centimeter ruler provided in the *Earth Science Reference Tables*, what is the length of line segment *X-Y*?

(1) 5.8 cm   (2) 6.1 cm   (3) 6.4 cm   (4) 7.1 cm

6. The diagram below represents the scale of a triple beam balance. What mass is indicated by this scale?

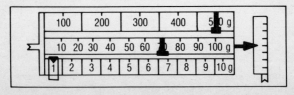

(1) 130 g   (2) 151 g   (3) 517 g   (4) 571 g

7. Substances *A*, *B*, *C*, and *D* are at rest in a container of liquid as shown in the accompanying diagram. Which substance probably has the same density as the liquid?

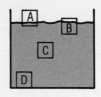

(1) *A*   (2) *B*   ● *C*   (4) *D*

8. A student determines the density of an ice cube to be 0.80 gram per cubic centimeter, when it is actually 0.90 gram per cubic centimeter. What is the percent deviation (percentage of error) in this calculation? [Refer to the *Earth Science Reference Tables*.]   (1) 6%   ● 11%   (3) 13%   (4) 88%

9. Substances *A*, *B*, *C*, and *D* are at rest in a container of liquid as shown by the diagram below. Which choice lists the substances in the order of lowest density to highest density?

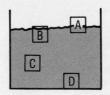

● *A*, *B*, *C*, *D*   (2) *A*, *D*, *C*, *B*   (3) *D*, *C*, *B*, *A*   (4) *C*, *B*, *A*, *D*

Base your answers to questions 10 through 14 on your knowledge of earth science, the *Earth Science Reference Tables*, and the diagrams below. Objects *A* and *B* are solid and made of the same uniform material.

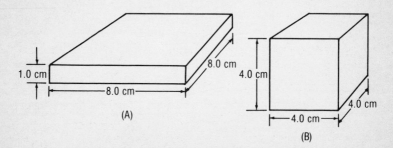

(A)

(B)

10. If object *B* has a mass of 173 grams, what is its density? (1) 0.37 g/cm³   (2) 2.7 g/cm³   (3) 3.7 g/cm³   (4) 5.7 g/cm³

11. Object *A* expands when it is heated. Which graph best represents the relationship between the temperature and the density of object *A?*

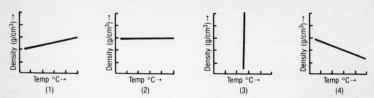

12. A student measures the mass of object *B* to be 156 grams, but the actual mass is 173 grams. The student's percent deviation (percentage of error) is approximately   (1) 1%   (2) 5%   (3) 10%   (4) 20%

13. A third object is made of the same uniform material as object *B*, but has twice the volume as object *B*. How does the density of this third object compare to the density of object *B?*   (1) It is one-half as dense as *B*.   (2) It is the same density as *B*.   (3) It is twice as dense as *B*.   (4) It is four times as dense as *B*.

Note that question 14 has only three choices.

14. How does the mass of object *B* compare to the mass of object *A?*   (1) The mass of *B* is less than the mass of *A*.   (2) The mass of *B* is greater than the mass of *A*.   (3) The mass of *B* is the same as the mass of *A*.

Base your answers to questions 15 through 19 on your knowledge of earth science and on the graph at the right, which shows the masses and volumes of four different earth materials.

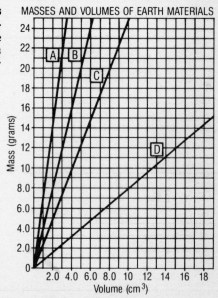

MASSES AND VOLUMES OF EARTH MATERIALS

15. Which material has the greatest density?

(1) *A*

(2) *B*

(3) *C*

(4) *D*

16. If the density of water is 1 g/cm³, which material will float on water?   (1) *A*   (2) *B*   (3) *C*   (4) *D*

17. What is the mass of sample *C* if its volume is 3.0 cubic centi-meters?   (1) 7.5 g   (2) 2.1 g   (3) 3.0 g   (4) 21 g

18. Which material has a density of 4.0 g/cm³?   (1) *A*   (2) *B*   (3) *C*   (4) *D*

19. The two solid blocks below are made of the same material and are under the same temperature and pressure conditions. If the mass of block *X* is 54 grams, what is the mass of block *Y*?

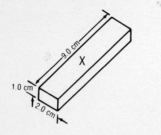
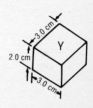

(1) 18 g   (2) 27 g   (3) 54 g   (4) 108 g

Additional Questions

1. Which of the following statements about a rock is *not* an observation?   (1) the rock is dark-colored   (2) the rock formed deep within the earth   (3) the rock has a bitter taste   (4) the rock feels rough

2. Which of the following statements about a rock is *not* an inference?   (1) the rock has large grains   (2) the rock has been weathered by chemical action   (3) the rock formed by the cooling of liquid rock over a long period of time   (4) the rock was once eroded by a glacier

3. The main reason for the use of instruments in scientific work is to   (1) eliminate errors in observation   (2) save time   (3) extend the human senses   (4) eliminate errors in measurement

4. What is the main reason why scientists classify objects and events?   (1) to make better observations   (2) to organize materials for easier study   (3) to make better measurements   (4) to eliminate errors in inferences

5. Which statement is *not* true about measurement?   (1) many measurements are made by comparison with a standard   (2) all measurements contain some error   (3) measurements with the best instruments contain no error   (4) all measurements are just an approximation of the absolute value

6. The maximum density of most materials occurs when the material is a   (1) high-temperature gas   (2) low-temperature gas   (3) liquid   (4) solid

7. As the temperature of a gas increases, the density   (1) increases   (2) decreases   (3) remains the same

8. As the pressure on a gas increases, the density   (1) increases   (2) decreases   (3) remains the same

CHARACTERISTICS OF CHANGE.   Observations reveal that many of the properties of the environment are undergoing **change** at all times. As a result, the description of a portion of the environment is never exactly the same in all details at two different times. The occurrence of a change in the properties of an object or a system is called an **event.** Events may be almost instantaneous, as in the case of a lightning flash, or they may occur over long periods of time, as in the building-up or wearing-down of a mountain.

FRAMES OF REFERENCE.   Change can be described with respect to time and space (location). Time and space are called the **frames of reference** for studying change. As an example, we say that the moon changes because we observe it in different locations and different phases at different times.

RATE OF CHANGE.   A change can be described in terms of the rate at which it occurs. To say that the moon moved so many degrees across the sky for each specific period of time is a more complete description than to just say it has moved. It is difficult to measure the rates of change of some earth processes. For example, the erosion of a mountain is too slow to be easily measured.

CYCLIC CHANGE.   Many changes in the environment occur in some orderly fashion in which the events constantly repeat themselves with reference to space and time. Such orderly changes are called **cyclic change,** and they include the movements of celestial objects (sun, moon, stars, planets), seasonal events, and the water and rock cycles.

PREDICTION OF CHANGE.   If a change is cyclic or if a trend can be inferred, the scope (amount and type) and direction of the change can often be predicted. Astronomers can predict the occurrence of solar and lunar eclipses many hundreds of years in the future because eclipses occur in a cyclic pattern.

ENERGY AND CHANGE.   All change involves a flow of energy from one part of the environment (which loses energy) to another part (which gains it). For example, in the movement of the water in a stream, friction causes the stream to lose energy, while the environment around the stream gains energy (in the form of heat). Energy is usually exchanged across an **interface,** which is the boundary between regions with different properties. In the case of the stream, there is an interface between the water and the air and another between the water and the stream bed.

ENVIRONMENTAL EQUILIBRIUM. Although change occurs continuously throughout the environment, certain general characteristics tend to remain constant. For example, the wooded shore of a lake tends to look the same from one day to the next. Although it may go through a cycle of seasonal changes, it tends to look the same each year at the same season. This is the result of a natural balance among all the changes taking place, called **environmental equilibrium.** This equilibrium is easily upset on a small scale, for example by the burrowing of a worm in the soil, but is normally not upset on a large scale. Human activities, however, often abruptly upset the natural environmental equilibrium. For example, a bulldozer may quickly clear a large area for the construction of a house, thus introducing change on a large scale.

POLLUTION OF THE ENVIRONMENT. **Pollution** of the environment occurs when the concentration of any substance or form of energy reaches a proportion that adversely affects people, their property, or plant or animal life.

CAUSES OF POLLUTION. Many forms of pollution are the result of human technology, which often produces substances and forms of energy in harmful quantities. Some forms of pollution are the results of natural events or processes and would occur without the presence of people. High concentrations of pollen in the air, and ash and gases from volcanic eruptions, are examples of natural pollution.

Pollutants (things that pollute) include solids, liquids, gases, biologic organisms, and forms of energy such as heat, sound, and nuclear radiation. People, through their technology, add pollutants by individual action, community action, and by industrial processes. Many forms of pollution vary with the time of day or season of the year because the causes are cyclic. Air pollution in cities, for example, may increase at the times people are going to and from work because the automobile is one of the greatest contributors to air pollution.

VOCABULARY

change	interface
event	environmental equilibrium
frames of reference	pollution
cyclic change	pollutants

QUESTIONS ON TOPIC II—THE CHANGING ENVIRONMENT

Questions in Recent Regents Exams (end of book)

June 1984:   2
June 1985:   3, 59
June 1986:   5
June 1987:   none

Questions from Earlier Regents Exams

1. People who live close to major airports are most likely to complain about which form of pollution?   (1) sound   (2) heat   (3) radioactivity   (4) particulates

2. Which graph represents the greatest rate of temperature change?

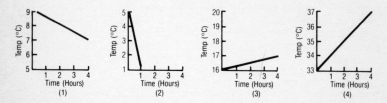

3. Future changes in the environment can best be predicted from data that are   (1) highly variable and collected over short periods of time   (2) highly variable and collected over long periods of time   (3) cyclic and collected over short periods of time   (4) cyclic and collected over long periods of time

4. Why were laws passed that made some insecticides, such as DDT, unavailable to the general public?   (1) Some insecticides were not effective against insects.   (2) Some insecticides' colors were causing a change in the environment's physical appearance.   (3) Some insecticides' concentration in the environment became harmful to other animal life as well as to insects.   (4) Some insecticides' effects were weakened when diluted by the atmosphere and hydrosphere.

Additional Questions

1. Which statement is *not* true about earth changes?   (1) most changes are cyclic   (2) the scope and direction of most changes are not predictable   (3) change is the natural state of the environment   (4) a change in the environment also involves a change in time and space quantities.

2. When a change occurs, energy is exchanged at   (1) a transition zone   (2) a transfer zone   (3) an isozone   (4) an interface

3. Which statement is true about the pollen, carbon monoxide, and sound found in an urban community?   (1) their concentrations change with time   (2) they are not forms of pollution because they can be caused by natural events   (3) they are always considered pollutants because they adversely affect the environment in any concentration   (4) they are produced by the technology of people and are thus considered form of pollution.

4. Most changes in the environment are   (1) cyclic   (2) destructive   (3) sudden   (4) unnatural

5. Which statement best describes the relationship between the interface and energy?   (1) energy is created at the interface   (2) energy is destroyed at the interface   ● energy is exchanged at the interface   (4) there is no exchange of energy at the interface

Refer to the graph shown below to answer questions 6–10.

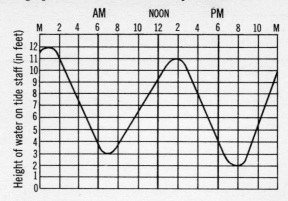

6. Which statement is true about the change in the height of the water? ⬤ it appears to be cyclic ⬤ it is noncyclic because tides are unpredictable   (3) it is noncyclic because the rate of tidal change cannot be measured   (4) it is noncyclic because the maximum height varies

7. The next low tide will occur the next day probably at   (1) 3 A.M.   (2) 7 A.M.   (3) 8 A.M.   (4) 9 A.M.

8. Which statement is true about the tidal changes shown?   (1) they involved no exchange of energy   (2) the scope and direction of the change are predictable   (3) there is no interface in tidal changes   (4) the space quantities in tidal changes cannot be measured

9. The amount of change in the height of the water from one high tide to the next low tide is   (1) 6 feet   (2) 9 feet   (3) 12 feet   (4) 18 feet

10. The approximate time interval between the high tide at 2 P.M. and the next low tide is   (1) 4 hours   (2) 6 hours   (3) 8 hours   (4) 12 hours

11. Which statement is true about the environment of most of the earth?   (1) it is usually greatly unbalanced   (2) it is usually in equilibrium and hard to change   (3) it is usually in equilibrium but easy to change on a small scale   (4) it is normally heavily polluted by natural occurrences

12. Why have humans been such a big factor in the pollution of the environment?   (1) they have had many wars   (2) they are larger in size than most animal forms   (3) their technology creates pollutants   (4) they are the only form of life that can adapt to almost all the environments on the earth's surface

13. An area is considered to be polluted when   (1) a species of life dies because of competition for a specific environment   (2) a part of the environment is adversely affected by the concentration of some substance or some form of energy   (3) there are a large number of people in any specific area   (4) people change the ecology of an area by introducing different plants and animals which replace the life forms that were once present

Measuring the Earth

SIZE AND SHAPE OF THE EARTH

THE EARTH'S SHAPE. The earth's shape is an **oblate spheroid;** that is, it is a sphere with a slight flattening at the polar regions and a slight bulging at the equatorial region. As a result, the equatorial diameter and circumference are larger than the polar diameter and circumference respectively, as Figure 3-1 shows.

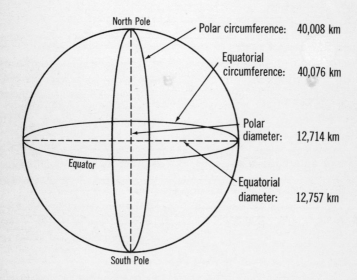

Figure 3-1. Polar and equatorial dimensions of the earth.

However, the differences are very small compared to the actual dimensions; for example, the difference between the two circumferences is only 68 kilometers. This variation from a spherical shape could not be detected in a model of the earth, such as an ordinary globe. Such models are therefore made in the shape of a sphere. (A **model** is any way of representing the properties of an object or system. A model may be an object, such as a globe to represent the earth, or it may be a drawing, diagram, graph, chart, table, or even a mathematical formula or equation. Scientists construct models of these various kinds as aids in studying and understanding the environment.) Besides being very close to a perfect sphere, the earth's surface is very smooth (has very little relief) compared to its diameter.

EVIDENCE FOR THE EARTH'S SHAPE

1. Altitude of Polaris. The **altitude** of an object in the sky is its angle above the horizon. The **latitude** of a point on the earth's surface is its angle north or south of the equator. The star **Polaris** (also called the *North Star*) is almost directly over the North Pole of the earth. From the geometry of a sphere, it can be shown that the altitude of Polaris at any point in the Northern Hemisphere should be the same as the latitude of that point. That is, the altitude of Polaris should change from 0° at the equator to 90° at the North Pole, always being equal to the observer's latitude. (See Figure 3-2).

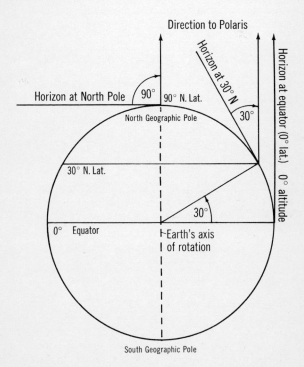

Figure 3-2. Showing that the altitude of Polaris should be the same as the latitude of the observer on a spherical earth. Note that the **geographic poles** are at the ends of the earth's **axis** of rotation.

The altitude of Polaris, however, does not vary exactly in step with latitude. The observed variation is evidence that the earth is not a perfect sphere but is slightly oblate.

2. Photographs from space. Extremely precise photographic observations of the earth taken from satellites and manned spacecraft confirm the oblateness of the earth's shape.

3. Gravity measurements. *Gravity* is the force that attracts all objects toward the center of the earth. The amount of this force on an object is called the object's *weight*. The law of gravitation states that this force in inversely proportional to the square of the distance between the centers of the earth and the object. That is, as the distance from the center of the earth increases, the weight of an object decreases. On a perfectly spherical earth, the weight of a body should be the same at any latitude, since all points on the surface of a sphere are the same distance from the center. However, measurements show that an object weighs more near the poles than near the equator. Part of the reason for this is the centrifugal effect of the earth's rotation. But when this is accounted for, there is still a greater gravity force at the poles than at the equator, indicating an oblate shape for the earth. (See Figure 3-3.)

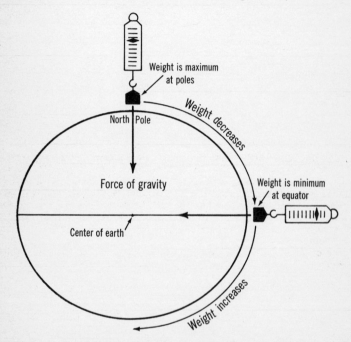

Figure 3-3. Gravity varies with latitude. Because of the flattening of the earth at the poles, the distance from the center of the earth is less at the poles than at the equator. As a result, the force of gravity is greater at the poles than at the equator. (Flattening greatly exaggerated in this drawing.)

MEASURING THE EARTH. In our space age, measurements of the earth's dimensions can be made from space. However, it has long been possible to estimate the earth's circumference quite accurately from earth by using fairly simple methods. One such method, developed by the ancient Greeks, involves measuring the altitude of the sun at two different locations at the same time and using simple geometry (see Figure 3-4). Once the circumference of the earth is estimated, its radius, diameter, surface area, and volume can be calculated (see Figure 3-5).

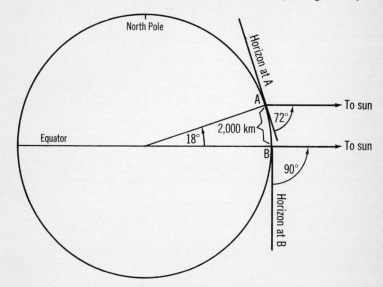

Figure 3-4. Determining the circumference of the earth. At the equinox, an observer at B measures the altitude of the sun at noon to be 90°. Another observer at A, at the same time and date, measures the altitude of the sun to be 72°. The difference between the two altitudes is 18°. Assuming the earth is a sphere, the two observers must be 18°/360° or 1/20 of the earth's circumference apart. If the distance between A and B is known to be about 2,000 km, the circumference of the earth must be about 20 × 2,000 km, or 40,000 km. Another way to determine the earth's circumference is to measure one degree of latitude (approximately 111 kilometers per degree) and multiply by 360°.

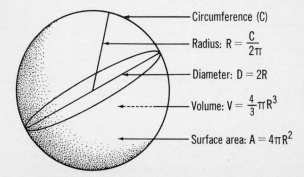

Figure 3-5. Relationships among the dimensions of a sphere.

THE OUTER PARTS OF THE EARTH

THE LITHOSPHERE. The **lithosphere** is a continuous layer of rock that forms the solid outer shell of the earth (see Figure 3-6). The lithosphere is approximately 100 km thick. The upper portion is called the crust.

THE HYDROSPHERE. The **hydrosphere** is the layer of water that rests on the lithosphere. It covers most (about 70%) of the earth's surface. The layer is relatively thin, averaging only 3.8 kilometers in thickness; in fact, even the thin line labeled "hydrosphere" in Figure 3-6 is too thick to show the hydrosphere in correct relation to the lithosphere and atmosphere.

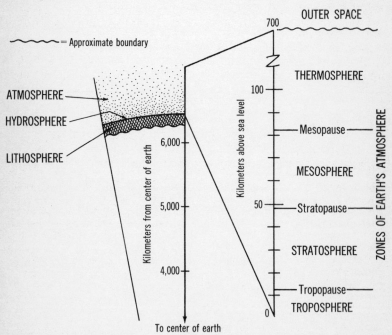

Figure 3-6. A cross section of the earth showing the three outer spheres. The drawing has not been made to scale, but the relative thicknesses of the parts of the earth are close to proportion.

THE ATMOSPHERE The **atmosphere** is the shell of gases that surrounds the earth. It extends out several hundred kilometers into space, but nearly all of its mass is confined to the first few kilometers from the earth's surface. The atmosphere is *layered,* or *stratified,* into zones (see Figure 3-6) with their own distinct characteristics, such as temperature and composition.

LOCATING POSITIONS ON THE EARTH

COORDINATE SYSTEMS. To fix the location of a point on any two-dimensional surface, such as the surface of the earth, two numbers, called *coordinates,* are needed. The system for determining the coordinates of a point is called a **coordinate system.** The *latitude-longitude system* is the one commonly used to locate points on the earth. However, it is not the only possible one that could have been devised.

LATITUDE. **Latitude** is an angular distance north or south of the equator. If a line is drawn from any point on the earth's surface to the center of the earth, the latitude of that point is the number of degrees in the angle between the line and the plane of the equator. All points that have the same latitude lie on a circle that is parallel to the equator. These circles are called **parallels** of latitude. The **equator** may be considered to be the parallel of latitude 0°. Latitude increases north and south of the equator to a maximum of 90° at each pole.

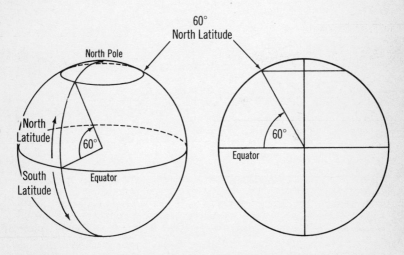

Figure 3-7. The meaning of latitude. Latitude is the angular distance north or south of the equator. On the left, the earth is shown as a sphere with the 60° parallel of North Latitude shown as a circle parallel to the equator. On the right, the earth is shown with the North-South axis vertical; the equator and the parallels of latitude then becomes horizontal lines.

MEASURING LATITUDE. An observer in the Northern Hemisphere can determine latitude by measuring the altitude of Polaris, as shown in Figure 3-2 on page 13. In the Southern Hemisphere, latitude can be determined by measuring the altitude of certain other stars. In both cases, astronomical tables are used to make adjustments for date and time if extreme precision is desired.

LONGITUDE.   Longitude is an angular distance east or west of the Prime Meridian. A **meridian** is any semicircle on the earth's surface connecting the North and South Poles. The meridian that passes through Greenwich, England, has been designated the *Prime Meridian,* or the meridian of zero longitude. The longitude of any point on the Prime Meridian is 0°. The longitude of any other point on the earth's surface is the number of degrees between the meridian that passes through the point and the Prime Meridian. This angle can be measured along the equator or along any parallel of latitude. Since a full circle is 360°, longitude increases east or west of the Prime Meridian from 0° at the Prime Meridian to 180° at the meridian that is the continuation of the Prime Meridian on the other side of the earth.

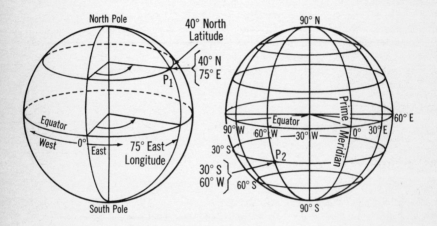

Figure 3-8. The meaning of longitude. Longitude is the angular distance east or west of the Prime Meridian, which is the meridian passing through Greenwich, England. Latitude and longitude together provide a system of coordinates for locating any point on the earth. The coordinates of Point P_1 are 40° N. Lat. and 75° E. Long. Those for Point P_2 are 30° S. Lat. and 60° W. Long.

MEASURING LONGITUDE.   *Local noon* (12:00 A.M.) at any point on the earth occurs when a line from the sun to the center of the earth cuts the meridian of that point. At that moment the sun reaches its highest altitude of the day, so that the instant of local noon can be determined by observing the sun. Since the earth rotates from west to east at the rate of one rotation per day, or 360° in 24 hours, it rotates 15° per hour. Therefore, the occurrence of local noon moves from east to west at the same rate of 15° per hour. Longitude can be calculated if, when local noon occurs, the observer knows what time it is at Greenwich, England. For example, if local noon occurs at 1:00 P.M. Greenwich time (G.M.T.), one hour has passed since the sun crossed the Prime Meridian; the local longitude is therefore 15° west. In general, longitude can be calculated by finding the time difference in hours between local sun time and Greenwich time, and multiplying by 15°. If local time is earlier than Greenwich time, the longitude is west; if later, it is east. Greenwich time can be determined if the observer has a clock that has been set to keep Greenwich time, or by means of radio signals that are broadcast regularly for that purpose.

FIELDS

DEFINITION. A **field** is any region of space or the environment that has some measurable value of a given quantity at every point. Examples of field quantities are gravity, magnetism, elevation or depth, atmospheric pressure, wind, and relative humidity.

VECTOR AND SCALAR FIELDS. Some fields need only an amount, or *magnitude,* to be completely described. These fields are called **scalar fields** and include such things as temperature, atmospheric pressure, and relative humidity. Other fields need a magnitude plus a *direction* to totally describe them. These fields are called **vector fields** and include such things as magnetism, gravity, and wind.

REPRESENTATION OF FIELDS. The varying values of a field are often represented on a map of the region by the use of lines, called **isolines,** which connect points of equal value. Some common examples of isolines are *isotherms* (which connect points of equal temperature), *isobars* (which connect points of equal air pressure), and *contour lines* (which connect points of equal elevation).

ISO-SURFACES. Isolines show field values over a *two-dimensional* field or surface. For example, isotherms on a weather map show temperatures at one level only (usually ground level). To show field values throughout a *three-dimensional* region or volume of space, it is necessary to use *iso-surfaces.* An **iso-surface** is a surface all of whose points have the same field value.

An example of the use of iso-surfaces to represent a field in three dimensions would be a model of the temperature field inside a classroom. Usually, the air in a room is colder near the floor and warmer near the ceiling. The iso-surfaces would then be a series of roughly horizontal planes, each successively higher iso-surface representing a higher temperature value. The iso-surfaces would bend upward near a cold window and bend downward near a heat source (see Figure 3-9). Note that the intersection of a plane with this three-dimensional field model produces a series of isolines (isotherms in this case) which show the temperature field in that plane.

CHANGES IN FIELDS. Since the environment is constantly changing, field characteristics usually change with time. This means that any model of a field, such as a weather map, shows the field for only one particular time.

GRADIENT.   The rate at which a field changes from place to place within the field is called the **gradient** or *slope*. It can be calculated from the following formula:

$$\text{gradient} = \frac{\text{amount of change in the field}}{\text{distance through which the change occurs}}$$

For example, if a contour map shows a change of elevation of 60 m between two points 3 km apart, the gradient between those two points is 20 m per km.

USING CONTOUR MAPS

CONTOUR MAPS.   A **contour map** (topographic map) is a commonly used model of the elevation field of the surface of the earth. The **contour lines** are isolines that connect points of equal elevation above sea level. Other symbols are models of other features on the earth's surface.

DISTANCE ON MAPS.   To find the horizontal distance between two places on a map, you compare the distance on the map with the map scale. For example, the length of the road with the number 84 on the map in Figure 3-10 is approximately 4 miles.

MAP DIRECTION.   Most maps, including contour maps, usually show directions by indicating north with some type of arrow. The map in Figure 3-10 indicates north by ★ which stands for "geographic north." In most maps, the top of the map faces north.

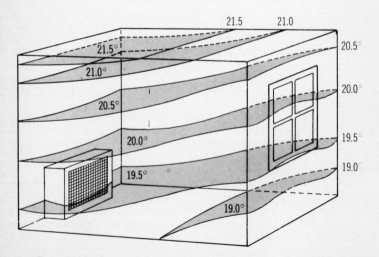

Figure 3-9. Isothermal surfaces in the 3-dimensional temperature field inside a room. All points in any of the iso-surfaces have the same temperature. Where the iso-surfaces meet the ceiling, a 2-dimensional field of isothermal lines is formed. A similar 2-dimensional field can be seen in the right-hand wall.

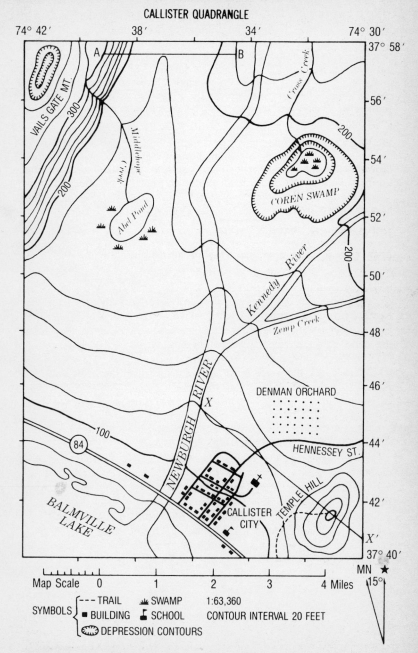

Figure 3-10. A topographic map.

MAP GRADIENT.   For practice, compute the gradient of the Newburgh River in Figure 3-10 from the 180-foot contour line to the 100-foot contour line. Your result should be 20 feet per mile. On any map of a field, the relative amount of gradient can be estimated by the distance between the isolines. The more closely spaced the lines, the greater the gradient. In the map example, the gradient is great, or steep, just to the east of Vails Gate Mountain because the contour lines are close together. In the area around the Denman Orchard, the gradient is small, or gentle, because the contour lines are far apart.

PROFILES.   The three-dimensional nature and the gradient of a field can be shown by drawing a profile. Profiles of contour maps are often drawn to show the shape of the earth's surface. The method of making a profile of a contour map is illustrated in Figure 3-11. The profile is drawn for the region between X and X' in the southeast corner of the map in Figure 3-10.

TOPOGRAPHIC MAP EXERCISE

Answer the following questions based on the map in Figure 3-10.

   1. What is the maximum altitude of Denman Orchard?   (1) 140 feet   (2) 150 feet   (3) 159 feet   (4) 161 feet

   2. What is the longitude of the middle of Coren Swamp?   (1) 37°53′ North   (2) 37°53′ West   (3) 74°32′ North   (4) 74°32′ West

   3. What is the total distance of Hennessey Street on the map from the margin of the map to where it meets Route 84?   (1) 2½ miles (2) 3 miles   (3) 3½ miles   (4) 4 miles

   4. What is the gradient of the Kennedy River from the 200-foot contour line to the contour line before the Kennedy River meets the Newburgh River?   (1) 5 to 10 feet/mile   (2) 15 to 20 feet/mile (3) 25 to 30 feet/mile   (4) 35 to 40 feet/mile

   5. What is the latitude of the school?   (1) 74°34′ North   (2) 74°34′ West   (3) 37°41′ West   (4) 37°41′ North

   6. Which side of Temple Hill has the steepest gradient?   (1) north (2) south   (3) east   (4) west

   7. The most gentle slope is found in the vicinity of   (1) Abel Pond   (2) Denman Orchard   (3) Temple Hill   (4) Zemp Creek

   8. What direction is Vails Gate Mountain from Callister City? (1) north   (2) northwest   (3) northeast   (4) west

   9. In what direction is the Kennedy River flowing?   (1) south (2) southwest   (3) north   (4) northeast

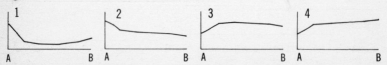

   10. Which of the profiles above represents the shape of the landscape from A to B on the map?   (1) 1   (2) 2   (3) 3   (4) 4

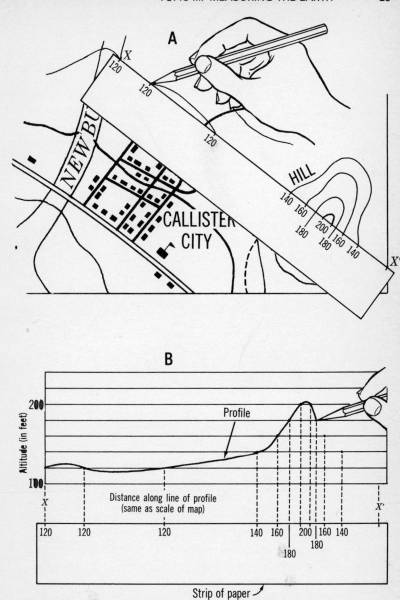

Figure 3-11. Constructing a profile along the line X-X′ on the contour map of Figure 3-10. The edge of a strip of paper is placed along the line, and a mark is made wherever the paper crosses a contour line. The marks are labeled with the corresponding altitude. The marks are then projected upward to locate the points of the profile on a chart as in Drawing B.

VOCABULARY

oblate spheroid	atmosphere	scalar field
model	coordinate system	vector field
altitude	latitude	isoline
Polaris	parallels	iso-surface
geographic poles	equator	gradient
axis	longitude	contour map
lithosphere	meridians	contour line
hydrosphere	field	

QUESTIONS ON TOPIC III—MEASURING THE EARTH

Questions in Recent Regents Exams (end of book)

June 1984: 4, 6, 7, 47, 76, 102, 103
June 1985: 5, 6, 7, 56, 57, 58, 60, 61, 62, 63, 64, 65, 87, 103
June 1986: 4, 6, 7, 8, 66, 69, 70
June 1987: 5–7, 54, 94

Questions from Earlier Regents Exams

1. In the diagram, what is the latitude of the observer?

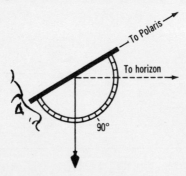

(1) 30°N   (2) 60°N   (3) 90°N   (4) 120°N

2. Which is a vector quantity?   (1) density of water   (2) speed of a seismic wave   (3) a magnetic force   (4) a temperature reading

3. In which sphere would a hurricane occur?   (1) lithosphere (2) hydrosphere   (3) atmosphere

4. In which sphere would an earthquake occur?   (1) lithosphere (2) hydrosphere   (3) atmosphere

5. Which sphere is most dense?   (1) lithosphere   (2) hydrosphere   (3) atmosphere

6. Measurements taken with gravity meters would be most useful in providing information concerning the   (1) magnetic field intensity (2) shape of the earth   (3) tidal range   (4) distance from the sun

7. Which could be calculated from the observations shown in the diagram?

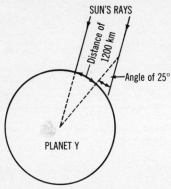

(1) circumference of planet Y   (2) density of planet Y   (3) distance to the sun from planet Y   (4) diameter of the sun

8. As a person travels due west, the altitude of the pole star will (1) decrease   (2) increase   (3) remain the same

Base your answers to questions 9 through 12 on the following contour map of a section of New Mexico and on your knowledge of earth science.

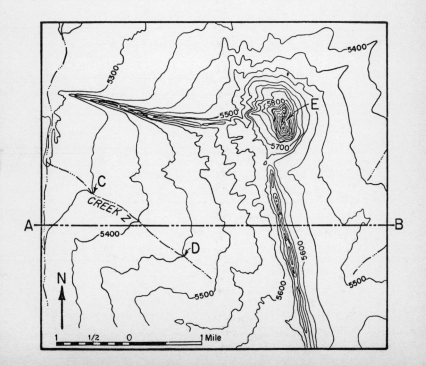

9. Which profile represents the shape of the landscape from A to B?

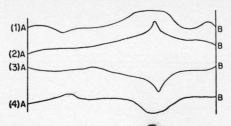

10. Creek Z flows toward the ⬤(1) northwest   (2) northeast
(3) southwest   (4) southeast

11. In which portion of the map is the total area of gentle slopes greatest?   (1) northeast   (2) northwest   (3) southeast   (4) southwest

12. The gradient of Creek Z between points C and D is approximately   (1) 130 ft/mile   (2) 100 ft/mile   (3) 65 ft/mile   (4) 50 ft/mile

To answer questions 13 through 17 refer to the temperature chart at the right and use your knowledge of earth science. The temperature data (°C) were taken at one time in a room and plotted as shown in the chart.

A   B
20•	21 •	22•	24•	26•
19•	20•	22•	25•	28•
18•	19 •	22•	27•	27 •
17•	18 •	24•	25•	24 •
16•	17 •	20•	22•	22•
15•	16 •	17 •	18 •	18•

D   C

13. A heat source would most probably be located nearest   (1) A
(2) B   (3) C   (4) D

14. Which diagram best represents the temperature field in the room?

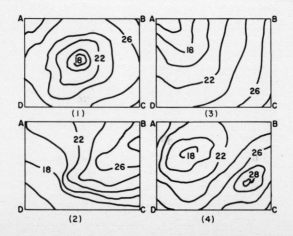

15. In which direction would a person have to walk in order to experience the most rapid temperature increase?   (1) *A* to *D*   (2) *D* to *C*   (3) *C* to *B*   (4) *B* to *A*

16. Which graph best represents the temperature profile if a person walks directly from *A* to *C*?

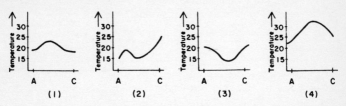

17. For every point in the room the temperature field shows (1) direction, only   (2) magnitude, only   (3) magnitude and direction (4) a combination of magnitude and direction varying with time

Additional Questions

To answer questions 1 and 2, refer to the diagram below which shows a manmade satellite in a polar orbit around the earth. Assume that the satellite contains photographic equipment.

1. Which of the following could not be easily determined from data from the satellite?   (1) the thickness of the lithosphere   (2) the circumference of the earth   (3) the shape of the earth (4) the surface area of the earth

2. If the satellite were in a perfectly circular orbit, which of the following statements would be true of its distance from the surface of the earth? (1) it would be constant   (2) it would be greatest at the poles   (3) it would be greatest at the equator   (4) it would sometimes be greatest at the poles and at other times greatest at the equator

3. Which of the following gives the spheres of the earth in order of increasing thickness?   (1) hydrosphere, lithosphere, atmosphere (2) hydrosphere, atmosphere, lithosphere   (3) lithosphere, hydrosphere, atmosphere   (4) atmosphere, hydrosphere, lithosphere

4. Which of the following cannot be determined about the earth when the only dimension known is the circumference?   (1) mass (2) volume   (3) diameter   (4) surface area

5. What is needed to determine the circumference of the earth? (1) the altitude of the sun at one location   (2) the altitude of Polaris at one location ● the altitude of the sun at two locations   (4) the altitude of the sun at three locations

6. As gradient increases, the distance between isolines   (1) increases ● decreases   (3) remains the same

Refer to the map of "Generalized Bedrock Geology of New York State" in the *Reference Tables* **to answer questions 7 and 8.**

7. Which is the latitude of the largest area of Triassic rocks in New York State?   (1) 41°W   ● 41°N   (3) 74°E   (4) 74°N

8. Which is the longitude of one location of Pennsylvanian and Mississippian rocks in New York State?   (1) 42°N   (2) 42°E   (3) 78°N   ● 78°W

9. Which statement is true about the shape of the earth?   (1) it is a perfect sphere   ● it is larger in circumference along the equator   (3) it is larger in circumference through the poles   (4) it is larger in the Northern Hemisphere because there is more lithosphere

10. Which of the following is the most accurate model of the earth's shape?   ● a basketball   (2) a football   (3) an egg   (4) a pear

11. How is a vector field described?   (1) by magnitude only   (2) by direction only   ● by both magnitude and direction   (4) by magnitude or direction

12. Which is a model?   ● a globe   (2) a ruler   (3) a hand lens   (4) a mineral specimen

The diagrams below illustrate systems that can be used to determine position on a sphere. Refer to them to answer questions 13 and 14.

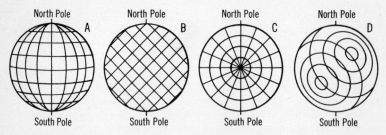

13. Systems of lines like those illustrated above are called   (1) latitude systems   ● coordinate systems   (3) great circle systems   (4) axis systems

14. Which of the systems illustrated is most like the latitude-longitude system used on the earth?   ● A   (2) B   (3) C   (4) D

15. Which statement is *not* true about fields?   ● they do not change with time   (2) they are often illustrated by the use of isolines   (3) any one place in a field has a measurable value at a specific time   (4) gradients indicate the degree of change from place to place in a field

16. Which makes up most of the earth's surface?   (1) the atmosphere   (2) the lithosphere   ● the hydrosphere

TOPIC IV   The Earth's Motions

APPARENT MOTIONS OF CELESTIAL OBJECTS

CELESTIAL OBJECTS. A **celestial object** is any object outside the earth's atmosphere. The stars, the sun, the planets, and the moon are examples of celestial objects.

DAILY MOTION. All celestial objects appear to move across the sky from east to west. The paths of these apparent motions are circular, and the motion occurs at a constant rate of approximately 15° per hour. This is called **daily motion.** The daily motion of stars as viewed from the mid-latitudes of the Northern Hemisphere is illustrated in Figure 4-1.

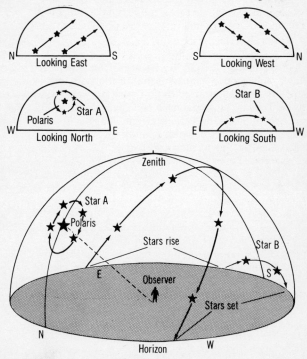

Figure 4-1. The apparent daily motion of the stars. To an observer in the mid-latitudes of the Northern Hemisphere, all stars appear to move from east to west in circular paths, or along parts of circles called **arcs,** at an angular rate of 360° in 24 hours (15° per hour). The center of these circular paths and arcs is very near the star Polaris. The complete circular path can be seen for stars in the northern part of the sky around Polaris. Other stars rise over the eastern horizon and set at the western horizon.

MODELS TO ACCOUNT FOR CELESTIAL OBSERVATIONS. The most obvious way to explain the daily motion of celestial objects is to assume that the earth is stationary and that the celestial objects are revolving around it at a rate of 15° per hour. This is called the *geocentric* ("earth-centered") model. It is the model that was employed by the ancient Greek scientists and that was accepted up to the 16th century. However, the geocentric model fails to explain certain observed **terrestrial motions** (motions related to the earth). In modern times it has been replaced by the *heliocentric* ("sun-centered") model. In this model the earth is rotating on its axis at the rate of 15° per hour and is revolving around the sun once per year. (**Rotation** of a body is the turning of the body on its own axis, in the manner of a spinning toy top. **Revolution,** or revolving, of a body is its movement around another body in a path called an **orbit.**) The heliocentric model accounts for all observed motions of celestial objects and terrestrial objects in a simpler way than the geocentric model. (Additional discussion of these two models will be found on pages 42–44.)

MOTIONS OF THE PLANETS. As seen from the earth, the planets also exhibit daily motion similar to that of the stars, but over extended periods of time they appear to change position with respect to the *star field* around them. This apparent movement relative to the stars is not uniform. According to the heliocentric model, the apparent motion of the planets is the result of the revolution of the earth and the planets around the sun at different rates (see Figure 4-2 on page 31).

The **apparent diameter** of an object is the diameter or size the object appears to have to an observer, not the actual diameter. The apparent diameter of each planet changes in a regular, or cyclic, manner. This occurs because the distance of the planets from the earth varies as the planets and earth revolve around the sun. The closer a planet is to the earth, the larger its apparent diameter, just as a distant object on earth seems to become larger as we approach it.

When observed over a period of time, identifiable features of several of the planets appear in different locations on the face of the planet. These changes in location occur in a uniform direction in a cyclic manner and therefore indicate that these planets rotate. Additional evidence indicates that all the planets rotate.

MOTIONS OF THE MOON. As viewed from the earth, the moon shares the daily motion of all celestial objects. In addition, it appears to move relative to the stars in an orbit around the earth at the rate of one revolution per 27⅓ days. The apparent diameter of the moon varies in a cyclic manner at the same rate. These observations are explained by the revolution of the earth and the moon in elliptical orbits around the center of mass of the earth-moon system, while the system as a whole revolves around the sun.* The results of this compound motion are illustrated in Figure 4-3 on page 32.

---

*Elliptical orbits are discussed on page 37.

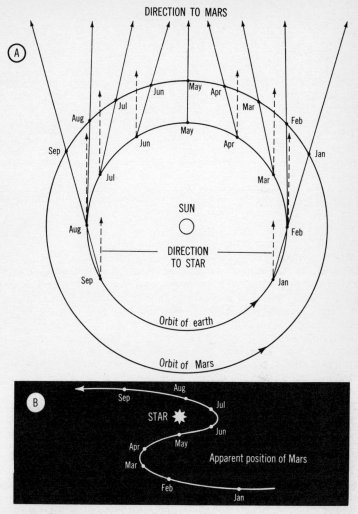

Figure 4-2. Apparent motion of a planet. Diagram A shows successive positions of the earth and Mars along their orbits at monthly intervals during part of a particular year. The dashed arrows show the sight lines from the earth to some fixed star. These sight lines are practically parallel because of the great distance of the star. The solid arrows are the sight lines toward Mars. As the diagram shows, the sight line in January was to the right of the star. From January to March, Mars appeared to move to the left. From March to June it appeared to move to the right. From June to September, it appeared to move to the left again. As a result, the apparent position of Mars changed with respect to the star as shown in Diagram B. Because the orbits of the earth and Mars are tilted with respect to each other, the altitude of Mars with respect to the fixed star also changed. In the following year, a similar motion would be observed, but in a different region of the heavens.

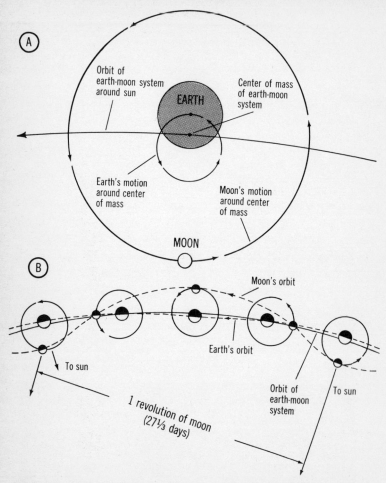

Figure 4-3. Motions of the earth-moon system as viewed from above the North Pole. Diagram A shows that the centers of the earth and the moon revolve around their common center of mass. This center of mass is so near the earth's center that it is actually inside the earth, about 1700 kilometers below the surface. Diagram B shows the motion of the earth-moon system as it revolves around the sun. The oscillations of the orbits are greatly exaggerated. If drawn to scale, the radius of the moon's orbit in Diagram B would be about 1/50 inch.

MOON PHASES. Half of the moon is always receiving light from the sun at any given time. However, the varying positions of the moon with respect to the earth cause an observer on earth to see varying amounts of that lighted half of the moon. Those varying amounts of the lighted moon are known as its **phases** (see Figure 4-4).

Because the revolution of the moon around the earth-moon focus is cyclic, the phases of the moon are also cyclic. However, because of the revolution of the earth-moon system around the sun, the cycle of phases is somewhat longer than the time of one revolution of the moon. The period from one full moon to the next is 29½ days, whereas the period of revolution is 27⅓ days. (See Figure 4-5.)

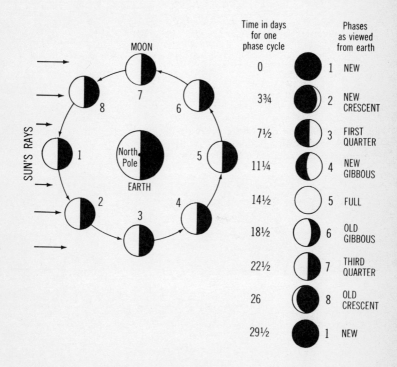

Figure 4-4. The phases of the moon. The half of the moon facing the sun at any given time is illuminated. The other half is dark. An observer on the earth sees varying portions of the illuminated half, depending on the position of the moon in its orbit. The appearance of the phases for eight positions in the cycle is illustrated.

MOTIONS OF THE SUN. Like all other visible celestial objects, the sun also goes through daily motion in the sky. The sun's apparent path, extending from sunrise to sunset, has the shape of an **arc** (part of a circle). As shown in Figure 4-6, that path changes position and length with the seasons. The greater the length of the path, the longer the daylight period. Figure 4-6 also shows how the position of the sun at sunrise and sunset varies predictably with the seasons.

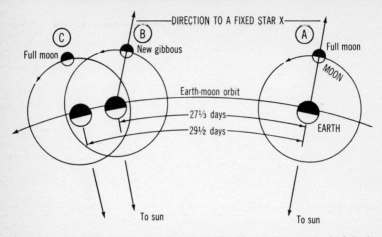

Figure 4-5. Period of one phase cycle. At Position A, the moon is full. At Position B, the moon has made one complete revolution about the earth. However, it is not full until it reaches Position C (about 2 days later).

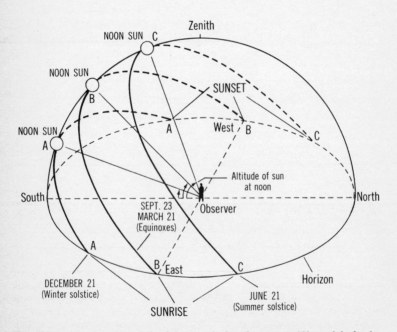

Figure 4-6. The changing path of the sun during the year at 42° north latitude. Note that the path of the sun is longest on June 21st and shortest on December 21st.

ALTITUDE OF THE NOON SUN.   The sun always reaches its highest position in the sky at local noon (see page 18). However, the altitude of the sun at noon depends on the time of year and the latitude of the observer. Only between latitudes 23½° N and 23½° S can the noon sun ever be directly overhead. Thus the noon sun is never directly overhead anywhere in the continental United States. Figure 4-7 shows how the latitude at which the noon sun is overhead changes in the course of a year.

If you know the latitude at which the noon sun is directly overhead on a particular date, you can calculate the altitude of the noon sun for any other location on that date. First find the number of degrees between the latitude of the observer and the latitude at which the noon sun is overhead. Then subtract that number of degrees from 90°. For example, to find the altitude of the noon sun at 40° N on December 21, first note that on December 21 the noon sun is directly overhead at 23½° S. The number of degrees between 23½° S and 40° N is 63½° (23½° S to 0°, plus 0° to 40° N). Now subtract 63½° from 90°. The result is 26½°. This is the altitude of the noon sun at 40° N on December 21.

Figure 4-7. The changes in latitude where the sun is directly overhead (at the zenith point) at noon in the course of one year. Point 1—June 21   Point 3—Dec. 21   Point 2—Sept. 23   Point 4—March 21

ROTATION OF THE EARTH

The main motions of the earth are its rotation and its revolution. The earth's rotation is the spinning of the earth on its axis, the imaginary line from the North Pole to the South Pole through the planet. The earth rotates from *west to east* 360 degrees in 24 hours, or 15 degrees an hour. The rotational speed of a point on the earth's surface depends on its latitude. As shown in Figure 4-8, the circumference of the circle of rotation increases as you go from the poles toward the equator. Therefore, the speed of rotation also increases in the same way.

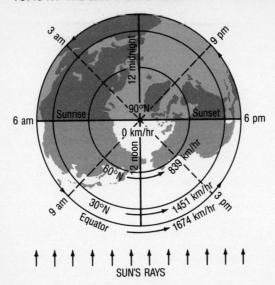

Figure 4-8. Circles of rotation showing linear rotation rates at different latitudes. Angular rotation rate is 15 degrees per hour at any latitude. Solar time changes 1 hour for each 15 degrees of longitude. When it is noon on the side of the earth facing the sun, it is midnight on the opposite side.

EVIDENCE OF ROTATION

1. The Foucault pendulum. When the Foucault pendulum is allowed to swing freely, its path will appear to change in a predictable way, as shown in Figure 4-9. This is evidence for the earth's rotation, because if the earth did not rotate, the pendulum would continue to swing in the original path (A-A'). What is really happening is that the earth is rotating under the pendulum, so that the pendulum's path appears to change.

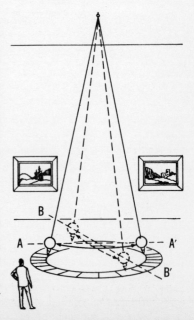

Figure 4-9. Apparent motion of Foucault pendulum. An observer sees a pendulum swing in the direction A-A'. Several hours later, the pendulum has changed its direction of swing to the line B-B'. Actually, the pendulum swings in a fixed direction in space, while the earth, carrying the observer with it, rotates under the pendulum.

2. The Coriolis effect. The **Coriolis effect (Coriolis force)** is the tendency of all particles of matter moving at the earth's surface to be deflected from a straight-line path. The deflection is to the right in the Northern Hemisphere and to the left in the Southern Hemisphere. The deflection occurs because the earth is rotating, and therefore the earth's surface is moving with respect to the path of the particles. The following example can help to explain the effect: You are at the center of a merry-go-round that is rotating counterclockwise. Your friend is near the rim of the merry-go-round. You throw a ball directly at your friend. By the time the ball reaches the rim of the merry-go-round, your friend has been carried to the left. The ball reaches the rim at a point that is now to the right of your friend. With respect to the moving merry-go-round, the ball has been deflected to the right. In a similar manner, ocean currents and winds are deflected with respect to the earth's surface.

REVOLUTION OF THE EARTH

A planet's revolution is its motion around the sun in a path called an **orbit.** The shape of the earth's orbit (and those of the other planets) is a closed curve called an **ellipse.** Within the ellipse are two fixed points called **foci** (singular, **focus**). The sum of the distances between any point on the ellipse and the two foci is a constant; that is, the sum of those distances for one point is equal to the sum for any other point on the curve. The sun is at one of the foci of each planetary orbit in the solar system (see Figure 4-10).

The flattening of an ellipse is measured by its **eccentricity.**

$$\text{eccentricity of an ellipse} = \frac{\text{distance between foci}}{\text{length of major axis}} = \frac{d}{L}$$

If you measure d and L in the ellipse of Figure 4-10 and apply the formula, you should find the eccentricity to be 0.25. As the foci of an ellipse are brought closer together, the ellipse becomes more like a circle and the eccentricity decreases toward zero.

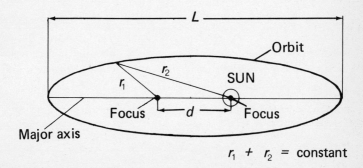

Figure 4-10. An elliptical orbit of a planet with the sun at one focus. Flattening of ellipse and separation of foci are greatly exaggerated.

VARYING DISTANCE OF PLANETS FROM THE SUN. The elliptical shape of planetary orbits causes the planets to vary in distance from the sun during a revolution. For example, the earth is 147,000,000 kilometers from the sun when closest (**perihelion,** January 3) and 152,000,000 kilometers from the sun when farthest away (**aphelion,** July 4). The difference between these two distances is the same as the distance between the two foci (5,000,000 km). Since this distance is relatively small compared to the major axis (299,000,000 km), the eccentricity of the orbit is small (0.017) and the orbit is very nearly a circle.

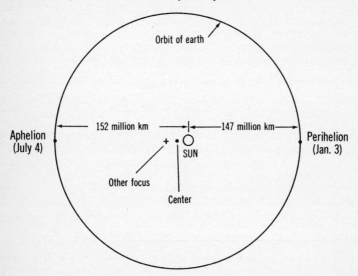

Figure 4-11. The earth's orbit. If drawn exactly to scale, the two foci would be about 1 mm apart.

The changing distance of the earth from the sun causes the sun's apparent diameter to change in a cyclic fashion during the year. The sun's apparent diameter is greatest on January 3 when the sun is closest to the earth and smallest on July 4 when it is farthest.

GRAVITATION. The earth and the other planets orbit the sun under the influence of **gravitation,** which is the attractive force that exists between any two objects in the universe. The gravitational force is proportional to the product of the masses of the objects and inversely proportional to the square of the distance between their centers. This can be expressed as

$$F \propto \frac{m_1 m_2}{d^2}$$

where m_1 and m_2 are the two masses, d is the distance between the *centers* of the two objects, and F is the gravitational force.

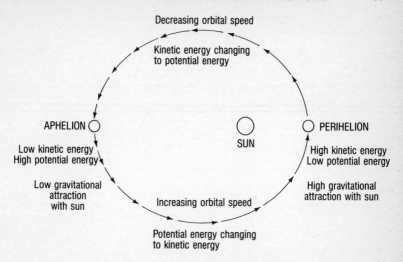

Figure 4-12. Cyclic energy transformation and changing orbital speed of a planet. Elliptical shape of orbit greatly exaggerated.

ORBITAL SPEED.   The force of gravitation between the sun and a planet is always pulling the planet toward the sun. The planet does not fall into the sun because of the centrifugal effect of its orbital motion. However, when the planet is in a part of its orbit that is bringing it closer to the sun, the force of gravitation is aiding the motion, causing the planet to speed up. The planet at such times is actually "falling" toward the sun, and some of its **potential energy** (stored energy or energy of position) is converted to **kinetic energy** (energy of motion). As the planet enters the part of its orbit that takes it away from the sun, the force of gravitation tends to oppose this motion. The planet's speed therefore decreases as it "climbs" to a higher distance from the sun. At such times its kinetic energy is being converted back to potential energy. Thus we see that there is a cyclic energy transformation between potential energy and kinetic energy as a planet revolves around the sun (see Figure 4-12). In the case of the earth, it is closest to the sun (perihelion) and has its greatest orbital speed around January 3. It is farthest from the sun (aphelion) and has its least orbital speed around July 4.

Changes in the orbital velocity of a planet always take place according to a definite principle: *An imaginary line connecting the sun and the planet always sweeps through equal areas during equal intervals of time.* This principle is illustrated in Figure 4-13. Since equal areas must be covered in equal intervals of time, the planet's orbital speed must be fastest at perihelion and slowest at aphelion.

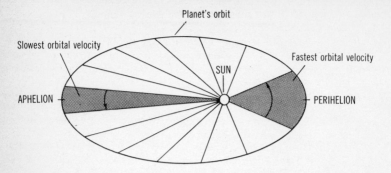

Figure 4-13. A line from the sun to a planet will sweep out each of these equal areas in the same time.

PLANET PERIOD. The **period** of a planet is the amount of time it takes the planet to make one orbit, or revolution, around the sun. This equals one **year** for that planet. The period of a planet is related to the planet's distance from the sun. The closer a planet is to the sun, the smaller its orbit, and the shorter its period. More precisely, for any planet the square of its period is proportional to the cube of its mean distance from the sun. The relationship is expressed symbolically as $T^2 \propto R^3$, where T is the period of the planet and R is the mean distance from the sun. When T is expressed in earth years and R in Astronomical Units, then $T^2 = R^3$. One Astronomical Unit is the mean distance of the earth from the sun or about 150 million kilometers.

The relationship of period to distance can be easily verified with the required data. Take Mars, for example. The period of Mars is 1.88 earth years and its distance from the sun is 1.52 times the average earth distance, or 1.52 Astronomical Units.

$$T = 1.88 \qquad\qquad R = 1.52$$
$$T^2 = 1.88 \times 1.88 \qquad R^3 = 1.52 \times 1.52 \times 1.52$$
$$= 3.53 \qquad\qquad\quad = 3.51$$

Although the results are not equal, they are close enough to verify the relationship.

TIME AND EARTH MOTIONS

THE YEAR. The length of the **year** is equal to the time it takes the earth to make one revolution around the sun.

THE APPARENT SOLAR DAY. As explained on page 35, the sun reaches its highest point in the sky once each day at noon. The time it takes for the earth to rotate from noon to noon on two successive days at any fixed location on the earth is called the **apparent solar day.** Time based on the actual motions of the sun in the sky is called **apparent solar time,** or **sundial** time, because a sundial is used to measure it. As shown by Figure 4-14, the apparent solar day is always longer than one rotation of the earth. If the earth did not move along its orbit, it would take exactly one rotation to bring a point on the earth into the same position with respect to the sun. However, because the earth does move along its orbit, it has to turn a small additional amount to bring the point into the same position relative to the sun.

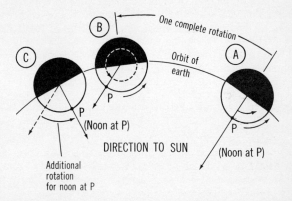

Figure 4-14. Length of apparent solar day. At Position A, it is noon at Point P on the earth. After one complete rotation, the earth is at Position B, but it is not yet noon at Point P. The earth must rotate an additional amount to bring Point P in line with the sun again, when it is again noon at P. The earth will have moved to Position C in this time. (The drawing is exaggerated to make the principle clear.)

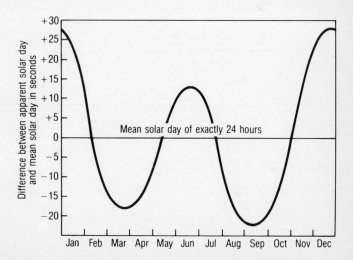

Figure 4-15. Variations in the length of the apparent solar day. This curve shows the difference between the apparent solar day and the mean solar day during the course of one year.

MEAN SOLAR DAY.   If the earth moved around the sun in a circular orbit at constant speed, the apparent solar day would have a constant length. However, the earth's speed around the sun varies in a cyclic manner in the course of the year. As a result, the length of the apparent solar day also varies during the year. The inclination of the earth's axis, and the varying curvature of its orbit, also have an effect on the apparent solar day. The combination of these effects produces the cyclic variation in the apparent solar day shown in Figure 4-15. For convenience in timekeeping, a solar day of average length, called the **mean solar day,** has been established. This mean solar day has been divided into exactly 24 hours. On most days of the year, the apparent solar day is either slightly more or slightly less than 24 hours in length (as already noted in Figure 4-15).

MODELS FOR EXPLAINING CELESTIAL MOTIONS

GEOCENTRIC MODEL.   An early concept of celestial objects and their motions is the **geocentric model** ("earth-centered"). In this model, the earth is stationary and all celestial objects revolve around it, as shown in Figure 4-16.

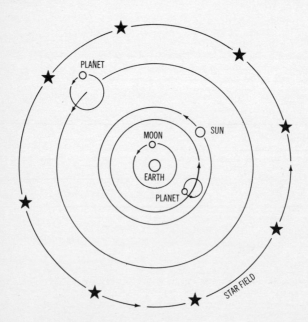

Figure 4-16. Geocentric model of celestial objects. The earth is stationary. The moon, sun, and fixed stars revolve about the earth in circular orbits at different speeds. The planets revolve in small circles, while the centers of these circles move about the earth in circular orbits. These additional circles for the planets are needed to explain their irregular motions.

Some of the major points about the geocentric model are:

1. It explains the apparent motions of celestial objects. The daily motion of the sun and stars is explained by their revolution around the earth. The irregular motion of the planets is explained by assuming that they move in small circular paths in addition to their revolution around the earth.

2. This model does not explain certain terrestrial motions, such as rotation of the Foucault pendulum and the Coriolis effect.

3. The need for auxiliary circles for the planetary motions makes the model complex.

HELIOCENTRIC MODEL. The modern concept of the motions of celestial objects is the **heliocentric model** ("sun-centered"). In this model, the earth and the planets revolve around the sun; in addition, the earth rotates on its axis. (See Figure 4-17.)

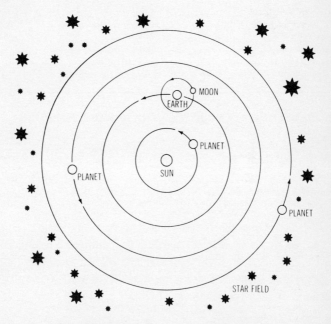

Figure 4-17. Heliocentric model. The sun is stationary. The earth and the planets revolve about the sun at different speeds in elliptical orbits. The stars are stationary and are located at great distances from the solar system.

The major points about the heliocentric model are:

1. It explains the apparent motions of celestial objects. The daily motion is the result of the earth's rotation. The irregular motion of the planets is the result of the revolution of the earth and the planets around the sun at different rates.

2. This model accounts for observed terrestrial motions, such as rotation of the Foucault pendulum and the Coriolis effect.

3. It is less complex than the geocentric model because each planet requires only one orbit.

VOCABULARY

celestial object	perihelion
daily motion	aphelion
arc	gravitation
terrestrial motions	orbital speed (or velocity)
rotation	potential energy
revolution (revolving)	kinetic energy
orbit	period (of revolution)
apparent diameter	year
phases (of the moon)	apparent solar day
Foucault pendulum	apparent solar time
Coriolis effect	sundial
ellipse (elliptical)	mean solar day
focus (of an ellipse)	geocentric model
eccentricity	heliocentric model

QUESTIONS ON TOPIC IV—THE EARTH'S MOTIONS

Questions in Recent Regents Exams (end of book)

June 1984: 8, 9, 10, 11, 61, 62, 63, 64, 65, 66, 70
June 1985: 8, 9, 10, 11, 12, 21
June 1986: 5, 9–12, 64, 71–75
June 1987: 8–11, 61–65, 101, 103

Questions from Earlier Regents Exams

Base your answers to questions 1 and 2 on the information below:

A student in New York State obtained the data below by noting the altitude of the sun at noon for 3 consecutive months.

Month	Altitude of sun at noon
X	27.0°
Y	23.5°
Z	25.5°

1. The data for month Y were obtained during   (1) March (2) June   (3) September   ● December

2. From month X to month Z, the length of a noontime shadow would (1) increase, only (2) decrease, only ● increase, then decrease (4) decrease, then increase

3. The Foucault pendulum provides evidence of the earth's ● rotation (2) revolution (3) precession (4) inclination

4. Planetary winds do not blow directly north or south because of ● the Coriolis effect (2) gravitational force (3) magnetic force (4) centripetal force

5. The star Sirius is observed in the evening sky during the month of January. At the end of three hours, Sirius will appear to have moved (1) 60° ● 45° (3) 3° (4) 0°

6. To a person located at 43° north latitude, the sun appears to rise due east on (1) December 22 (2) March 1 ● March 21 (4) June 22

7. As the distance between two objects in the universe increases, the attraction between these two objects ● decreases (2) increases (3) remains the same

Base your answers to questions 8 through 10 on the diagram below, which represents a portion of the earth with specific sections lettered A through F, and on your knowledge of earth science. Write the number preceding the term that best completes each statement or answers each question.

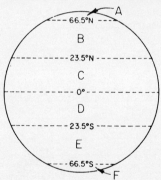

8. During October, the vertical ray of the sun will always be in section (1) E (2) B (3) C (4) D

9. At noontime on June 21, the sun will make an angle of 23.5° with an observer's zenith if the observer is located at ● 0° (2) 23.5°N (3) 23.5°S (4) 66.5°N

10. In which direction will a projectile be deflected if it is fired due south from a point at 23.5° north latitude to 10° north latitude? (1) north (2) south (3) east (4) west

11. When the orbital velocity of the earth is greatest, what is the season in the Northern Hemisphere? (1) spring (2) summer (3) fall (4) winter

For questions 12 and 13, write the number of the graph, chosen from those shown below, which best illustrates the relationship between the two variables mentioned in that question. The first variable mentioned is on the Y-axis and the second is on the X-axis. (A number may be used more than once.)

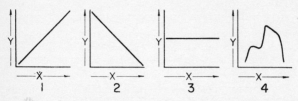

12. Number of hours of daylight vs. latitude south of the Equator on June 21

13. The time it takes a planet to make one revolution around the sun vs. the distance of the planet from the sun

Base your answers to questions 14-18 on the adjoining diagram and your knowledge of earth science.

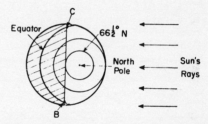

14. On this day, in which direction would an observer at the North Pole look to see the sun?   (1) north   (2) east   (3) south   (4) west

15. The time at point C is closest to   (1) 12 noon   (2) 9 A.M. (3) 6 A.M.   (4) 6 P.M.

16. The length of the daylight period for a point at 66½°N would be   (1) 24 hours   (2) 18 hours   (3) 12 hours   (4) 0 hours

17. Which month is represented by the diagram?   ● June (2) December   (3) March   (4) September

18. At point B, the approximate number of daylight hours is (1) 24   (2) 18   ● 12   (4) 0

On the adjoining diagram of the earth, there are five locations numbered from 1 to 5. For each of the statements 19 to 22, choose the number of the location that best fits the statement.

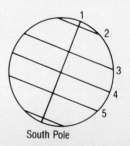

19. This location is farthest from the center of the earth. 4

20. The North Star can never be seen from this location.

21. Gravitational attraction should be greatest at this location. $|$

22. At this location the altitude of the North Star is 23.5°.

23. As one moves from the poles toward the equator, the linear velocity in km/hr of the earth's surface caused by the earth's rotation (1) decreases ● increases (3) remains the same

24. If the earth rotated from north to south, the North Star would appear to (1) set in the south ● set in the north (3) move in a circle in the sky (4) remain stationary

Base your answers to questions 25 through 29 on the *Earth Science Reference Tables*, your knowledge of earth science, and the diagram below. The diagram represents the Earth, Moon, and Sun on a particular day as viewed from a point in space. Positions *A* through *D* are located along the Earth's Equator and *E* is at the North Pole. Positions *F* and *G* are located on the surface of the Moon.

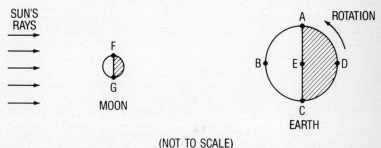

(NOT TO SCALE)

25. At the time of year represented by the diagram, rays of the Sun would strike perpendicular to the Earth's surface at (1) the North Pole (2) the Equator (3) 23½° North of the Equator (4) 23½° South of the Equator

26. Sunrise on Earth would be occurring at the position marked ● *A* (2) *B* (3) *C* (4) *D*

27. To an observer at position *B*, what percentage of the Moon appears to be lighted by the Sun's rays? ● 0% (2) 25% (3) 50% (4) 100%

28. Which statement best explains why an observer on the Moon sees varying amounts of the illuminated side of the Earth (phases of the Earth) during a one-year period? (1) The Earth rotates on its axis. (2) The Sun revolves on its axis. (3) The Moon rotates on its axis. (4) The Moon revolves around the Earth.

29. The actual diameter represented by the line *F-G* is (1) 1.74 × 10³ km (2) 3.48 × 10³ km (3) 6.37 × 10³ km (4) 12.74 × 10³ km

30. The diagrams below represent photographs of the Moon taken from Earth at different times. Which photograph was taken when the Moon was closest to the Earth?

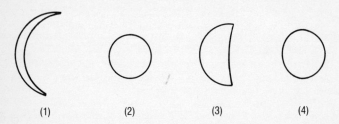

(1)   (2)   (3)   (4)

31. An observer in New York State took a time exposure photograph from 10 P.M. until midnight of the stars over the *northern* horizon. Which diagram best represents this photograph?

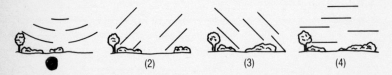

(2)   (3)   (4)

32. Which motion causes the Moon to show phases when viewed from the Earth?   (1) the rotation of the Moon on its axis   (2) the revolution of the Moon around the Earth   (3) the rotation of the Sun on its axis   (4) the revolution of the Sun around the Moon

33. If the distance between the Earth and the Sun were increased, which change would occur?   (1) The apparent diameter of the Sun would decrease.   (2) The amount of insolation received by the Earth would increase.   (3) The time for one Earth rotation (rotation period) would double.   (4) The time for one Earth revolution (orbital period) would decrease.

34. The graph below shows the time of apparent solar noon (maximum altitude of the Sun) and the time of mean solar noon (clock time) during the year. How does the time of apparent solar noon compare with the time of mean solar noon?

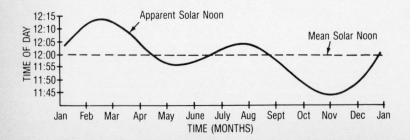

(1) Apparent solar noon always occurs after mean solar noon. (2) Apparent solar noon and mean solar noon never occur at the same time. ● The time of apparent solar noon changes with the seasons. (4) The time of mean solar noon changes during the year.

35. Based on the diagram below and the *Earth Science Reference Tables,* what is the eccentricity of the ellipse shown below?

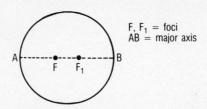

F, F₁ = foci
AB = major axis

(1) 1.0   (2) 0.5   (3) 0.25   (4) 0.13

Base your answer to question 36 on the diagram below, the metric scale in the *Earth Science Reference Tables,* and the equation for gravitational force.

36. Which would represent the change in gravitational force between sphere 1 and sphere 2 after sphere 2 is moved from position A to position B?   (1) ⅙ as great   (2) ½ as great   (3) ⅓ as great   (4) ⅑ as great

37. An observer took a time-exposure photograph of Polaris and five nearby stars. How many hours were required to form these star paths?

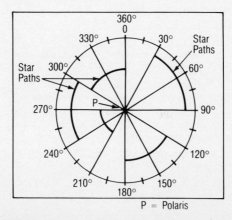

P = Polaris

(1) 6   (2) 2   (3) 8   (4) 4

Additional Questions

1-10. Refer to the diagram below, which represents the solar system of the star Abel, which is very similar to our own solar system. Objects A, C, D, E, and F are planets revolving around the star Abel. Object B is a satellite of planet A and is very similar to the earth's moon. Objects A and B are shown in four different positions in their orbits.

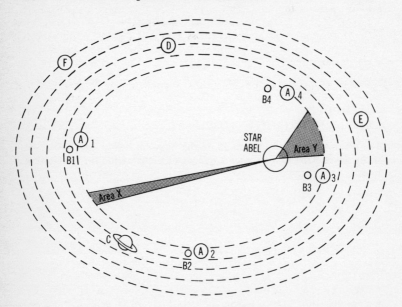

1. In which position of planet A would the satellite B have the smallest apparent diameter?   (1) A-1   (2) A-2   (3) A-3   (4) A-4

2. In which position of planet A would satellite B look like the drawing at the right?   (1) A-1   (2) A-2   (3) A-3   (4) A-4

3. In which position of planet A would the satellite probably not be visible?   (1) A-1   (2) A-2   (3) A-3   (4) A-4

4. How would the apparent size of planet F change as observed for a period of many years from planet A?   (1) planet F would stay the same size   (2) planet F would constantly increase in size   (3) planet F would constantly decrease in size   (4) planet F would increase and decrease in size in a cyclic fashion

5. In terms of the orbit of planet A, where would it have its greatest potential energy?   (1) A-1   (2) A-2   (3) A-3   (4) A-4

6. In terms of the orbit of planet A, where would it have its greatest kinetic energy?   (1) A-1   (2) A-2   (3) A-3   (4) A-4

7. The shapes of the orbits of all the planets in the Abel system are   (1) spheres   (2) oblate spheroids   (3) circles   (4) ellipses

8. In order from planet A to planet F, the length of the planet's period of revolution would   (1) increase   (2) decrease   (3) remain the same

9. Which position in the system would the star Abel have?   (1) the epicenter   (2) the barycenter   (3) the axis   (4) the focus

10. On the diagram, area X equals area Y. How much time would it take planet A to cross area X compared to the time to cross area Y? (1) it would take the same time   (2) it would take longer to cross area X   (3) it would take longer to cross area Y   (4) you cannot tell the times because you do not know the force of gravity between planet A and the star Abel

11-13. Refer to the diagram below, which shows the position of the sun at five different dates or locations at 12:00 noon apparent solar time.

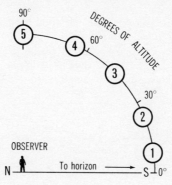

11. At which of the following latitudes is the sun never seen as shown in position 5 in the diagram?   (1) 0°   (2) 23½°N   (3) 23½°S (4) 42°N

12. In New York State, in which position would the sun be when it rises farthest south?   (1) 5   (2) 2   (3) 3   (4) 4

13. What would be the position of the sun at 23½° north latitude on June 21?   (1) 5   (2) 2   (3) 3   (4) 4

14. How many degrees does the sun appear to move across the sky in two hours?   (1) 15°   (2) 30°   (3) 45°   (4) 60°

15. In New York State, when is the sun the highest in the sky? (1) 11 A.M.   (2) noon   (3) 1 P.M.   (4) 2 P.M.

16. Which is *not* true about the geocentric model?   (1) it can explain the apparent daily motion of the sun   (2) it does not explain rotation of the Foucault pendulum   (3) it is less complicated than the heliocentric model   (4) the sun revolves about the earth

17. What is *not* true about the heliocentric model?   (1) it is less complicated than the geocentric model   (2) it includes rotation of the earth   (3) the sun revolves about the earth   (4) it explains the apparent daily motion of the sun

18. Given only the mean distance of a planet from the sun, which of the following can be computed?   (1) the planet's period of revolution   (2) the planet's period of rotation   (3) the eccentricity of the planet's orbit   (4) the amount of gravitational attraction between the planet and the sun

19. At 40° north latitude, for how many days a year is the sun in the zenith (directly overhead) position at noon?   (1) 1   (2) 2   (3) 3   (4) 0

20. In New York State, to see the sun at noon, one would look towards the   (1) north   (2) south   (3) east   (4) west

21. Astronomers have concluded that the planets rotate because (1) the earth rotates   (2) features on the planets appear to change position in a cyclic fashion   (3) movements of sunspots indicate the sun rotates   (4) the rate of a planet's rotation is related to its distance from the sun

22. If after a star rises, it moves 30° from the horizon in two hours, how far will it travel in five hours?   (1) 60°   (2) 75°   (3) 90°   (4) 150°

23. What is true about the mean solar day?   (1) it is the same as the apparent solar day   (2) it always is 24 hours in length   (3) it is often more or less than 24 hours in length   (4) it is determined by using a sundial

ENERGY. All earth processes result from the transfer of energy. **Energy** is the ability to do work.

ELECTROMAGNETIC ENERGY

Electromagnetic energy is energy that is radiated in the form of waves. All matter gives off electromagnetic energy unless it is at **absolute zero,** which is theoretically the lowest possible temperature and one at which the particles of matter have no motion. Electromagnetic energy has **transverse wave** properties, which means that the waves vibrate at right angles to the direction in which they are moving (see Figure 5-1). As an example, when a rope tied to a solid object is shaken, the particles making up the rope move up and down, but a transverse wave travels along the length of the rope.

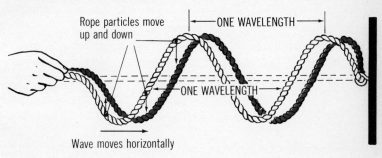

Figure 5-1. A transverse wave in a rope at two moments a short time apart. As the particles of the rope move up and down, the form of the wave moves to the right. In an electromagnetic wave, there are no moving particles. Instead, there are varying electric and magnetic forces at right angles to the direction of propagation of the wave.

The different types of electromagnetic energy are distinguished by their different *wavelengths*. The **wavelength** is the distance from one crest of the wave to the next crest or between corresponding points on successive cycles. Figure 5-2 lists various forms of electromagnetic energy in order of increasing wavelength. This group of electromagnetic radiations is known as the **electromagnetic spectrum.**

INTERACTION OF ELECTROMAGNETIC ENERGY WITH AN ENVIRONMENT. When electromagnetic energy interacts with a material, it can be (1) **refracted,** which means bent in its passage through the material; (2) **reflected,** which means turned aside to a new course; (3) **scattered,** which means refracted and/or reflected in various directions; or (4) **absorbed,** which means taken into the material.

SURFACE PROPERTIES AND ABSORPTION. The characteristics of a surface determine the quantity and type of electromagnetic energy that can be absorbed. For example, the darker and rougher the surface of a material, the more visible light will be absorbed. A forest will absorb more energy than a grassy plain because the forest is actually a darker, rougher "surface" to the incoming radiation.

METHODS OF ENERGY TRANSFER

The three methods of energy transfer are *conduction, convection,* and *radiation.* Conduction and convection refer to the transfer of heat energy in matter (solids, liquids, and gases). Radiation refers to the transfer of energy by electromagnetic waves in space and in matter.

CONDUCTION. **Conduction** is the transfer of heat energy from atom to atom or molecule to molecule through contact when atoms or molecules collide. Generally, in any one substance, conduction is most effective in the solid phase, because the atoms or molecules are closer together than in the gas and liquid phases.

CONVECTION. **Convection** is the transfer of heat by movements in fluids (gases and liquids) caused by *differences in density* within the fluid. Warmer portions of the fluid usually have lower density and tend to rise above cooler portions. The result is a circulatory motion called a **convection cell** or **convection current** which transfers heat energy from one place to another. Convection currents transfer heat through the earth's atmosphere, hydrosphere, and perhaps in parts of the mantle zone below the lithosphere.

RADIATION. In **radiation,** no medium is needed to transfer the transverse waves that carry electromagnetic energy; such energy can radiate from its source across empty space, moving in straight lines at the speed of light (which is the visible form of electromagnetic energy). This is the method by which the sun's electromagnetic energy gets through space to the other objects in the solar system.

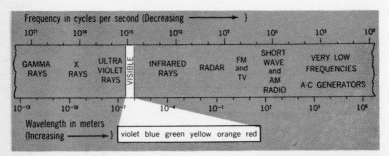

Figure 5-2. The electromagnetic spectrum. Wavelengths are indicated on a logarithmic scale, in which each mark indicates a wavelength 10 times as great as the preceding one. There is no zero point on such a scale.

TRANSFER OF ENERGY WITHIN A CLOSED SYSTEM

SOURCE AND SINK.   Energy moves away from an area of high concentration, called a **source,** to an area of low concentration, called a **sink.** The energy will continue to move from the source to the sink until their energies are equal, establishing a **dynamic equilibrium.** At dynamic equilibrium an object loses and gains equal amounts of energy. If the dynamic equilibrium is between all forms of energy, then the temperature of the object or system will remain constant.

CONSERVATION OF ENERGY.   In any energy system that is closed, or isolated, the total amount of energy remains the same. Thus the amount of energy lost by a source must equal the amount of energy gained by a sink. This concept, that energy is not created or destroyed but stays the same in amount in a closed system, is called the principle of **conservation of energy*.**

KINETIC AND POTENTIAL ENERGY.   An object in motion has a kind of energy called **kinetic energy.** Objects or systems can also have a kind of energy called **potential energy,** which is energy related to position or state. It may be thought of as "stored" energy. Either of these two kinds of energy can be transformed into the other. For example, water at the top of a waterfall has potential energy because of its position with respect to the earth's center of mass. As the water falls to a lower level, some of its potential energy is transformed to kinetic energy, resulting in an increase in speed. In a swinging pendulum, there is a cyclic exchange of kinetic and potential energy. At the top of its swing, the pendulum has zero kinetic energy and maximum potential energy. As it passes through the low point of its swing, it has its maximum kinetic energy and minimum potential energy.

FRICTION AT INTERFACES.   Transformations of energy occur when there is *friction.* For example, as a stream flows, some of its kinetic energy is transformed into heat energy at the interface between the stream and its bed. This transformation occurs because of friction between the moving water and the bed.

WAVELENGTH CHANGE.   A good absorber of electromagnetic energy is also a good radiator. Often when electromagnetic energy is absorbed by an object, it is reradiated at a longer wavelength. This is very common at the earth's surface, where the relatively short-wavelength ultraviolet and visible radiations from the sun are absorbed and reradiated as longer-wavelength infrared radiations.

---

*Einstein's theory of relativity states that mass (or matter) and energy are equivalent, and that one can be converted to the other. The release of energy by radioactivity is an example of the conversion of mass to energy. The energy radiated by the sun and the other stars is also generated by the conversion of mass to energy within the stars.

TEMPERATURE AND HEAT

TEMPERATURE.   According to the modern theory of matter, the particles of every material are in continuous, random motion. The particles therefore have kinetic energy. At any moment, some of the particles have large kinetic energies, some have small kinetic energies, and some have intermediate kinetic energies. **Temperature** is a measure of the *average kinetic energy* of the particles of a body of matter. The greater the average kinetic energy of the particles, the higher the temperature of the body. If two bodies have the same temperature, the average kinetic energy of their particles is also the same. This is true regardless of the substances in the bodies.

TEMPERATURE SCALES.   The human senses respond to temperature by the sensations called "hot" and "cold." Temperature can be measured more accurately by instruments called *thermometers*. Thermometers indicate temperature on a scale marked off in *degrees*. There are several different temperature scales in use, with different sizes of degrees and different zero points. Relationships among three common temperature scales are given in the *Earth Science Reference Tables*.

HEAT.   If two bodies at different temperatures are placed in contact, some of the kinetic energy of the particles of the hotter body will be transferred to the particles of the cooler body. As a result, the particles of the cooler body will acquire more kinetic energy on the average, and its temperature will therefore rise. The particles of the hotter body will lose kinetic energy and its temperature will fall. This transfer of energy will continue until both bodies have the same temperature.

Energy that is transferred from a hotter body to a cooler one because of the difference in temperature is called **heat energy,** or more simply **heat.** For example, if a stone at a temperature of 80°C is placed in a container of water at 20°C, heat will flow from the stone into the water until both arrive at the same temperature. The heat transfer in this example occurs by conduction and convection.

QUANTITY OF HEAT.   Since an increase in temperature requires an increase in kinetic energy of the particles of a body, it takes twice as much heat energy to raise the temperature of a body 2° as to raise it 1°. It also takes twice as much heat energy to raise the temperature of 2 grams of a substance 1° as to raise the temperature of 1 gram of the same substance by this amount. In general, the quantity of heat involved in a temperature change of a given substance is directly proportional to the amount of temperature change and the mass of the substance.

When a substance "cools off," that is, when its temperature decreases, it releases the same amount of heat energy that was needed to raise its temperature by the same number of degrees. This is an example of the conservation of energy as applied to heat.

THE CALORIE.   The relationship between quantity of heat, mass of material, and temperature change can be used to define a unit of heat called the *calorie*. For this purpose, water is used as the standard material. One **calorie** is defined as the quantity of heat needed to raise the temperature of one gram of liquid water by one degree Celsius. Since one calorie is needed for each gram of water and for each degree Celsius of temperature change, the number of calories needed to change the temperature of a given mass of water by a given number of degrees can be calculated by the following formula:

No. of calories =
      mass of water in grams × temperature change in °C × 1 cal/g/°C

Example

How many calories of heat must be added to 10 grams of liquid water to raise its temperature 15°C?

Solution:

$$\text{No. of cal} = 10 \text{ g} \times 15°C \times 1 \text{ cal/g/°C}$$
$$= 150 \text{ cal}$$

SPECIFIC HEAT. We have seen that it takes one calorie to raise the temperature of one gram of water one degree Celsius. It takes only about 0.2 calorie (1/5 as much) to raise the temperature of one gram of a typical rock one degree Celsius. The quantity of heat needed to raise the temperature of one gram of any substance one degree Celsius is called the **specific heat** of that substance. The specific heat of the rock is 0.2 cal/g/°C. The specific heat of water is 1.0 cal/g/°C.

Liquid water has the highest specific heat of naturally occurring substances (1.0 cal/g/°C). All other naturally occurring substances have a specific heat less than 1 (see *Earth Science Reference Tables*, page 238). Therefore, for equal masses, the same amount of heat causes them to heat up or cool off faster than water.

HEAT LOST OR GAINED. The amount of heat lost or gained by a substance (in calories) equals the mass (in grams) times the temperature change (in °C) times the specific heat of the substance.

Example

How much heat is needed to heat 15 grams of granite from 15°C to 20°C if the specific heat of the granite is 0.19 cal/g/°C?

Solution:

$$\text{Temperature change} = 20°C - 15°C = 5°C$$
$$\text{No. of cal} = 15 \text{ g} \times 5°C \times 0.19 \text{ cal/g/°C}$$
$$= 14.25 \text{ cal}$$

HEAT ENERGY AND CHANGES OF PHASE

LATENT HEAT. Matter may exist in the solid, liquid, or gaseous phase. As long as a material is in a single one of these phases, its temperature rises as heat is added to it. If, however, the material begins to *change* phase, for example, from solid to liquid, its temperature *remains the same* as heat is added to it. During the phase change, the added heat energy is not increasing the kinetic energy of the molecules, and therefore the temperature does not change. The added heat energy is being converted to a kind of *potential energy* called **latent heat.**

HEAT LOST OR GAINED IN PHASE CHANGE.   When the change of phase is from a solid to a liquid or from a liquid to a gas, latent heat must be gained by the substance. When the phase change is from a gas to a liquid or from a liquid to a solid, latent heat must be lost by the substance. The heat gained (or lost) in a phase change is equal to the product of the mass times the latent heat (change in potential energy) per unit mass. The latent heat varies with the particular substance and type of phase change.

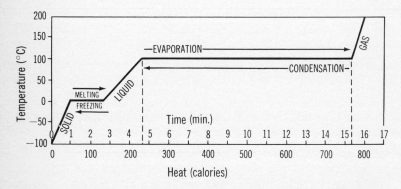

Figure 5-3. Heating curve for water. The graph shows the temperature change of one gram of water as heat is added at a constant rate (50 calories per minute). If read from right to left, the graph is the corresponding cooling curve.

LATENT HEAT AND PHASE CHANGE OF WATER.   Figure 5-3 shows how the temperature of a fixed amount of water changes as it is heated at a constant rate from ice at $-100°C$ to gaseous water (water vapor) at $200°C$. The temperature is plotted against time in minutes (upper scale of the graph) and the corresponding amount of heat added (lower scale of the graph). It can be seen that the temperature remains constant at $0°C$ for almost 2 minutes while the water is changing from the solid phase (ice) to the liquid phase. There is another constant-temperature interval of more than 10 minutes at $100°C$ while the water is changing from the liquid phase to the gaseous phase. The reason for these intervals of constant temperature is that the heat being added at those times is being changed to latent heat (potential energy). The latent heat for the change from solid to liquid water is 80 calories per gram; for the change from liquid to gas, the latent heat is 540 calories per gram.

THE EARTH'S ENERGY SUPPLY

SOLAR ENERGY.   Most of the energy of the earth comes from electromagnetic radiations from the sun. The sun gives off (radiates), and the earth receives, a wide range of electromagnetic energy radiations of various wavelengths. This solar electromagnetic spectrum includes X rays, ultraviolet rays, visible light, and infrared rays. Of all the types of electromagnetic radiations from the sun, the one of greatest intensity is visible light (see Figure 6-1 on page 65).

RADIOACTIVE DECAY.   The atoms of certain elements, such as uranium and radium, are unstable and tend to break down into more stable atoms of other elements. This natural, spontaneous breakdown of unstable atoms is called **radioactivity** or **radioactive decay.** It is a process that releases energy and that continues at a constant rate for any particular radioactive element, unaffected by changes in temperature, pressure, or other environmental conditions. Radioactive decay of elements within the earth is an additional source of energy for many earth processes, such as mountain building and volcanic activity.

VOCABULARY

energy	source
electromagnetic energy	sink
absolute zero	dynamic equilibrium
transverse wave	conservation of energy
wavelength	kinetic and potential energy
electromagnetic spectrum	dynamic equilibrium
refraction	temperature
reflection	heat energy
scattering	calorie
absorption	specific heat
conduction	phase change
convection cell or	latent heat
convection current	radioactivity or radioactive
radiation	decay

QUESTIONS ON TOPIC V—ENERGY IN EARTH PROCESSES

Questions in Recent Regents Exams (end of book)

June 1984:   12, 13, 49, 71, 72, 73, 74, 75, 104
June 1985:   3, 13, 14, 15, 66, 67, 68, 69, 105
June 1986:   13, 15, 16, 62, 67, 68
June 1987:   12, 14, 16, 66–70

Questions from Earlier Regents Exams

1. Two identical towels are hanging on a clothesline in the sun. One towel is wet; the other is dry. The wet towel feels much cooler than the dry towel because the   (1) dry towel receives more heat energy from the sun   (2) dry towel has more room for heat storage than the wet towel   (3) presence of water in the wet towel requires an additional amount of heat energy to bring about a temperature change   (4) water in the wet towel prevents absorption of heat energy

2. The primary source of energy for ocean currents and waves is (1) rotation of the earth   (2) motions of the atmosphere   (3) crustal movements   (4) incoming solar radiation

3. Which would absorb the most solar radiation, if you assume that each covers an equal geographic area?   (1) a freshwater lake (2) a snowfield   (3) a sandy beach   (4) a forest

4. Equal volumes of soil and water, at equal temperatures, are placed near a radiant heater. After ten minutes of heating, the soil temperature is 34°C and the water temperature is 27°C. Ten minutes after the source of heat is withdrawn, the soil temperature is 32°C and the water temperature is 26°C. Which conclusion is most logical?   (1) a good reflector of heat is a good absorber of heat   (2) a good reflector of heat is a good radiator of heat   (3) a good absorber of heat is a good radiator of heat   (4) a good absorber of heat is a poor radiator of heat

Questions 5–9 refer to the diagram below. A student is using the apparatus shown to perform an investigation. The two calorimeters contain equal amounts of water, and the metal bar is touching the water inside each calorimeter. At the beginning of the investigation, the temperature of the water was 100°C in calorimeter A and 20°C in calorimeter B. The room temperature is 20°C.

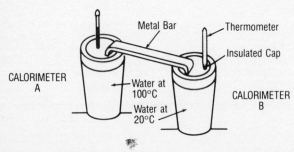

5. At the start of the investigation, which could be considered a heat source?   (1) the water in calorimeter A (2) the water in calorimeter B (3) the air surrounding the calorimeters   (4) the metal bar between the calorimeters

6. If this were a closed system, what would be the temperature when the system reaches equilibrium?   (1) 100°C   (2) 75°C   (3) 60°C (4) 40°C

7. Which conclusion should the student make after actually performing this investigation? (1) The energy gained by the cold water equaled the energy lost by the hot water. (2) The energy gained by the cold water was less than the energy lost by the hot water. (3) The change in temperature of the cold-water thermometer equaled the change in temperature of the hot-water thermometer. (4) Energy was transferred between the two calorimeters primarily by radiation.

8. Which procedure would increase the amount of heat energy that is actually gained by calorimeter *B*? (1) increasing the length of the metal bar (2) increasing the thickness of the metal bar (3) circulating air over the metal bar (4) placing insulation around the metal bar

9. Which graph best represents the probable relationship between the temperatures of the two calorimeters and the time for this heat transfer investigation?

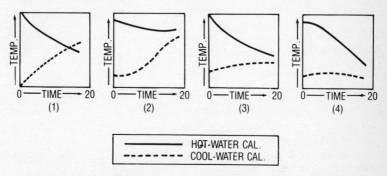

10. By which method is energy transferred by density differences? (1) absorption (2) conduction (3) convection (4) radiation

11. The environment is in dynamic equilibrium when it is gaining (1) less energy than it is losing (2) more energy than it is losing (3) the same amount of energy as it is losing

12. According to the *Earth Science Reference Tables*, how many calories of heat energy must be added to 5 grams of liquid water to change its temperature from 10°C to 30°C? (1) 5 cal (2) 20 cal (3) 100 cal (4) 150 cal

13. At which temperature will an object radiate the greatest amount of electromagnetic energy? [Refer to the *Earth Science Reference Tables*.] (1) 0° Fahrenheit (2) 5° Celsius (3) 10° Fahrenheit (4) 230° Kelvin

14. According to the *Earth Science Reference Tables*, how many calories of heat energy must be added to 10 grams of iron to raise its temperature 10°C? (1) 0.11 cal (2) 1.1 cal (3) 11 cal (4) 110 cal

15. Which characteristics of a material have the greatest effect on the amount of insolation that the material will absorb? (1) density and hardness (2) hardness and age (3) age and roughness (4) roughness and color

16. Based on the *Earth Science Reference Tables,* what is the total amount of energy required to melt 100 grams of ice at 0°C to liquid water at 0°C?   (1) 5,400 cal   (2) 8,000 cal   (3) 54,000 cal   (4) 80,000 cal

17. Equal masses of lead, granite, basalt, and water at 5°C are exposed to equal quantities of heat energy. Which would be the first to show a temperature rise of 10°C?   (1) lead   (2) granite   (3) basalt   (4) water

18. Which model best represents equal masses of water in various phases (states) showing the phase with the greatest stored energy (latent heat) at the top and lowest stored energy at the bottom?

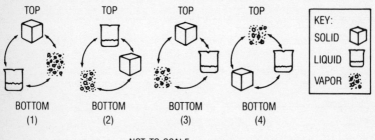

NOT TO SCALE

Additional Questions

1. At which temperature would an object *not* radiate electromagnetic energy?   (1) 100° Celsius   (2) 0° Fahrenheit   (3) 0° Celsius   (4) absolute zero

2. Electromagnetic energy can be   (1) refracted   (2) refracted and reflected   (3) refracted, reflected, and scattered   (4) refracted, reflected, scattered, and absorbed

3. When electromagnetic energy strikes an object that is a good radiator of electromagnetic energy, most of the energy will be   (1) refracted   (2) reflected   (3) scattered   (4) absorbed

4. Which is the major source of energy for earth processes?   (1) earthquakes   (2) electrical storms   (3) radioactive decay within the earth   (4) the sun

5. The solar electromagnetic spectrum consists of   (1) no wavelengths   (2) a single wavelength   (3) a narrow range of wavelengths   (4) a wide range of wavelengths

6. The maximum intensity of the solar electromagnetic spectrum occurs in which region?   (1) infrared   (2) ultraviolet   (3) visible   (4) X ray

7. The temperature of an object is determined by the   (1) average kinetic energy of its molecules   (2) average potential energy of its molecules   (3) total kinetic energy of the object   (4) total potential energy of the object

8. The transfer of heat energy by means of collisions of adjacent atoms or molecules is called   (1) conduction   (2) convection   (3) radiation   (4) insolation

9. Changes in phase involve   (1) only loss of energy   (2) only gain of energy   (3) either loss or gain of energy   (4) neither loss nor gain of energy

10. Which change of phase requires the addition of the most energy?   (1) liquid water to water vapor   (2) water vapor to liquid water   (3) ice to liquid water   (4) liquid water to ice

11. During a volcanic eruption, a rock is thrown into the air and returns to earth. Which best describes what happened to the potential energy of the rock?   (1) it increased   (2) it decreased   (3) it increased then decreased   (4) it decreased then increased

12. Which surface would absorb the most electromagnetic energy?   (1) dark and smooth   (2) dark and rough   (3) light and smooth   (4) light and rough

13. If equal masses of the following substances experienced an equal increase in temperature, which absorbed the most energy?   (1) iron   (2) rock   (3) soil   (4) liquid water

14. What is true about the amount of energy gained by the environment around the sun compared to the energy lost by the sun?   (1) it is about the same   (2) the environment gains much more than is lost by the sun   (3) the environment gains much less than is lost by the sun   (4) the relative amounts lost by the sun and gained by the environment vary greatly with time

15. Which statement best describes the electromagnetic radiations given off by the sun?   (1) they consist mostly of short-wave radiations   (2) they consist mostly of heat waves   (3) they are transverse waves   (4) they are longitudinal waves

16-20. Refer to the following diagram.

SUN

Meteorite

(Not drawn to scale)

16. By what method does the electromagnetic energy get from the sun to the meteorite?   (1) reflection   (2) convection   (3) conduction   (4) radiation

17. What must be true about the meteorite if it is a good absorber of electromagnetic energy?   (1) it must produce large amounts of electromagnetic energy of the same wavelength it absorbs   (2) it must be a good radiator of electromagnetic energy   (3) it cannot be a good radiator   (4) it cannot reflect any energy from the sun

18. How would you classify the energy relationship between the sun and the meteorite?   (1) they are both sinks   (2) they are both sources   (3) the sun is the source   (4) the meteorite is the source

19. When the short-wavelength electromagnetic energy absorbed by the meteorite is reradiated, its wavelength will   (1) increase   (2) decrease   (3) remain the same

20. As electromagnetic energy reached the meteorite, it could *not* be   (1) destroyed   (2) refracted   (3) reflected   (4) absorbed

To answer questions 21-25, refer to the graph below, which illustrates data for the heating of 50 grams of water from −50°C to 200°C. The amount of heat being added to the water per minute remains constant.

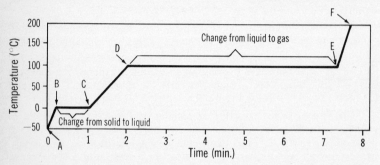

21. What is happening to most of the energy being added from D to E?   (1) it is causing an increase in temperature   (2) it is being transformed into potential energy   (3) it is being transformed into kinetic energy   (4) it is being lost due to poor insulation

22. The most energy is needed to cause the change from   (1) A to B   (2) C to D   (3) D to E   (4) E to F

23. The least energy is needed to cause the change from   (1) B to C   (2) C to D   (3) D to E   (4) E to F

24. How many changes of phase are indicated on the diagram?   (1) one   (2) two   (3) five   (4) none

25. Heat energy within the water between A and B would be transferred by   (1) an interface   (2) radiation   (3) convection   (4) conduction

26. A concrete play area is resurfaced with blacktop. Compared with the amount of heat energy that was absorbed by the concrete surface, the amount of heat energy absorbed by the blacktop surface will most probably be   (1) less   (2) greater   (3) sometimes the same and sometimes less   (4) sometimes greater and sometimes less

INSOLATION

SOLAR RADIATION.   As stated on page 53, every body of matter that is not at absolute zero radiates electromagnetic energy. This energy is radiated over a portion of the electromagnetic spectrum, with more of the energy radiated at some wavelengths than at others. The rate at which energy is radiated is called the *intensity* of the radiation. The higher the temperature of the matter, the shorter the wavelength at which the maximum intensity of radiation occurs. At the temperature of the sun, the maximum intensity of radiation occurs in the range of visible wavelengths.

INSOLATION.   Insolation (INcoming SOLar radiATION) is the portion of the sun's radiation that is received by the earth. Figure 6-1 shows how the intensity of insolation varies with wavelength. The maximum intensity occurs in the visible range, but about 50% of the total energy received is infrared, a type of long-wave radiation.

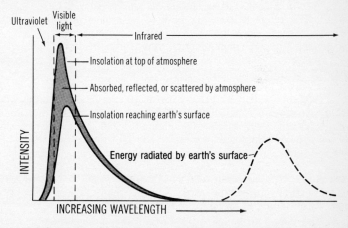

Figure 6-1. Intensity of insolation received and radiated by the earth's surface. Total amount of energy is proportional to the area under the curves. About 50% of the insolation received at the surface is in the infrared range of wavelengths, but 100% of the radiated energy is in this range. (The terrestrial radiation curve is not drawn to the same scale as the insolation curves. If drawn to the same scale, it would be much flatter and would extend much farther to the right.)

EFFECTS OF THE ATMOSPHERE ON INSOLATION.   Figure 6-1 also shows that the insolation reaching the earth's surface is different from the insolation entering the earth's upper atmosphere because of *absorption, reflection,* and *scattering* by the atmosphere. Some of the specific effects of the atmosphere on insolation are as follows:

1. Nearly all the ultraviolet radiation is absorbed by the atmosphere.

2. Most of the visible light passes through the atmosphere because the atmosphere is transparent to it.

3. Much infrared radiation is absorbed by water vapor (gaseous water) and carbon dioxide.

4. When clouds are present, much of the incident (incoming) insolation is reflected. For the earth as a whole on a typical day, it is estimated that about 25% of incident insolation is reflected by the cloud cover.

5. *Aerosols* cause random reflection, or scattering, of insolation. **Aerosols** are finely dispersed solids and liquids suspended in air. The dispersed materials include dust, ice crystals, liquid water droplets, and various air pollutants. As the concentration of aerosols increases, the scattering of insolation also increases, thus reducing the amount of insolation that reaches the earth's surface.

ABSORPTION AND RADIATION OF INSOLATION. When insolation reaches the earth's surface, some of it is reflected and some is absorbed, as explained in the next section. Insolation that is absorbed by the earth's surface is converted to heat and tends to raise the temperature of the surface. However, since the earth's surface is not at absolute zero, it also radiates electromagnetic energy, thus tending to lower its temperature. This energy emitted at the earth's surface is called **terrestrial radiation,** or ground radiation. Over a period of time, the amount of energy absorbed from insolation is equal to terrestrial radiation, and a temperature (or radiative) balance exists (see page 72). Because the earth's temperature is much lower than the sun's, the earth radiates energy at much longer wavelengths. Figure 6-1 indicates the relationship between the wavelengths of insolation and radiation emitted from the earth's surface.

INTERACTION OF INSOLATION AT THE EARTH'S SURFACE. When insolation reaches the earth's surface, many factors affect what happens to it. Some of these are as follows:

1. The darker or rougher the surface, the more insolation is absorbed and the less is reflected.

2. Ice and snow reflect almost all of the insolation, keeping areas with ice and snow cooler than they would otherwise be.

3. The altitude of the sun in the sky determines the **angle of insolation,** that is, the angle at which insolation will hit the earth's surface. The lower the angle of insolation, the more insolation is reflected and the less is absorbed.

4. The evaporation of water and the melting of ice and snow transform insolation into latent potential energy which does not raise the temperature of the surface. The more evaporation or melting occurring in an area, the smaller will be the amount of insolation available to heat the area; thus the temperatures will be lower than would otherwise be the case.

LAND AND WATER HEATING.   With equal amounts of insolation, an area consisting largely of water will heat up and cool off more slowly than an equal area of land. There are several reasons for this:

1. Water has a much higher specific heat than land.

2. Water is highly transparent to insolation: therefore the insolation is absorbed to a greater depth.

3. Convection can occur in water, thus distributing the absorbed energy through a much larger volume than is the case with land.

THE GREENHOUSE EFFECT.   Although the atmosphere allows most of the insolation entering it to pass through to the earth's surface, it absorbs most of the energy radiated by the surface. The reason for this is that the longer infrared radiations are absorbed to a large extent by the carbon dioxide and water vapor in the atmosphere. This absorption warms the atmosphere and causes it to act as a heat "blanket," which reduces the loss of energy to outer space and makes the earth's surface warmer than it would otherwise be. This process by which the atmosphere transmits short-wave energy and absorbs radiated long-wave energy (preventing its immediate escape into space) is called the **greenhouse effect.**

VARIATIONS OF INSOLATION

INTENSITY OF INSOLATION.   The **intensity of insolation** is the rate at which solar energy is received by a given area per unit of time. For example, intensity of insolation can be measured in calories per square meter per second.

EFFECT OF ANGLE OF INSOLATION ON INTENSITY.   When insolation is perpendicular to a surface (that is, striking the surface at an angle of 90°) its intensity is a maximum, because the insolation is concentrated in the smallest possible area. As the angle of insolation decreases from 90° toward zero, the same amount of insolation is spread out over greater and greater areas, as shown by Figure 6-2 (page 68). Therefore the intensity of insolation becomes smaller as the angle becomes smaller.

EFFECT OF INTENSITY OF INSOLATION ON TEMPERATURE.   As insolation falls upon a surface, the temperature of the surface gradually increases because it is absorbing energy. For the same type of surface, the heating effect of insolation will vary with the intensity of insolation. If the intensity is greater, the surface temperature will rise more rapidly, since there is then more energy reaching each unit of area.

EARTH'S SHAPE AND INTENSITY OF INSOLATION. The sun's energy reaches the earth as a bundle of parallel rays. If the earth were flat and perpendicular to these rays, the intensity of insolation would be the same everywhere on the earth's surface. However, the earth's surface is nearly a sphere. As a result, at any given time there is just one place where the insolation is perpendicular to the surface; at all other places, the angle of insolation is less than 90°. Therefore the intensity of insolation varies over the earth because of the curvature of its surface.

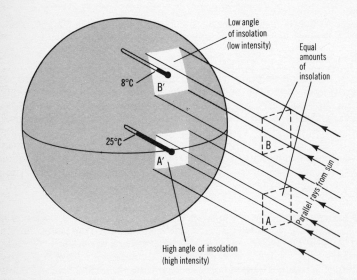

Figure 6-2. Because of the spherical shape of the earth, the parallel rays from the sun strike different parts of the surface at different angles. In high latitudes, where the angle is lower, the same amount of insolation spreads out over a larger area, thus resulting in a lower intensity than where the angle is higher.

INTENSITY OF INSOLATION IN RELATION TO LATITUDE. As shown in Fig. 6-3, insolation is perpendicular to the earth's surface at the equator at each of the **equinoxes** (March 21 and September 23). The rays of **perpendicular insolation** are known as **direct** or **vertical rays.** At each equinox, the intensity of insolation is maximum at the equator, where the direct rays strike, and it decreases with increasing latitude. At the **summer solstice** (June 21), the direct rays strike the earth at 23½°N latitude (the Tropic of Cancer). This is then the latitude of maximum intensity, and the intensity is less at any other latitude. At the **winter solstice** (December 21), the direct rays and the maximum intensity are at 23½°S latitude (the Tropic of Capricorn).

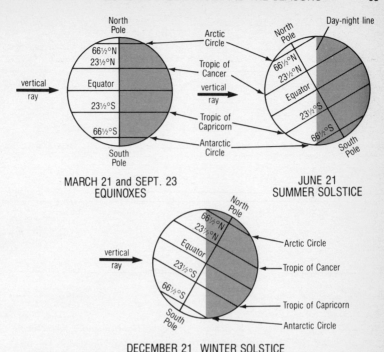

Figure 6-3. Intensity of insolation in relation to latitude. At any given time, intensity of insolation is a maximum at the latitude of the vertical rays, and is less at other latitudes.

INTENSITY OF INSOLATION IN RELATION TO SEASON. As the earth travels along its orbit around the sun, the angle of insolation at any given latitude varies with the seasons, depending on how far from the direct rays the given latitude is. The seasonal change in the maximum angle of insolation for a location at 42°N latitude is shown in Figure 6-4.

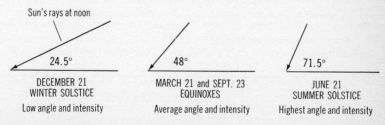

Figure 6-4. Maximum angle of insolation (at noon) at 42° north latitude at different seasons.

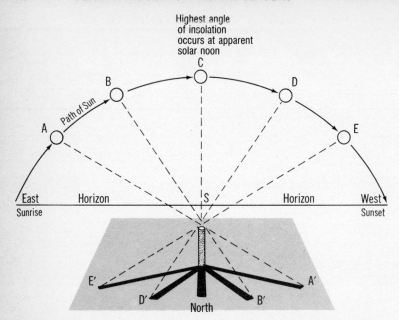

Figure 6-5. The shadow of a vertical post indicates how the angle of insolation varies during the day. The higher the angle of insolation, the shorter the shadow and the greater the intensity. Maximum angle and intensity occur at apparent solar noon.

INTENSITY OF INSOLATION IN RELATION TO TIME OF DAY. The angle of insolation is the same as the altitude of the sun. On any given day, the altitude of the sun varies from zero at sunrise, to a maximum at apparent solar noon, and back to zero again at sunset. The angle of insolation, and hence the intensity of insolation, also vary during the day in the same way, as shown by the changing length of the shadow in Figure 6-5.

DURATION OF INSOLATION. **Duration of insolation** is the length of time that insolation is received each day. That is, it is the number of hours that the sun is visible each day. The duration of insolation varies with latitude and with the seasons. Figure 4-6 on page 34 shows how the length of the sun's path through the sky varies during the year. The duration of insolation is proportional to the length of the path. There is one hour of insolation for each 15° of path. Thus, the longer the path, the greater the duration of insolation. Duration of insolation is greatest in the continental United States at the summer solstice (June 21), least at the winter solstice (December 21), and an average length, 12 hours, at the equinoxes (March 21 and September 23). See Table 6-1.

TEMPERATURES IN RELATION TO INSOLATION. The surface of the earth continuously radiates energy, mostly in the infrared wave-

TABLE 6-1. ANGLE AND DURATION OF INSOLATION

Latitude	SUMMER SOLSTICE JUNE 21		EQUINOXES MARCH 21 SEPTEMBER 23		WINTER SOLSTICE DECEMBER 21	
	Angle of Insolation at 12 Noon	Duration of Insolation	Angle of Insolation at 12 Noon	Duration of Insolation	Angle of Insolation at 12 Noon	Duration of Insolation
90°N	23½°	24 Hours	0°	12 Hours	—	0 Hours
80°N	33⅓°	24	10°	12	—	0
70°N	43½°	24	20°	12	—	0
66½°N	47°	24	23½°	12	0°	0
60°N	53½°	18½	30°	12	6½°	5½
50°N	63½°	16¼	40°	12	16½°	7¾
40°N	73½°	15	50°	12	26½°	9
30°N	83½°	14	60°	12	36½°	10
23½°N	90°	13½	66½°	12	43°	10½
20°N	86½°	13¼	70°	12	46½°	10¾
10°N	76½°	12½	80°	12	56½°	11½
0°	66½°	12	90°	12	66½°	12
10°S	56½°	11½	80°	12	76½°	12½
20°S	46½°	10¾	70°	12	86½°	13¼
23½°S	43°	10½	66½°	12	90°	13½
30°S	36½°	10	60°	12	83½°	14
40°S	26½°	9	50°	12	73½°	15
50°S	16½°	7¾	40°	12	63½°	16¼
60°S	6½°	5½	30°	12	53½°	18½
66½°S	0°	0	23½°	12	47°	24
70°S	—	0	20°	12	43½°	24
80°S	—	0	10°	12	33½°	24
90°S	—	0	0°	12	23½°	24

lengths. The rate of radiation depends on the temperature, being greater when the temperature of the surface is higher, and less when it is lower. The temperature of the earth's surface at any particular location varies through the day, and the average daily temperature varies through the year. This variation depends on the balance between the energy being gained from insolation and the energy being lost by terrestrial radiation. When the energy is being gained at a greater rate than it is being lost, the temperature rises. When energy is being lost faster than it is being gained, the temperature falls. Temperatures are generally higher when the intensity of insolation is greater; they are also higher when the duration of insolation is longer.

TIMES OF MAXIMUM AND MINIMUM TEMPERATURES.

1. During the year. It might be thought at first that the time of maximum temperature would occur at the time of maximum insolation, and the minimum temperature at the time of minimum insolation. This

is not the case, however. The times of maximum and minimum temperature occur somewhat later than the times of maximum and minimum insolation. In latitudes north of 23½°N, for example, the maximum intensity of insolation and the maximum duration of insolation occur on June 21, but the time of highest daily temperatures occurs toward the end of July or early in August. (See Figure 6-6.)

The reason for this is that as the intensity and duration of insolation increase during the spring, each day the surface receives more energy of insolation than it loses by radiation. Consequently, each day the average temperature goes up slightly. On June 21, more energy is gained than is lost; the temperature is still rising as a result. On June 22, a little less energy is received than on June 21. However, the amount received is still more than the amount lost. Therefore the temperature continues to go up. This continues until the rate of incoming energy finally drops below the rate of energy loss by radiation. At that time (usually in late July or early August) the surface temperature begins to drop.

Similarly, the earth north of 23½°N is not at its coolest during the time of minimum angle and duration of insolation on December 21. This occurs because the area continues to lose more energy than is gained by insolation until some time in January or February, when the region reaches its coolest temperature.

2. During the day. The hottest part of an average day is some time in midafternoon, not at apparent solar noon when insolation is greatest (see Figure 6-7). The coolest part of an average day is slightly after sunrise because the earth continues to lose heat during nighttime until after insolation begins at sunrise.

RADIATIVE BALANCE. If an object is in **radiative balance,** it gains the same amount of energy that it gives off, and average temperatures remain the same. Points X and Y in Figure 6-6 indicate the times when a given place on earth is in radiative balance. The graph (Figure 6-8)

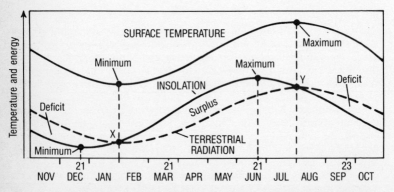

Figure 6-6. Average daily temperatures, insolation, and terrestrial radiation for mid-latitudes of the Northern Hemisphere during a year.

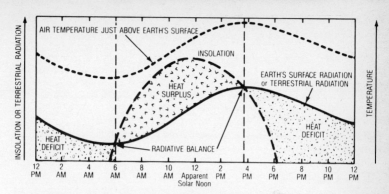

Figure 6-7. Typical variation in air temperature just above surface, insolation, and terrestrial radiation in the course of one day.

can be used to illustrate average temperatures for the eastern United States, which we will assume reflect average temperature changes of the earth. This graph illustrates the following points:

1. Annual measurements of temperature indicate (by changing) that the earth is not in radiative balance on a yearly basis.

2. Intermediate measurements (decades) indicate little change in average decade temperatures; thus the earth is in radiative balance over periods of decades.

The graph in Figure 6-9 on page 74 illustrates that the earth is not in radiative balance over very large periods of time. At different times during the earth's history, the earth has cooled off and glaciers have covered large portions of the earth's surface.

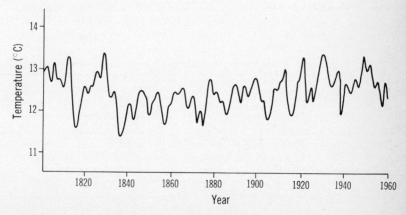

Figure 6-8. Estimated annual temperatures of the eastern seaboard of the United States, centered on Philadelphia, for a period of several decades.

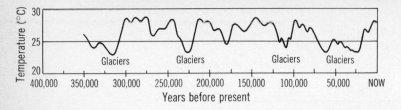

Figure 6-9. Estimated average temperature of the earth during the Pleisto-cene Ice Age.

SEASONS

The **seasons** are the four divisions of the year that are characterized by different types of weather conditions. For most of the earth, the major difference in the seasons is difference in temperature.

DIRECT CAUSE OF THE SEASONS. The seasonal changes in temperature and other weather conditions are the *direct* result of the cyclic variations in intensity and duration of insolation that occur during the year. These variations were described on pages 68–70.

INDIRECT CAUSES OF THE SEASONS. The variations in insolation that cause the seasons are themselves the result of factors that may be called the *indirect* causes of the seasons. These indirect causes are the following:

    1. Tilt of the earth's axis. As Figure 6-10 (page 75) shows, the earth's axis is inclined at an angle of 23½° with respect to a line perpendicular to the plane of its orbit.

    2. Parallelism of the earth's axis. Regardless of the position of the earth in its orbit, its axis always points in the same direction in space. The direction of the axis at any given time is always parallel to its direction at any other time.

    3. Revolution of the earth. As the earth revolves around the sun, the direction of the axis with respect to the sun varies, because of the first two factors described above. For example, on June 21 the North Pole is inclined *toward* the sun at an angle of 23½° from the perpendicular. On December 21, the North Pole is inclined *away* from the sun at this angle. On March 21 and September 23, the axis is still inclined 23½° from the perpendicular, but *neither* toward *nor* away from the sun. This cycle of variations causes the variations in angle and duration of insolation through the year.

SMALL EFFECT OF ELLIPTICAL ORBIT. The variation in distance between the earth and the sun as the earth travels along its orbit is too small to have a significant effect on the seasons. For example, winter in the Northern Hemisphere occurs at a time when the earth is actually nearest the sun.

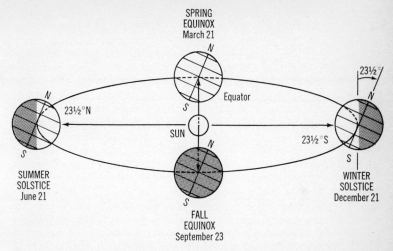

Figure 6-10. Causes of the seasons. The tilt of the earth's axis and parallelism of the axis result in varying angles and duration of insolation through the year.

VOCABULARY

insolation
aerosols
terrestrial radiation
angle of insolation
greenhouse effect
intensity of insoaltion

equinox
perpendicular insolation
solstice
duration of insolation
radiative balance
seasons

QUESTIONS ON TOPIC VI—INSOLATION AND THE SEASONS

Questions in Recent Regents Exams (end of book)

June 1984: 13, 14, 15, 50, 66, 67, 68, 69, 70, 77
June 1985: 9, 16, 17, 54, 69
June 1986: 14, 17, 18, 76, 78, 79, 80
June 1987: 13, 15, 17, 61, 66, 67

Questions from Earlier Regents Exams

1. Which locality has the greatest annual range of temperature? (1) Seattle, Washington   (2) Bismarck, North Dakota   (3) New York City   (4) Miami, Florida

2. At the time of the fall equinox, the number of hours of daylight in New York City is generally about   (1) nine   (2) twelve   (3) fifteen (4) eighteen

3. As nighttime cloudiness increases, the amount of heat lost by radiation from the earth   (1) increases   (2) decreases   (3) remains the same

4. Which is the main cause of seasons on the earth?   (1) difference in the earth-sun distance at perihelion and aphelion   (2) inclination of the earth's axis of rotation in relation to the plane of its orbit   (3) change of inclination of the earth's axis of rotation in relation to the plane of its orbit   (4) increase in velocity of the earth as it approaches the sun

5. Which change would occur if the earth's axis were inclined at an angle of 33½° instead of 23½°?   (1) the equator would receive fewer hours of daylight on June 21   (2) the sun's direct ray would move over a larger area of the earth's surface   (3) the altitude of the Pole Star would be increased by 10 degrees   (4) the celestial equator would be farther from the zenith

6. There are greater extremes of temperature at the South Pole than the North Pole because the   (1) continent of Antarctica is primarily a land mass   (2) Gulf Stream flows around the continent of Antarctica   (3) North Pole is inclined toward the sun   (4) South Pole is inclined toward the sun

7. As the number of degrees of latitude from the equator increases, the yearly average temperature generally   (1) decreases   (2) increases   (3) remains the same

8. Adding more carbon dioxide to the atmosphere increases the amount of   (1) radiant energy reflected by the earth   (2) radiation from the sun absorbed by the oceans   (3) radiation from the earth absorbed by the atmosphere   (4) ultraviolet rays striking the earth

9. Which is *not* a cause of our change of seasons?   (1) revolution of the earth   (2) inclination of the earth's axis   (3) variation of the distance to the sun   (4) parallelism of the earth's axis

To answer questions 10 to 14, refer to the graph below, which illustrates the relationship between insolation (energy received from the sun) and ground-radiation during a 24-hour period in New York State on March 21.

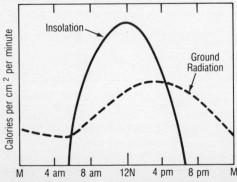

10. From the graph the most logical conclusion that can be made concerning the relationship between insolation and ground-radiation is that, as the insolation   (1) increases, the ground-radiation decreases   (2) increases, the ground-radiation increases   (3) increases, the ground-radiation remains the same   (4) remains the same, the ground-radiation decreases

11. The most logical conclusion that can be made from the relationship between the altitude of the sun throughout the day and the amount of insolation is that, as the sun's altitude   (1) increases, the insolation increases   (2) increases, the insolation decreases   (3) decreases, the insolation increases   (4) decreases, the insolation remains the same

12. According to the graph, the time period in which the energy gained by the soil is greater than the energy lost by the soil is approximately from   (1) midnight to noon   (2) 6 A.M. to 6 P.M.   (3) 6 A.M. to 4 P.M.   (4) noon to midnight

13. At which times are insolation and ground-radiation approximately equal?   (1) midnight and 6 A.M.   (2) 6 A.M. and 4 P.M.   (3) 6 A.M. and 6 P.M.   (4) 6 P.M. and midnight

14. How would the insolation curve be affected if only the latitude were decreased?   (1) the width (time) of the insolation curve would decrease   (2) the width (time) of the insolation curve would increase   (3) the height (energy received) of the insolation curve would decrease   (4) the height (energy received) of the insolation curve would increase

Base your answers to questions 15 through 19 on your knowledge of earth science and the diagrams below. The diagrams represent models of the apparent path of the Sun across the sky for observers at four different locations A through D on the Earth's surface. The observer is located at X in each diagram.

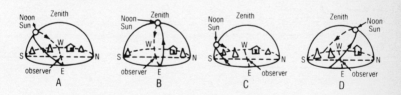

15. At location *A,* on which side of an observer would his shadow fall at local noon?   (1) south side   (2) north side   (3) east side   (4) west side

16. Which location would have the *shortest* duration of insolation for the day shown in the diagrams?   (1) *A*   (2) *B*   (3) *C*   (4) *D*

17. If the model of location *B* represents the apparent path of the Sun observed at the Equator, what is the date at location *B?*   (1) March 21   (2) June 21   (3) October 21   (4) December 21

18. If the model of location *D* represents the apparent path of the Sun on December 21, where is location *D?*   (1) the North Pole (2) 45°N. latitude   (3) the Equator   (4) 45°S. latitude

19. At location *B* three months later, how would the altitude of the noon Sun compare to its present altitude?   (1) The altitude would be less than shown.   (2) The altitude would be greater than shown. (3) The altitude would be the same as shown.

20. In the diagram below, the direct rays of the Sun are striking the Earth's surface at 23½°N. What is the date shown in the diagram?

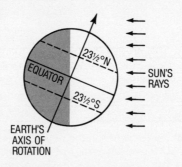

(1) March 21   (2) June 21   (3) September 23   (4) December 21

21. In New York State, summer is warmer than winter because in summer, New York State has   (1) more hours of daylight and is closer to the Sun   (2) more hours of daylight and receives more direct insolation   (3) fewer hours of daylight but is closer to the Sun   (4) fewer hours of daylight but receives more direct insolation

22. If an object with a constant source of energy is in radiative balance, the temperature of the object will   (1) decrease   (2) increase (3) remain the same

23. Which position in the diagram below best represents the Earth on the first day of summer in the Northern Hemisphere?

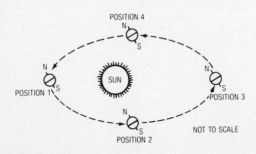

(1) 1   (2) 2   (3) 3   (4) 4

24. Which model best represents how a greenhouse remains warm as a result of insolation from the Sun?

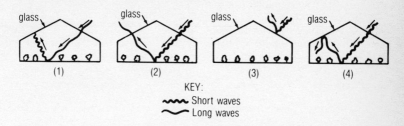

KEY:
~~~ Short waves
~~ Long waves

Base your answers to questions 25 through 29 on your knowledge of earth science and on the diagram below. The diagram represents the Earth at a specific time in its orbit with dash lines indicating radiation from the Sun and points *A* through *H*, locations on the Earth's surface.

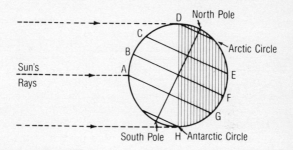

25. Which line represents the Equator?   (1) *AG*   (2) *BF*   (3) *CE* (4) *DH*

26. What is the season in the Northern Hemisphere when the earth is in the position shown in the diagram?   (1) spring   (2) summer (3) fall   (4) winter

27. When the Sun is in the position shown in the diagram, how many hours of daylight would occur at the North Pole during one complete rotation?   (1) 0   (2) 8   (3) 12   (4) 24

28. In which direction would a person located at position *H* have to look to see the Sun at the time shown in the diagram?   (1) north (2) east   (3) south   (4) west

29. Six months after the date indicated by the diagram, which point would receive the Sun's vertical rays at noon?   (1) *A*   (2) *B*   (3) *C* (4) *D*

30. On a hill in New York State in April, remaining winter snow would most likely be found on the side of the hill facing   (1) north (2) south   (3) east   (4) west

31. The graph at the right represents the relationship between the altitude of the Sun at solar noon at various times during the year for a given location on the Earth's surface. What latitude would have that data shown in the graph?

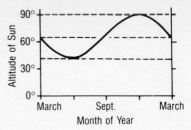

Month of Year

(1) 23½°N.   (2) 23½°S.   (3) 66½°N.   (4) 66½°S.

32. In New York State at 3 P.M. on September 21, the vertical pole shown in the diagram casts a shadow. Which line best approximates the position of that shadow?

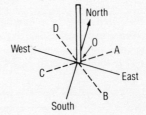

(1) *OA*   (2) *OB*   (3) *OC*   (4) *OD*

Additional Questions

1. Maximum insolation in northern mid-latitudes occurs about (1) June 21   (2) July 3   (3) August 1   (4) September 21

2. The atmosphere   (1) allows most of the visible radiation to pass through   (2) does not absorb ultraviolet radiation   (3) absorbs all of the infrared radiation   (4) reflects most visible radiation

3. For the earth as a whole, about what percent of the incoming insolation do clouds reflect?   (1) 0%   (2) 25%   (3) 50%   (4) 75%

4. When do the highest temperatures occur in the mid-latitudes of the Northern Hemisphere?   (1) at the time of greatest intensity of insolation   (2) before the time of greatest intensity of insolation   (3) after the time of greatest intensity of insolation, because the earth continues to receive more energy from the sun than it loses   (4) after the time of greatest intensity of insolation, because the earth continues to get closer to the sun until July 4

5. If the aerosol pollution in the atmosphere increases, the amount of insolation reaching the earth's surface will   (1) increase   (2) decrease   (3) remain the same

6. Most of the energy radiated from the earth's surface is in the form of   (1) visible light   (2) infrared rays   (3) ultraviolet rays   (4) energy from radioactive decay

7. Carbon dioxide and water vapor help keep the earth warm by (1) absorbing infrared energy   (2) forming clouds   (3) reflecting the radiations from the earth's surface back to the earth's surface (4) converting visible light and ultraviolet rays into infrared energy

To answer questions 8 to 10, refer to the diagram below. It shows five positions of the sun in its path across the sky as seen by an observer looking south. The location is in the continental United States and the date is March 21.

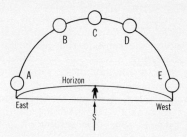

8. The maximum temperature will occur about when the sun is at position   (1) B   (2) C   (3) D   (4) E

9. The duration of insolation on this date is   (1) the greatest it can be   (2) the least it can be   (3) average

10. The greatest intensity of insolation on this date occurs when the sun is in position   (1) A   (2) B   (3) C   (4) D

Energy Exchanges in the Atmosphere—Weather

Variations in insolation (discussed in Topic VI) cause heat energy to be unevenly distributed in the atmosphere. This heat energy tends to move toward a condition of more uniform distribution. That movement of heat energy results in the constant changes in the atmosphere that are a major cause of *weather*.

Weather is the state or condition of the variables of the atmosphere at a location for any given short period of time. **Atmospheric variables** include temperature, pressure, wind, and moisture. Most of the weather changes occur in the troposphere, the part of the atmosphere immediately above the earth's surface. (For the location of the divisions of the atmosphere, see Figure 3-6, page 16.)

ATMOSPHERIC TEMPERATURE

Temperature data is often shown on maps by the use of isolines called **isotherms.**

HEATING OF THE ATMOSPHERE. The sun is the original source of heat for the atmosphere. Generally, the more insolation at a location, the warmer will be the earth's surface and the atmosphere above it. The atmosphere acquires much of its heat directly from the earth's surface, but it also gains energy in other ways. The many ways in which the atmosphere is heated (gains energy) include the following:

1. Conduction by contact with the earth's surface.

2. Direct absorption of insolation from the sun.

3. Absorption of radiations from the earth's surface. (Much of the heat absorption by the atmosphere is due to the presence of water vapor and carbon dioxide; the larger the amounts of water vapor and carbon dioxide, the more heat is absorbed by the atmosphere.)

4. Condensation (change of water vapor to liquid water) and **sublimation** (change of water vapor directly to ice) release large amounts of latent heat, directly heating the atmosphere.

5. The Coriolis effect, resulting from the rotation of the earth, causes a **frictional drag** at the interface of the atmosphere and the earth's surface; this friction produces heat, some of which is added to the atmosphere.

TRANSFER OF HEAT IN THE ATMOSPHERE. Differences in air density cause differences in air pressure. Air pressure differences in turn cause air to move parallel to the earth's surface *(wind)* and in vertical circular patterns called *convection cells* or *currents*. These air movements transfer heat energy within the atmosphere.

ADIABATIC HEATING AND COOLING. When a gas expands, its temperature decreases; when a gas is compressed, its temperature increases. This automatic change in the temperature of a gas due to expansion or compression is called an **adiabatic temperature change.** Thus when air rises in the atmosphere, it expands and its temperature decreases adiabatically; similarly, when it descends, it is compressed and its temperature increases. In the troposphere, temperatures generally decrease with altitude as a result of adiabatic processes. (See "Physical Properties of the Atmosphere" in the *Earth Science Reference Tables*.)

ATMOSPHERIC PRESSURE AND DENSITY

The more dense the atmosphere, the greater the weight of a given volume and therefore the greater the air pressure exerted by it; thus air pressure and density are directly related. **Atmospheric pressure,** also called **barometric pressure** and **air pressure,** is the pressure due to the weight of the overlying atmosphere pushing down on any given area. Standard air pressure (one atmosphere) at sea level is 29.92 inches of mercury or 1013.2 millibars. Barometric pressure in millibars can be converted to inches of mercury using the scale in the *Earth Science Reference Tables*. Air pressure is measured by an instrument called a barometer. Air pressure is often shown on weather maps by the use of isolines called **isobars.**

EFFECT OF TEMPERATURE ON PRESSURE. Changes in the temperature of the air cause changes in air pressure. As the temperature of air increases, the air expands, so that its density and pressure decrease. Decreasing temperature has the reverse effect.

EFFECT OF MOISTURE ON PRESSURE. The greater the amount of water vapor in the air (called **moisture** content, absolute humidity, and vapor pressure), the lower the air density and pressure. The reason for this is that each water molecule in the atmosphere *replaces* a molecule of air, usually oxygen or nitrogen. Since a water molecule weighs less than either an oxygen or a nitrogen molecule, the greater the amount of water vapor in the air, the less dense the air as a whole becomes.

EFFECT OF ALTITUDE ON PRESSURE. As altitude increases, atmospheric density and pressure decrease. (See "Physical Properties of the Atmosphere" in the *Earth Science Reference Tables*.)

To summarize, as either altitude, temperature, or moisture content in the atmosphere increases, air density and air pressure decrease.

WIND

Horizontal movement of air parallel to the earth's surface is called **wind.** Wind is a vector field, because it requires a magnitude and direction to describe it.

WIND SPEED. Winds are caused by differences in air pressure. The difference in air pressure for a specific distance is called the **pressure gradient.** The closer together the isobars on a weather map are, the greater (steeper) the pressure gradient. The greater the pressure gradient is, the greater the wind speed (see Figure 7-1).

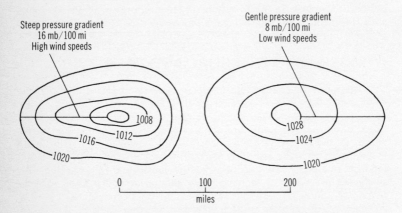

Figure 7-1. Pressure gradient as indicated by closeness of isobars on a weather map. The greater the pressure gradient, the greater the wind speed.

WIND DIRECTION. Air (wind) moves from areas of high pressure to areas of low pressure. However, the Coriolis effect (caused by the earth's rotation) modifies that pattern of movement, deflecting winds to the right in the Northern Hemisphere and to the left in the Southern Hemisphere. Figure 7-2 illustrates how the wind directions are modified by the Coriolis effect.

A wind is named for the direction from which it comes; for example, a wind blowing *from* the south *toward* the north is called a *south* wind.

Figure 7-2. Deflection of winds by the Coriolis effect. The dashed arrow in each case shows the direction the wind would flow if there were no Coriolis effect. The solid arrow shows the actual path of the wind. If you face with the wind, it is always deflected to the right in the Northern Hemisphere and to the left in the Southern Hemisphere.

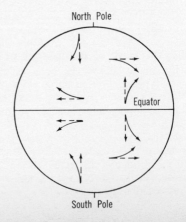

CIRCULATION OF THE ATMOSPHERE

CONVECTION CELLS. The unequal distribution of insolation on the earth results in unequal heating and differences in air pressure. Cooler air, being denser, sinks toward the earth under the influence of gravity, causing the less dense warmer air to rise. The result is a series of convection cells around the earth at various latitudes, as shown in Figure 7-3. As indicated by the solid arrows, there are upward currents in the vicinity of 0° latitude (the equator) and 60° north and south latitudes. Downward currents exist near 30° and 90° north and south latitudes. Regions where air comes together to form vertical currents are called regions of **convergence** (labeled "C" in Figure 7-3). Regions where air spreads out from the vertical currents are called regions of **divergence** (labeled "D").

PLANETARY WINDS. At the earth's surface, winds flow horizontally away from regions of divergence and toward regions of convergence. Because of the Coriolis effect, these winds are deflected to the right in the Northern Hemisphere and to the left in the Southern Hemisphere, as indicated by the dashed arrows in Figure 7-3. The result is a series of **planetary wind belts** within which the winds move generally in a specific direction much of the time.

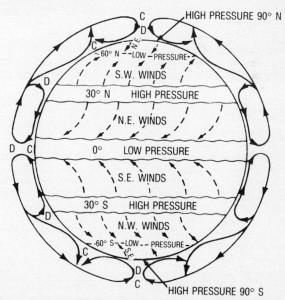

Figure 7-3. Planetary wind and pressure belts in the troposphere. The drawing shows the locations of the belts near the time of an equinox. The locations shift somewhat with the changing latitude of the sun's vertical ray. In the Northern Hemisphere the belts shift northward in summer and southward in winter.

WEATHER MOVEMENT.   Much of the continental United States is affected by planetary winds that blow from the southwest. Therefore, weather changes in the United States move generally from a southwesterly direction to a northeasterly direction.

SURFACE OCEAN CURRENTS.   The surface ocean currents are caused by wind blowing over the oceans and transferring energy to the water. The direction of these currents is affected by the direction of the planetary winds.

ATMOSPHERIC MOISTURE

Atmospheric moisture exists in three states of matter: liquid, solid, and gas. Gaseous water in the atmosphere is commonly called **water vapor.**

SOURCES OF ATMOSPHERIC MOISTURE.   Moisture in the form of water vapor enters the atmosphere by *evaporation* and *transpiration*. **Evaporation** is the process by which a liquid changes to a gas; **transpiration** is the process by which plants release water vapor as part of their life functions. Collectively, evaporation and transpiration are called **evapotranspiration.** The oceans, which cover about 70% of the earth's surface, are the primary source of most atmospheric moisture.

ENERGY OF EVAPORATION AND TRANSPIRATION.   Large amounts of energy (approximately 540 calories/gram) are required to change liquid water into water vapor during processes of evaporation and transpiration. When evapotranspiration occurs, the more energetic water molecules leave the liquid and form water vapor. Since the molecules leaving the liquid are the more energetic ones, the average kinetic energy of the molecules remaining in the liquid decreases. As a result, the temperature of an evaporating liquid is somewhat lower than its surroundings.

FACTORS AFFECTING EVAPORATION RATE.   The net evaporation rate at a location is determined by (1) *the amount of energy available—* the more energy available, that is, the higher the temperature, the faster the evaporation of available water; (2) *surface area of the water—*the more spread out the water, the greater the air-water interface and the faster the evaporation; (3) *vapor pressure of the air over the water—* the higher the vapor pressure (moisture content), the closer the air is to being saturated and the slower the net evaporation rate.

PROCESS OF EVAPORATION.   Figure 7-4 helps to explain what happens when water—or any other liquid—evaporates. Diagram A shows a closed container of air into which some water has just been added. We assume there are no water vapor molecules in the air at this moment. However, as soon as water is placed in the container, some of its more energetic molecules begin to escape into the air above and mingle with the other gas molecules that are present. Diagram B shows the situation a short time later. There are now some water molecules in the air, represented by the four molecules shown. We see two more molecules in the process of leaving the water. However, one of the other four is about to enter the water, so that there will be five molecules in the air after this happens. Diagram C shows the situation some time later. There are now eight water molecules in the air. Again, two more are about to leave the water. But now *two* of the eight are about to return to the water. The net result will be eight molecules in the air—the same number as before. We have a condition of *dynamic equilibrium,* in which the rate at which water is entering the gaseous state (evaporation) equals the rate at which water vapor is returning to the liquid state (condensation).

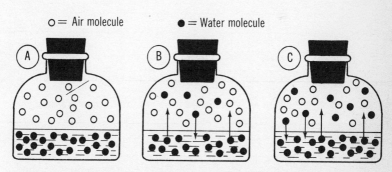

○ = Air molecule   ● = Water molecule

Figure 7-4. The saturation of the air over an evaporating liquid. At A, no evaporation has occurred. At B, evaporation is proceeding faster than condensation. At C, equilibrium has been reached. The air is **saturated** with vapor, and evaporation and condensation are occurring at the same rate. The pressure of the vapor under these conditions is called the **saturation vapor pressure.** The higher the temperature, the greater the saturation vapor pressure.

SATURATION VAPOR PRESSURE.   In the equilibrium condition described above, the air contains the maximum amount of water vapor it can hold (represented by eight molecules). This condition is called **saturation.** Water vapor, being a gas, exerts a pressure, which is called **vapor pressure.** When the air is saturated with water vapor (at capacity), the vapor pressure is called the **saturation vapor pressure.**

SATURATION VAPOR PRESSURE AND TEMPERATURE.   The saturation vapor pressure (and capacity) increases rapidly with an increase in temperature, as shown in the graph in Figure 7-5 (page 88). This means that the moisture capacity of the air increases with an increase in temperature.

ABSOLUTE HUMIDITY.   Humidity, like moisture, is a general term that refers to the water vapor content of the atmosphere. The amount of water vapor in each unit volume of air is called the **absolute humidity.**

There is a definite vapor pressure corresponding to each value of absolute humidity. The vapor pressure increases in direct proportion to the absolute humidity, so that vapor pressure can be used as a measure of absolute humidity.

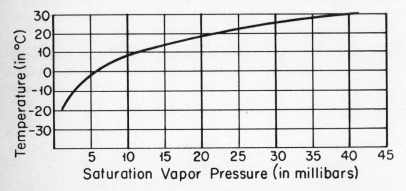

Figure 7-5. Relationship of temperature and saturation vapor pressure.

RELATIVE HUMIDITY.   **Relative humidity** is the ratio of the amount of water vapor in the air to the maximum amount it can hold (its **moisture capacity**). It is also the ratio of the actual vapor pressure to the saturation vapor pressure. The closer the vapor pressure is to the saturation vapor pressure, the higher the relative humidity. (Be sure to understand that relative humidity is a percentage of saturation, *not* a percentage of the volume of air present.)

RELATIVE HUMIDITY AND TEMPERATURE.   At any given time and place, the air has a certain absolute humidity, with a corresponding vapor pressure. If the temperature of the air changes, but the amount of water vapor (that is, the absolute humidity) remains the same, the relative humidity will change. For example, if the temperature increases, the relative humidity will decrease. This occurs because the saturation vapor pressure increases with the increase in temperature, while the actual vapor pressure remains the same. On the other hand, if the temperature decreases, while the absolute humidity and vapor pressure remain the same, the relative humidity will increase.

RELATIVE HUMIDITY AND VAPOR PRESSURE.   If the temperature of the air remains constant, but more water vapor is added to it (for example, by evapotranspiration), the absolute humidity, the vapor pressure, and the relative humidity will all increase.

DEW POINT TEMPERATURE.   If the temperature of the air decreases, while the vapor pressure remains the same, the temperature will eventually reach a point at which the saturation vapor pressure equals the actual vapor pressure. At this temperature, the relative humidity will be 100%, that is, the air will be saturated. This temperature is called the **dew point temperature,** or simply the **dew point.** Any further drop in temperature will result in condensation or sublimation of water, since there would then be more water vapor in the air than it can hold.

DEW POINT AND VAPOR PRESSURE.   The dew point temperature depends only on the absolute humidity or vapor pressure of the air, and not on the relative humidity. As the vapor pressure or the amount of water vapor in the air increases, the dew point rises.

MEASURING RELATIVE HUMIDITY.   It is difficult to measure vapor pressure or determine saturation vapor pressure directly. Relative humidity is therefore measured by indirect methods. One such method uses an instrument called a *psychrometer.* This instrument contains an ordinary thermometer called the **dry-bulb thermometer,** and another thermometer with a wick around its bulb, called the **wet-bulb thermometer.** When the wick is moistened and the thermometers are whirled in the air, the temperature of the wet-bulb drops because of the cooling effect of the evaporation of the water. The amount of cooling depends on the rate of evaporation, and is therefore related to the relative humidity. A chart like the "Dew-point Temperature Chart" in the *Earth Science Reference Tables* can then be used to determine the relative humidity from the wet and dry bulb readings.

USING THE DEW-POINT TEMPERATURE CHART.   To explain the use of the dew-point temperature chart, we will use a specific example. We will assume that the dry bulb reads 11°C, and the wet bulb reads 8°C. The difference between these two readings, which is 3°C in this case, is called the **wet bulb depression.** To simplify the procedure, we will use Figure 7-6 on page 90, which reproduces only that part of the dew-point temperature chart required for this example.

Step 1. Find the dry bulb reading (11°C) along the left side of the chart. Note that a dry bulb thermometer reading is the same as a regular temperature reading.

Step 2. Note the saturation vapor pressure that corresponds to this temperature. For 11°C, the saturation vapor pressure is 13.0 millibars.

Step 3. Find the wet bulb depression (3°C) along the lower right side of the chart.

Step 4. Follow the horizontal line for the dry bulb reading to the right until it meets the vertical line running up from the wet bulb depression.

Step 5. Note the line running diagonally through this intersection. This line tells you the dew point corresponding to the wet and dry bulb readings. In this case it is one of the heavy diagonal lines. It is labeled "5," which means that the dew point is 5°C.

Step 6. Follow this dew point line down to the left until it meets the dry bulb scale. You will notice that it meets the dry bulb scale at the same value of 5°C. All the dew point lines do the same thing. This is to be expected, since if the air temperature is at the dew point, the dry bulb will read the dew point temperature directly.

Step 7. Now note the saturation vapor pressure corresponding to the dew point. It is 8.7 millibars in this case. This is the actual vapor pressure of the air, since the dew point is the temperature at which the saturation vapor pressure equals the actual vapor pressure.

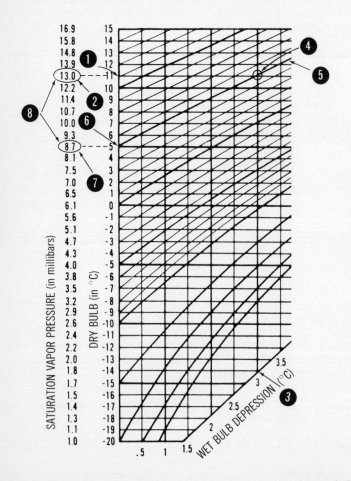

Figure 7-6. Using the dew-point temperature chart to determine relative humidity. See text for explanation. The complete chart will be found in the *Earth Science Reference Tables.*

Step 8. Calculate the relative humidity in percent by dividing the actual vapor pressure (8.7) by the saturation vapor pressure (13.0) and multiplying by 100:

$$\frac{8.7}{13.0} \times 100 = 67\% \text{ (approx.)}$$

CONDENSATION, SUBLIMATION, AND CLOUDS. If the temperature of the air cools (often adiabatically) below the dew point, the water vapor will usually condense, changing to microscopic liquid water droplets or ice crystals. In the atmosphere, if the temperature is above 0°C, condensation produces water droplets which as a group appear as a *cloud*. Some clouds are composed of ice crystals, which form when water vapor "condenses" below 0°C by the process of sublimation. A **cloud** is therefore a collection of liquid water droplets and/or ice crystals suspended in the atmosphere.

At the earth's surface, condensation produces dew, and sublimation produces frost.

CONDENSATION SURFACE. Besides needing saturated air, condensation requires a surface upon which the vapor can condense. This is called the **condensation surface.** In the formation of clouds, the condensation surfaces are aerosols.

PRECIPITATION. **Precipitation** is the falling of liquid or solid water from clouds toward the surface of the earth. The forms in which precipitation occurs are rain, snow, sleet, and hail. For precipitation to occur, the ice crystals or water droplets in clouds must become big enough so that they will fall.

ATMOSPHERIC TRANSPARENCY AND PRECIPITATION. The more pollutants added to the atmosphere by the activities of nature and people, the more aerosols are present. The more aerosols in the air, the less transparent the atmosphere is to insolation. Condensation in cloud formation incorporates some of the aerosols, and these aerosols are removed from the atmosphere during precipitation. The falling liquid or solid water also collects other aerosols on the way down, thus lowering air pollution levels and cleaning the atmosphere.

AIR MASSES AND FRONTS

Much of the weather of the continental United States is the result of the invasion of *air masses* and their interactions. An **air mass** is a large body of air in the troposphere with similar characteristics of pressure, moisture, and temperature.

SOURCE REGIONS. An air mass forms when a large mass of air stagnates over a part of the earth's surface for a period of time and thus acquires some of the characteristics of that surface. The geographic regions in which air masses are formed are called **source regions.** The source regions for the air masses that invade the United States are shown in Figure 7-7.

If the source region is at a high latitude, the air mass will have a low temperature; if the source region is at a low latitude, the air mass will have a high temperature. If the source region is land, the air mass will be dry; if the source region is water, the air mass will be moist. Air masses are described as arctic (A), polar (P), or tropical (T), depending on whether they originate at high or low latitudes. Air masses are also described as either continental (c) or maritime (m), depending on whether they originate over land or water. These air mass symbols are found in the *Earth Science Reference Tables.* When an air mass remains stationary over its source region for a period of time, it tends to acquire relatively uniform temperature and moisture conditions at any one altitude within it.

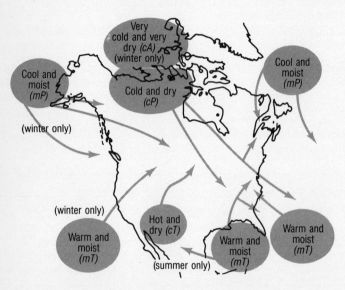

Figure 7-7. Source regions and tracks of air masses that affect the weather of the continental United States.

LOWS AND HIGHS.   Portions of the troposphere are divided into two types according to pressure and direction of circulation of winds. **LOWS,** also called **cyclones,** have low pressure. The pressure in a LOW is lowest at its center, and thus winds blow toward the center. The winds are deflected by the Coriolis effect, so that in the Northern Hemisphere a counterclockwise circulation occurs within LOWS, as shown in Figure 7-8. **HIGHS,** or **anticyclones,** have high pressure. The pressure in a HIGH is greatest at its center, and thus winds blow out from the center. The general circulation around HIGHS is clockwise in the Northern Hemisphere.

FRONTS. Where two air masses of different characteristics meet, an interface called a **front** develops (see Figure 7-9 on page 94). A **cold front** is the interface between an advancing cold air mass and a warmer air mass, where the underlying cold air pushes forward like a wedge. A **warm front** is a front between an advancing warm air mass and a retreating wedge of a cooler air mass; because the cool air is heavier, the warm air mass is forced to rise as it advances. An **occluded front** is the interface between opposing wedges of cold air masses formed when a cold front overtakes a warm front, lifting the warm air mass off the ground. Occluded fronts are important because they are associated with the formation of mid-latitude cyclones (LOWS), as shown in Figure 7-9. When two adjacent air masses of different characteristics remain in the same positions, they form a **stationary front.**

At fronts between air masses of different temperatures the warmer air, being less dense, is forced to rise. This results in the unstable conditions that are characteristic of fronts and that produce much of the precipitation of the continental United States.

FRONTS AND WEATHER MAPS. On weather maps half-circles and/or triangles are used on the lines representing fronts to indicate the type of front. See Figure 7-8 for specific front symbols. The triangles and half-circles point in the direction the fronts and associated air masses are moving.

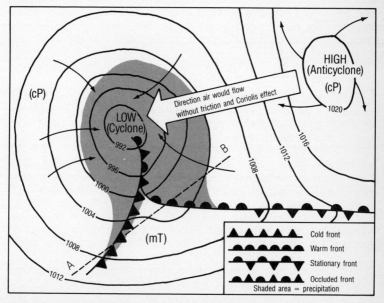

Figure 7-8. Circulation of winds and interaction of high and low pressure air masses in the Northern Hemisphere. Air circulates clockwise in a HIGH and counterclockwise in a LOW.

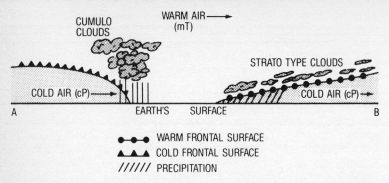

WARM FRONTAL SURFACE
COLD FRONTAL SURFACE
PRECIPITATION

Figure 7-9. Cross-sectional view of the ---- line in Figure 7-8. The conditions of the cold front at left are: steep slope, cumulo (puffy) clouds, and precipitation just before and after the point where the front meets the earth's surface. The conditions of the warm front at right are: gentle frontal surface, strato (layered) clouds, and a broad band of precipitation preceding the point where the front meets the earth's surface.

TRACKS OF AIR MASSES AND FRONTS. In the United States, the **tracks** (paths) and rate of movement of air masses and fronts can be predicted on the basis of past observations. Thus, the succession of weather changes that accompanies such movements can be reasonably forecasted. The direction of some of these tracks is indicated by the arrows in Figure 7-7. Most of the tracks follow a westerly to easterly route in the United States because of our location in the southwest planetary winds.

WEATHER PREDICTION AND PROBABILITY

Most weather predictions, or forecasts, are based on the **probability** (chance) of occurrence of weather variables based on relationships between weather variables. As an example, suppose that in a twenty-day period the air pressure drops on ten days and that the air temperature increases on eight of those ten days. What is the probability that air temperature will increase if air pressure is decreasing? Based on the data above, there is an 8/10 or 80% chance of increasing temperature. In actual cases of computing probability, the Weather Service uses large amounts of data collected over many years on which to base predictions.

Probabilities have been worked out for a vast number of possible relationships between variables. Many of the relationships are very complex, but some of them are simple direct or inverse relationships. Some of the simple relationships are listed below:

1. Air pressure is related to temperature changes: As temperature increases, pressure decreases, and vice versa.

2. The chance of precipitation increases as the air temperature gets closer to the dew point temperature. This is the case because the smaller the difference between the air temperature and the dew point temperature, the nearer the air is to saturation, condensation, and precipitation.

3. The greater the pressure gradient in an area, the faster is the speed of the winds.

STATION MODELS.   On weather maps the weather conditions for each weather station are shown by symbols arranged in order around a small circle. These symbols and the circle make up a **station model,** which gives the latest readings for all the weather variables. For a sample of a station model see Figure 7-10 below.

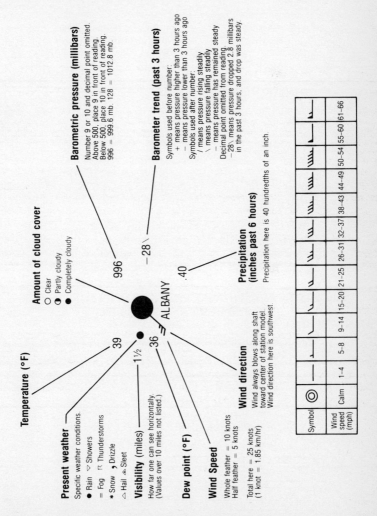

Figure 7-10. Sample Station Model For Weather Map. (Also see the charts of weather map symbols in the *Earth Science Reference Tables*.)

VOCABULARY

weather	relative humidity
atmospheric variables	moisture capacity
isotherm	dew point temperature
condensation	cloud
sublimation	condensation surface
frictional drag	precipitation
adiabatic temperature change	air mass
atmospheric pressure	continental polar air mass (cP)
barometric pressure	continental tropical air mass (cT)
air pressure	maritime tropical air mass (mT)
isobar	maritime polar air mass (mP)
moisture	source region
wind	LOW
pressure gradient	cyclone
convergence	HIGH
divergence	anticyclone
planetary wind belts	front
water vapor	cold front
evaporation	warm front
transpiration	occluded front
evapotranspiration	stationary front
saturation	track
vapor pressure	probability
saturation vapor pressure	visibility
absolute humidity	present weather

QUESTIONS ON TOPIC VII—ENERGY EXCHANGES IN THE ATMOSPHERE AND WEATHER

Questions in Recent Regents Exams (end of book)

June 1984: 5, 16, 17, 18, 19, 21, 51, 79, 81, 82, 83, 84, 85, 105
June 1985: 7, 17, 18, 19, 20, 21, 22, 23, 70, 71, 72, 73, 74, 75, 101
June 1986: 19–24, 76, 81–85
June 1987: 18–21, 24, 25, 53; 71–75, 104, 105

Questions from Earlier Regents Exams

1. Planetary winds do *not* blow directly north or south because of (1) the Coriolis effect (2) gravitational force (3) magnetic force (4) centripetal force

2. Adding more carbon dioxide to the atmosphere increases the amount of (1) radiant energy reflected by the earth (2) radiation from the sun absorbed by the oceans (3) radiation from the earth absorbed by the atmosphere (4) ultraviolet rays striking the earth

3. During which part of the day is the relative humidity usually *lowest?*   (1) morning   (2) midafternoon   (3) evening   (4) late night

4. As the air descends on the leeward side of the mountain (the side sheltered from the wind), its temperature will   (1) decrease due to expansion   (2) increase due to expansion   (3) decrease due to compression   (4) increase due to compression

5. The dry-bulb temperature is 20°C. The wet bulb temperature is 17°C. What is the dew point?   (1) 12°   (2) 13°   (3) 14°   (4) 15°

6. The air temperature is 7°C and the dew point is 2°C. What is the approximate relative humidity?   (1) 30%   (2) 50%   (3) 70%   (4) 90%

7. Methods of rainmaking are usually directed toward attempts to   (1) increase the temperature of the air   (2) increase the moisture in clouds   (3) raise the height of the cloud base   (4) provide nuclei for condensation

8. Air molecules have the greatest average kinetic energy at a temperature of   (1) 0°C   (2) 0°K   (3) 0°F   (4) 200°K

9. If the air temperature is 10°C and the dew point temperature is 0°C, what is the approximate relative humidity?   (1) 100%   (2) 50%   (3) 35%   (4) 0%

10. If each of the following covered an area of 1 square kilometer of the earth's surface, which would transfer the most moisture to the atmosphere on a warm summer day?   (1) a lake   (2) a city   (3) a forest   (4) a glacier

11. Which instrument is used in detecting the interface between two air masses?   (1) barometer   (2) seismometer   (3) spectrometer   (4) photometer

12. Which is the primary source of energy for ocean currents and waves?   (1) the moon   (2) the atmosphere   (3) the continents   (4) the sun

13. Because the equator receives the greatest amount of the sun's energy during the year, the equator is generally an area of   (1) high pressure and high precipitation   (2) high pressure and low precipitation   (3) low pressure and high precipitation   (4) low pressure and low precipitation

14. At a dew point temperature of −10°C, the saturation vapor pressure is   (1) 1.4 millibars   (2) 2.6 millibars   (3) 10 millibars   (4) 12.2 millibars

15. When the dry-bulb temperature reading is 10°C and the wet-bulb temperature reading is 2°C, the dew point temperature of the air is   (1) −15°C   (2) −8°C   (3) 2°C   (4) 10°C

16. In a parcel of air, the saturation vapor pressure is 15.8 millibars at the dry-bulb temperature reading and 11.4 millibars at the dew point temperature reading. What is the relative humidity of the parcel of air? (1) 17%   (2) 34%   (3) 72%   (4) 90%

17. As the rate of molecular activity of a liquid increases, the rate of evaporation of that liquid   (1) decreases   (2) increases   (3) remains the same

18. As the exposed area of a moist object decreases, the rate of evaporation of the liquid from that object   (1) decreases   (2) increases (3) remains the same

19. As the amount of light energy striking a moist object increases, the rate of evaporation of the liquid from that object   (1) decreases (2) increases   (3) remains the same

20. As the amount of water vapor in a given volume of air increases, the rate of evaporation from a moist object   (1) decreases   (2) increases   (3) remains the same

21. As the temperature of a given volume of saturated air decreases, the condensation   (1) decreases   (2) increases   (3) remains the same

To answer questions 22 through 25, refer to the graph below, which shows the hourly surface air temperature, dew point, and relative humidity for a twenty-four-hour period during the month of May at Washington, D.C.

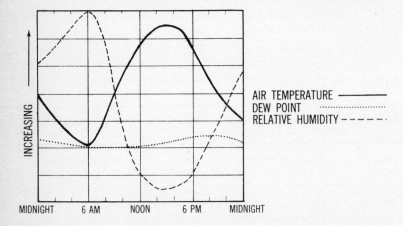

22. The greatest net change in air temperature occurred during the period from   (1) midnight to 6 A.M.   (2) 6 A.M. to noon   (3) noon to 6 P.M.   (4) 6 P.M. to midnight

23. Which conclusion concerning the relationship between the dew point and air temperature is best justified by the data shown?   (1) changes in dew point do not necessarily occur when air temperature changes (2) the dew point increases in proportion to an increase in air temperature   (3) the dew point increases in proportion to a decrease in air temperature   (4) changes in dew point are caused by air temperature changes but not in proportion to these changes

24. The graph indicates that as the air temperature increases, the relative humidity   (1) increases   (2) decreases   (3) sometimes increases and sometimes decreases   (4) remains the same

25. Condensation is most likely to occur at approximately   (1) 6 A.M.   (2) 9 A.M.   (3) 7 P.M.   (4) 10 P.M.

26. To say that the relative humidity on a given day is 70 percent means that the air   (1) is composed of 70 percent water vapor   (2) holds 70 percent of its water vapor capacity   (3) contains 70 parts of water to 100 parts of dry air   (4) contains the same amount of water that it would contain at 70°F

27. During a given year in Albany, New York, the relative humidity for a certain day in February is exactly the same as that for a certain day in June. Which is the most probable explanation?   (1) an unusually high pressure in February   (2) an unusually high pressure in June   (3) a difference in the dew points   (4) a turbulent air mass in June

28. On a certain day in Syracuse, New York, there is a high-pressure center directly north and a low-pressure center directly south. Because of the effect of the Coriolis force, the air in Syracuse will   (1) blow directly to the south   (2) blow directly to the north   (3) be deflected toward the southwest   (4) be deflected toward the northeast

29. As the air temperature rises, the relative humidity   (1) increases   (2) decreases   (3) remains the same

30. As the amount of condensation increases, the rate of cooling of a rising parcel of air   (1) increases   (2) decreases   (3) remains the same

31. As a parcel of air increases in altitude, its pressure will   (1) decrease   (2) increase   (3) remain the same

32. The energy supply of a hurricane comes from   (1) heat released by condensation   (2) evaporation of tropical waters   (3) the tradewinds   (4) discharge of lightning

33. During the summer a warm, moist air mass moved over Texas. This air mass probably originated over   (1) northern Canada   (2) the Pacific Ocean   (3) southern Arizona   (4) the Gulf of Mexico

34. Which best describes the movement of air in a high pressure air mass (anticyclone) in the Northern Hemisphere?   (1) clockwise and away from the center   (2) clockwise and toward the center   (3) counterclockwise and away from the center   (4) counterclockwise and toward the center

35. As the pressure gradient increases, wind velocity   (1) decreases   (2) increases   (3) remains the same

36. Air at a temperature of 60°F and a relative humidity of 51% was warmed to a temperature of 70°F, but the relative humidity remained at 51%. What change occurred in the moisture content?   (1) the moisture content decreased   (2) the moisture content increased   (3) the moisture content remained the same

37. The transfer of heat energy within the troposphere occurs primarily by   (1) insolation   (2) conduction   (3) radiation   (4) convection

38. The original characteristics of an air mass are determined by   (1) surface over which it is formed   (2) pressure of the air mass   (3) insolation it receives   (4) rotation of the earth

39. In the Northern Hemisphere, a wind blowing from the south will be deflected toward the   (1) northwest   (2) northeast   (3) southwest   (4) southeast

Refer to the weather map below to answer questions 40 through 50.

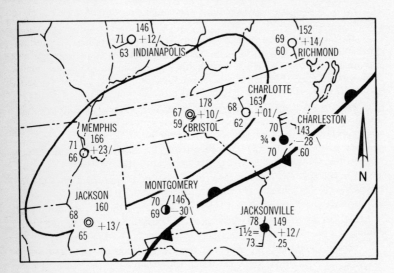

40. Which of the following locations has the highest wind velocity? (1) Jacksonville   (2) Charlotte   (3) Indianapolis   (4) Jackson

41. What type of front is found between Montgomery and Jacksonville?   (1) cold   (2) warm   (3) stationary   (4) occluded

42. The barometric reading in millibars of the isobar that passes through Jackson, Miss., is   (1) 160   (2) 1,016   (3) 1,060   (4) 1,600

43. Which station has the highest relative humidity?   (1) Montgomery   (2) Jackson   (3) Bristol   (4) Richmond

44. Which is characteristic of most weather stations within the closed isobar?   (1) low velocity winds   (2) overcast skies   (3) a barometer now lower than three hours ago   (4) poor visibility

45. At which location is visibility the lowest?   (1) Charleston   (2) Jacksonville   (3) Montgomery   (4) Bristol

46. If the front started moving in a northwesterly direction, in a few hours temperatures at Montgomery would most likely   (1) increase   (2) decrease   (3) remain the same

47. At Charlotte wind is blowing from what compass direction? (1) South   (2) Northeast   (3) Northwest   (4) Southeast

48. The most precipitation in the six hours before the time of the map was reported at which station?   (1) Memphis   (2) Charleston   (3) Jacksonville   (4) Richmond

49. The air mass found south and east of the front would most likely be classified as a(n)   (1) cP   (2) cT   (3) mT   (4) mP

50. What was the barometric pressure at Indianapolis 3 hours before the time of the map?   (1) 1014.6 mb   (2) 1015.8 mb   (3) 1013.4 mb   (4) 1026.6 mb

51. A barometer indicates a pressure of 30 inches of mercury at sea level; at 3½ miles above sea level, it indicates a pressure of 15 inches. What is the best conclusion to be drawn from these data?   (1) humidity affects the pressure   (2) temperature affects the pressure   (3) of the total mass of air, about 99 percent is within 3½ miles of sea level   (4) of the total mass of air, about 50 percent is more than 3½ miles above sea level

52. In order for a large mass of air to acquire uniform characteristics, it must   (1) stagnate over a large land or water surface   (2) descend from the upper troposphere   (3) move rapidly with the prevailing westerlies   (4) move in the general planetary circulation

53. As moving air descends the leeward side of a mountain, its moisture-holding capacity   (1) increases   (2) decreases   (3) remains the same

54. According to the *Earth Science Reference Tables,* an air pressure of 30.15 inches of mercury is equal to   (1) 1017 mb   (2) 1019 mb   (3) 1021 mb   (4) 1023 mb

55. Which diagram shows the *usual* paths followed by low-pressure storm centers as they pass across the United States?

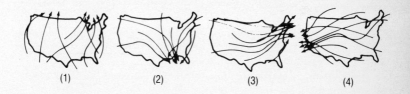

(1)   (2)   (3)   (4)

56. Which process is most likely to remove pollutants from the air?   (1) precipitation   (2) evaporation   (3) transpiration   (4) runoff

57. A temperature of 104° Fahrenheit is equal to a temperature of (1) 40°C   (2) 72°C   (3) 104°C   (4) 136°C

Additional Questions

1. Which best describes the relationship of the pressure field gradient and wind speed?   (1) the closer the isobars, the steeper the gradient and the greater the wind speed   (2) the farther apart the isobars, the steeper the gradient and the greater the wind speed   (3) the closer the isobars, the steeper the gradient and the less the wind speed   (4) the closer the isobars, the less steep the gradient and the less the wind speed

2. Which is *not* true about wind?   (1) wind direction is named for the direction toward which the wind blows   (2) wind moves from regions of higher pressure to lower pressure   (3) the steeper the gradient, the greater the wind speed   (4) wind is horizontal movement of air

3. At any given altitude within an air mass, which fields are nearly uniform?   (1) wind speed and amount of water vapor   (2) wind direction and pressure   (3) temperature and amount of water vapor   (4) temperature and wind speed

4. Where is precipitation the most probable?   (1) at the center of an anticyclone   (2) near the interface between air masses of different temperatures   (3) in areas of descending air   (4) in regions of low relative humidity

5. Which is required to cause evaporation and transpiration? (1) increase in vapor pressure   (2) decrease in temperature   (3) addition of wind   (4) addition of energy

6. As the average molecule in liquid water becomes more energetic, the rate of evaporation of water   (1) increases   (2) decreases (3) remains the same

7. Dynamic equilibrium exists when   (1) evaporation and condensation stop   (2) condensation occurs only   (3) saturation vapor pressure is reached   (4) evaporation occurs only

8. As the vapor pressure of the air increases at constant temperature, the rate at which water is lost by evaporation at an air-water interface   (1) increases   (2) decreases   (3) remains the same

9. Suppose the air is at saturation vapor pressure and the air is being cooled. The water vapor will begin to   (1) change to a gas (2) precipitate   (3) evaporate   (4) condense

10. Air moves from regions of   (1) low density to high density (2) low pressure to high pressure   (3) high temperature to low temperature   (4) low humidity to high humidity

11. As air rises, its temperature   (1) increases   (2) decreases (3) remains the same

12. As air descends,   (1) the pressure increases, the air expands, the air becomes cool   (2) the pressure increases, the air contracts, the air becomes cool   (3) the pressure decreases, the air contracts, the air becomes warm   (4) the pressure increases, the air contracts, the air becomes warm

13. The process by which water vapor changes directly to ice is called   (1) evaporation   (2) sublimation   (3) transpiration   (4) condensation

14. At which temperature will water vapor change directly to ice? (1) 100°C   (2) 32°C   (3) 10°C   (4) −10°C

15. Water vapor forms clouds by means of   (1) evaporation and transpiration   (2) evaporation and condensation   (3) condensation and sublimation   (4) condensation and transpiration

16. Precipitation occurs (1) whenever air cannot support the droplets or ice crystals (2) whenever the dew point is reached (3) whenever air is rising in large quantities (4) whenever the clouds are thick and dark

17. In approaching the center of a cyclone on a weather map, the numerical values of the isobars (1) increase (2) may increase or decrease (3) decrease (4) remain the same

18. What is *not* true when the vapor pressure of the air equals the saturation vapor pressure? (1) condensation can occur (2) precipitation must begin (3) the relative humidity is 100% (4) a dynamic equilibrium is reached

19. Moisture enters the atmosphere from plants by a process called (1) hydration (2) evaporation (3) condensation (4) transpiration

20. When air rises, the rate of cooling of the air with increasing altitude decreases when condensation begins. Why? (1) condensation requires energy (2) condensation gives off energy (3) rising air expands (4) the clouds formed reduce the amount of insolation

21. The more carbon fuels people use, the greater the chance that temperatures on the earth will increase. Why? (1) the burning of carbon fuels increases the amount of radioactive decay of carbon (2) the burning of carbon fuels forms carbon dioxide (3) the smoke produced by the burning of carbon fuels increases the amount of aerosols in the atmosphere (4) the burning of carbon fuels decreases the amount of oxygen in the atmosphere

22. Which of the following would most easily result in condensation? (1) pure dry air rising (2) pure moist air rising (3) dry air with dust rising (4) moist air with dust rising

23. A change in which of the following would have the least effect on air density? (1) elevation (2) temperature (3) wind (4) moisture

24. The direct source of energy for ocean currents is (1) the sun (2) differences in insolation (3) differences in air pressure (4) wind

25. Which of the following directly leads to precipitation? (1) condensation (2) water droplets combining (3) air rising so that vapor pressure equals saturation vapor pressure (4) adiabatic cooling of air

26. Which could *not* form if the dew point were below 0°C? (1) snow (2) frost (3) hail (4) rain

27. Suppose that during five days in which pressure decreased, it rained on four of the days. Based on that data, what is the probability of rain when there is a pressure decrease? (1) 10% (2) 12.5% (3) 50% (4) 80%

28. Weather predictions are expressed as a probability of occurrence based on many variables of the atmosphere, but many predictions are incorrect. This would indicate that the majority of atmospheric variables are (1) related in a direct fashion (2) related in an indirect fashion (3) not related (4) related in a complex fashion

To answer questions 29 through 34 refer to the adjoining diagram, which shows movement of air in the lower part of the atmosphere around the time of an equinox.

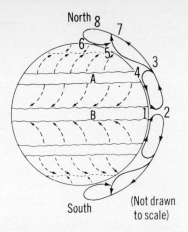

29. The movement of air from 1 to 2 to 3 to 4 to 1 would be called a(n)

(1) advection cell

(2) adiabatic cell

(3) convection cell

(4) Coriolis cell

30. What is the basic underlying reason for the movement of air shown?   (1) differences in insolation   (2) differences in air density   (3) differences in pressure gradient   (4) differences in Coriolis effect

31. How does the movement of air at position 2 compare to the movement of air at position 4?   (1) they both have converging air   (2) they both have diverging air   (3) position 2 is diverging and position 4 is converging   (4) position 2 is converging and position 4 is diverging

32. What would be the most likely cause of the movement of air at position 1?   (1) low moisture content and low temperature   (2) high moisture content and high temperature   (3) low moisture content and high temperature   (4) high moisture content and low temperature

33. The air moves at the surface of the earth, from position A to position B, because   (1) positions A and B have low pressure   (2) positions A and B have high pressure   (3) position A has low pressure and position B has high pressure   (4) position A has high pressure and position B has low pressure

34. Condensation would most likely occur at position   (1) 3   (2) 4   (3) 6   (4) 7

35. The vapor pressure of the atmosphere most often increases   (1) at air-water interfaces   (2) during condensation   (3) during adiabatic cooling   (4) when water droplets are combining

36. The most energy is required to cause   (1) evapotranspiration   (2) condensation   (3) precipitation   (4) change from water vapor to ice

37. Suppose in a ten-day period there were clouds in the sky five days and during those cloudy days it rained on three days. Based on this data, what is the probability of rain when there are clouds in the sky?   (1) 30%   (2) 50%   (3) 60%   (4) 90%

38. If the temperature increases and the dew point remains the same, the probability of rain   (1) increases   (2) decreases   (3) remains the same

39. The four station models below show the weather at the same place but at different times during the approach and passing of a cold front. Which grouping places the four models in their correct order of occurrence?   (1) 1, 3, 4, 2   (2) 1, 2, 4, 3   (3) 4, 2, 1, 3   (4) 4, 3, 2, 1

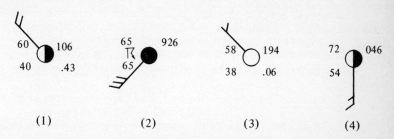

(1)   (2)   (3)   (4)

40. Which best describes the movement of the leading edge of a cold air mass?   (1) warm air pushes under cold air   (2) cold air pushes under warm air   (3) cold air flows over warm air   (4) the cold and warm air masses mingle to form one moderate air mass

To answer questions 41-47, use the diagram below, which shows four station models, at the same instant in time, identified by letters *A–D*. The stations are located on a west-east line at fifty mile intervals in the United States.

A   B   C   D

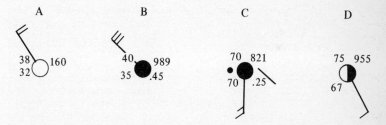

41. The strongest wind is reported at station   (1) *A*   (2) *B*   (3) *C* (4) *D*

42. Station *B* has just experienced the passage of a   (1) warm front   (2) cold front   (3) stationary front   (4) hurricane

43. At station *D* the wind is blowing from the   (1) northeast (2) northwest   (3) southeast   (4) southwest

44. The temperature at station *A* is   (1) 6°F   (2) 16°F   (3) 32°F (4) 38°F

45. The relative humidity at station *C* is   (1) 0%   (2) 25% (3) 70%   (4) 100%

46. Heaviest rainfall in the past 6 hours was reported from station (1) *A*   (2) *B*   (3) *C*   (4) *D*

47. Clear skies are reported from station   (1) *A*   (2) *B*   (3) *C* (4) *D*

Water, Energy, and Climate

THE WATER CYCLE

The **water cycle** is a model used to illustrate the movement and the phase changes of water at and near the earth's surface (see Figure 8-1). Below are some of the important aspects of the water cycle:

1. The ultimate source of most water on land is the oceans.

2. The moisture gets to the land from the oceans by way of the atmosphere.

3. When precipitation falls on the land, four things can happen to it:

a. Storage. It can be stored on the land surface as ice or snow.

b. Infiltration. It can infiltrate, or seep into, the earth. The water beneath the earth's surface is called **subsurface water.**

c. Runoff. It can flow on the surface of the land, and is then called **runoff.**

d. Evapotranspiration. Usually a large percentage of precipitation is evaporated or transpired back into the atmosphere.

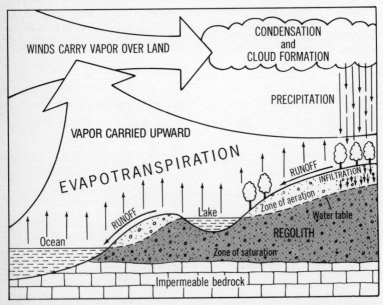

Figure 8-1. The water cycle: a model of the movement and phase changes of water at and near the earth's surface. The water table is an interface of changing position between the zone of saturation, where the pores of the regolith are filled with water (ground water), and the zone of aeration, where the pores are only partly filled with water (capillary water).

FACTORS AFFECTING INFILTRATION. Most infiltration occurs in the *regolith,* which is the unconsolidated material (including soil) at the earth's surface. The amount of water that can infiltrate when precipitation occurs depends on several variables:

1. *The slope of the land.* The steeper the slope (gradient), the less the infiltration.

2. *The degree of saturation of the regolith.* The more saturated the regolith, the less the infiltration. Figure 8-1 shows that the regolith is divided into two zones: the **zone of saturation,** where the pores between solid particles are filled with water; and the **zone of aeration,** where the air spaces are partly filled with water (capillary water). Water infiltrates until it meets the interface between the zone of saturation and the zone of aeration. This interface is called the **water table.** The height of the water table varies with the amount of infiltration. The portion of the subsurface water below the water table is called **ground water.**

3. *The porosity of the regolith.* **Porosity** is the percentage of open space (pores) in a material compared to its total volume. Generally, the greater the porosity of the regolith, the greater the amount of infiltration that can occur.

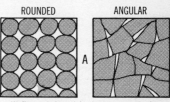

Well-rounded particles have more porosity than particles with angular shapes.

The porosity of a material is determined by the *shape, packing,* and *sorting* of the particles composing it. (See Figure 8-2.)

a. *Shape.* Well-rounded particles have greater porosity than particles with angular shapes, because the round ones do not fit together so well.

b. *Packing.* The more closely packed the particles, the lower the porosity.

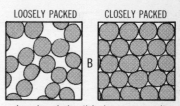

Loosely packed particles have more porosity than closely packed particles.

c. *Sorting.* If all the particles in a material are about the same size, they are called **sorted;** if the particles are of mixed sizes, they are **unsorted.** The more unsorted the particles, the lower the porosity, because the small particles can fit into the spaces between the larger particles. It should be noted that size by itself does not affect porosity. For example, a material with large particles may have about the same porosity as one with smaller particles if the shape, packing, and sorting of both particle sizes are about equal.

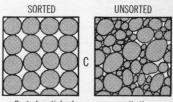

Sorted particles have more porosity than unsorted particles.

Figure 8-2. Effect of particle or sediment shape, packing, and sorting on porosity of the regolith.

4. *The permeability of the regolith.* **Permeability** is the ability of a material to allow fluids such as water to pass through it. The **permeability rate** is the speed at which fluids will flow through a material. A material can be porous and yet impermeable (not permeable). Impermeability may be due to tight packing or cementing of particles, which seals off the pores from one another so that water cannot enter them. In the winter the cementing is often due to ice. In loose particles, the larger the particle size, the faster the permeability rate. The reason is that the size of the pores increases with the size of the particles, thus reducing the amount of friction.

5. *Capillarity.* During infiltration, some water is stopped from moving downward by the attractive force between water molecules and the surrounding earth materials. This attractive force is called **capillarity.** The water that is thus stored in small openings in the zone of aeration is called **capillary water.**

Capillarity also causes water to move up from the water table toward the earth's surface in the zone of aeration. This upward movement is called **capillary migration.**

When the particle size of loose particles becomes smaller, the capillarity becomes greater.

FACTORS AFFECTING RUNOFF AND STREAM DISCHARGE.

Surface runoff can occur when (1) rate of precipitation exceeds the permeability rate (or infiltration rate) of the earth's surface, (2) the regolith pore space is saturated, or (3) the slope of the surface is too great to allow infiltration to occur.

Most runoff gets to streams, which eventually carry the water to the oceans. The greater the runoff, the greater the amount of *stream discharge* in local streams. **Stream discharge** is the volume of water flowing past a certain spot in a stream in a specific amount of time, and is expressed in such units as cubic meters/second.

WATER, OR HYDROSPHERIC, POLLUTION

SOURCES OF WATER POLLUTANTS. Pollutants are added to the hydrosphere by individuals, community action, and industrial processes. Generally, as the population density of an area increases, the concentration of pollutants in local lakes, streams (rivers), and ground water increases.

TYPES OF POLLUTANTS IN THE HYDROSPHERE. Water pollutants include dissolved and suspended materials, organic and inorganic wastes, outflow from industrial processes, radioactive substances, larger than normal concentrations of certain life forms, and thermal (heat) energy.

Excessive heat energy is considered a source of pollution because of its effects on oxygen content of water. The higher the temperature of water, the less the amount of dissolved oxygen it can hold. Furthermore, high temperatures increase the activity of the **aerobic bacteria** that are normally present. These bacteria use oxygen for their life processes, and their increased activity reduces the oxygen content of the water still further, thus killing many of the other forms of life that are present. Eventually, the aerobic bacteria are replaced by **anaerobic** varieties (types of bacteria that live without free oxygen). These bacteria and their wastes then become pollutants.

Power generating plants, including nuclear reactor types, are a major source of *thermal* (heat) pollution of bodies of water.

LONG-RANGE EFFECTS OF WATER POLLUTION.   As water pollution increases, more and more water becomes unfit for human use. Purification of unfit water is a very complex and costly process.

LOCAL WATER BUDGET

The **local water budget** is a numerical model of a local area's water supply by months during a year. The water budget is useful to help determine an area's climate type and has practical applications in flood and irrigation control.

SYMBOLS AND MEANING OF TERMS IN LOCAL WATER BUDGET.   To understand the local water budget, one must know the meaning of the terms used and how they relate to one another. The list below shows the symbols and the meaning of each of the terms used in the local water budget. Quantities of water per unit of area are expressed in millimeters. This is the depth to which the water would fill a pan covering the area involved.

1. Precipitation *(P)*. The moisture source for the local water budget is precipitation.

2. Potential evapotranspiration *(E_p)* is the amount of water that would evapotranspire if the water were available. The E_p of an area is directly related *(a)* to the amount of energy (heat) available to the area (which for most places is largely determined by the amount of insolation—thus E_p generally decreases as latitude increases), and *(b)* the amount of evaporation surface area. An area of forest has more evaporation surface area for evapotranspiration, thus it has a higher E_p than an equal area of lawn receiving the same insolation. Figures 8-3 and 8-4 on page 110 show the relationships between insolation and latitude and between insolation and potential evapotranspiration.

3. The difference between precipitation and potential evapotranspiration *($P - E_p$)*. Its value can be negative, positive, or zero.

4. The amount of change in the water stored in the ground *(ΔSt)*. Its value can be negative, positive, or zero. If ΔSt is positive, it is called **recharge.** Recharge occurs when the soil is not saturated and P is greater than E_p. Negative ΔSt is called **usage.** Water usage occurs when E_p is greater than P and soil storage is greater than zero.

5. Soil storage *(St)* is the amount of water stored in the soil. Each area has a specific maximum amount of soil storage, but for most areas it is assumed to be 100 millimeters.

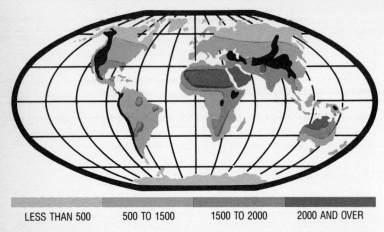

| LESS THAN 500 | 500 TO 1500 | 1500 TO 2000 | 2000 AND OVER |

Figure 8-3. World map of insolation at the earth's surface in thousands of calories/cm²/year. Note how yearly insolation generally increases with decreasing latitude. Due to many factors, however, especially differences in cloud coverage, it is not a perfect correlation. (Darkest areas have very high elevation.)

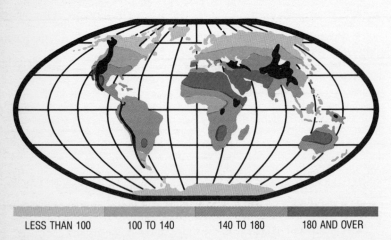

| LESS THAN 100 | 100 TO 140 | 140 TO 180 | 180 AND OVER |

Figure 8-4. World map of potential evapotranspiration in centimeters per year. Note the very good comparison to the yearly insolation map above. It is not a perfect correlation, because local heat values are affected by many other factors such as surface ocean currents and tropospheric convection currents. (Darkest areas have very high elevation.)

6. Actual evapotranspiration (E_a). E_a can never be greater than E_p. When there is a deficit, E_a is less than E_p, and at all other times E_a equals E_p.

7. Water deficit (D). A water deficit exists when E_a does not equal E_p because there is not enough water in the combination of P and St. The deficit is the amount of water that would be necessary for E_a to equal E_p, that is, it is E_p minus E_a. A deficit can occur only when the combined St and P are not as great as E_p.

8. Water surplus (S). There is a surplus when the soil is saturated (maximum St) and P is greater than E_p. Surplus water eventually becomes runoff.

EXAMPLES OF LOCAL WATER BUDGETS. To understand how a water budget is worked out, study the procedure that is described for the water budget of Syracuse, New York (Figure 8-6 on page 112). Then use the procedure to complete the water budget for El Paso, Texas (Figure 8-7 on page 113). Graph your results and see if they agree with the graph in Figure 8-7.

STREAM DISCHARGE AND WATER BUDGET. The discharge of a local stream is usually a measure of the amount of surplus water in the local drainage area of the stream. Figure 8-5 shows the discharge of a stream in Syracuse, New York. Comparison of this data with the water budget of Syracuse shows that the stream discharge is greatest when the surplus is the largest and least when the surplus is smallest.

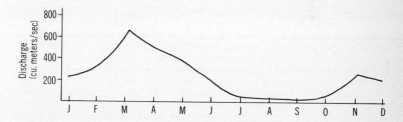

Figure 8-5. Discharge of a stream in Syracuse, New York, which is dependent on local precipitation. Compare with the water budget of Syracuse (Fig. 8-6). Much of the surplus in the winter months is stored temporarily as snow and ice, and does not contribute to stream discharge until early spring. The discharge during the period of deficit (August and September) is due to depletion of ground water at levels too deep to be available to plants.

Note that the stream is still flowing when Syracuse has a deficit in the water budget. If a local stream is still flowing during a deficit period, the source of the water is ground water depletion.

	J	F	M	A	M	J	J	A	S	O	N	D	Totals
P	72	68	81	75	74	87	84	82	72	76	68	72	911
E_p	0	0	3	34	83	115	134	122	84	46	15	0	636
$P-E_p$	72	68	78	41	−9	−28	−50	−40	−12	30	53	72	
ΔSt	0	0	0	0	−9	−28	−50	−13	0	30	53	17	
St	100	100	100	100	91	63	13	0	0	30	83	100	
E_a	0	0	3	34	83	115	134	95	72	46	15	0	597
D	0	0	0	0	0	0	0	27	12	0	0	0	39
S	72	68	78	41	0	0	0	0	0	0	0	55	314

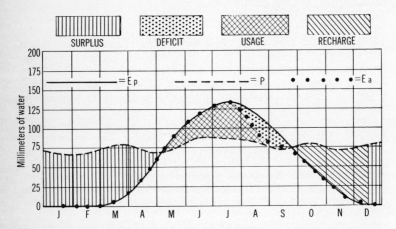

Figure 8-6. The water budget for Syracuse, New York. The data for P and E_p in the first two rows of the table are given. To complete the table, first enter all the values of P − E_p in the third row. This is done by simple subtraction. If E_p is greater than P, the result is entered with a minus sign. The next step is to find a month in which storage (St) is either 0 or 100. When the total P is greater than the total E_p (a humid climate), look for a storage of 100. This will occur whenever there is a series of months in which positive values of P − E_p add to more than 100. This happens in October to December (30 + 53 + 72 = 155). Therefore, St for December must be 100 (the assumed maximum storage). We now go on to the next month, January. Since storage is full, and P − E_p is positive, there is no change in storage ($\Delta St = 0$), and all of P − E_p (72 mm) is surplus. We also make E_a equal to E_p. (It is zero in this month because the ground is frozen and plants are dormant.) For the next three months, St remains at 100, $E_a = E_p$, and all of P − E_p is surplus.

In May, P − E_p is negative. However, the difference can come out of storage. Thus, $\Delta St = -9$, St becomes 91, and $E_a = E_p$ because there is enough water available. But there is no surplus this month. This continues until August. In August, P − $E_p = -40$, but there is only 13 mm in storage. Therefore E_a is only 95 (P of 82 plus 13 from St). St drops to zero, and there is a deficit of 27 ($E_p − E_a$). In September there is another deficit. E_a equals P, because there is no water in storage. In October, P − E_p becomes positive, and recharge begins ($\Delta St = 30$). In November, $\Delta St = 53$, bringing St up to 83. In December, St becomes 100 (as already noted), and there is a surplus of 55.

	J	F	M	A	M	J	J	A	S	O	N	D	Totals
P	10	11	8	7	8	18	40	41	33	17	13	12	218
E_p	11	18	37	75	117	163	171	152	111	62	24	10	951
$P-E_p$	-1	-7	-29	-68	-109	-145	-131	-111	-78	-45	-11	2	
ΔSt													
St				0									
E_a													
D													
S													

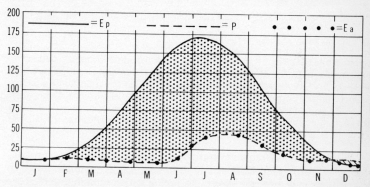

Figure 8-7. The water budget for El Paso, Texas. Since P is less than E_p, this is an arid climate. To complete the table, look for a series of months in which negative values of $P - E_p$ add to -100. From January to April, the total is -105. Therefore, St for April must be 0. This can be your starting point.

CLIMATE

Climate is the overall view of weather conditions of a region over a long period of time. The two major aspects of climate are *temperature* and *moisture conditions*. The factors that determine climate include latitude, planetary wind and pressure belts, oceans and other large bodies of water, ocean currents, mountains, and elevation.

TEMPERATURE AND CLIMATE. In terms of climate, two characteristics of the temperatures of a region are important: (1) the average temperature over the year, and (2) the range of average monthly temperatures from lowest to highest during the year.

MOISTURE AND CLIMATE. A climate is called **arid,** or dry, if the total precipitation during the year is less than the potential evapotranspiration, that is, if P is less than E_p. A climate is called **humid** if P is greater than E_p. Thus, whether a climate is said to be arid or humid depends not on the amount of precipitation but on the difference between the amount of moisture available and the potential need. As illustrated in Figure 8-8 on page 114, a region can have very little precipitation and still have a humid climate.

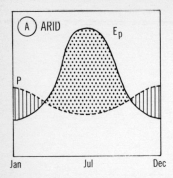
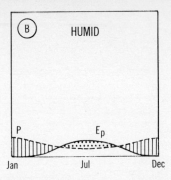

Figure 8-8. Examples of an arid and a humid climate. Graph A shows the relationship between P and E_p for a region of moderate rainfall but high values of E_p. Since there is a net moisture deficit for the year, the region has an arid climate. Some regions around 30° latitude have climates of this type. Graph B represents a climate in which there is little precipitation, but even smaller values of E_p. Since there is a moisture surplus for the year, the climate is humid. Many polar regions have climates of this type.

Regions with extreme moisture deficits (large yearly negative values of $P - E_p$) are called **deserts**. The term *semi-arid* is sometimes used to describe the moisture conditions of a region with a moderate deficit.

LATITUDE AND TEMPERATURE. Latitude is a major factor in determining climates because of its influence on both temperature and moisture conditions. Temperature characteristics vary with latitude because of the relationships between insolation and latitude discussed in Topic VI. At low latitudes, where the maximum angle of insolation is always high, average temperatures are high throughout the year. Because the duration of insolation is fairly constant at about 12 hours per day, there is little temperature variation during the year. At high latitudes, where the maximum angle of insolation is never large and in some months remains zero, average temperatures are low. Since the duration of insolation varies from zero to 24 hours a day, and is longest at the times of greatest angle of insolation, temperatures vary over a wide range from winter lows to summer highs.

LATITUDE AND MOISTURE. Moisture conditions vary with latitude because of the location of the planetary wind and pressure belts (see page 85). Where there is low pressure, such as near the equator and in mid-latitudes, the air rises. The cooling of that rising air results in large amounts of precipitation and humid climates. When air falls in high-pressure belts, such as around 30° latitude, it warms and there is little precipitation. Such areas have arid climates.

LATITUDINAL CLIMATE PATTERNS. The combination of the temperature and moisture effects of latitude results in a basic distribution of climate types around the world, called **latitudinal climate patterns** (see Figure 8-9).

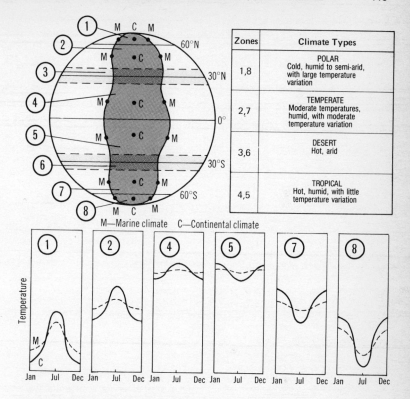

M—Marine climate   C—Continental climate

Figure 8-9. Basic latitudinal climate pattern on an imaginary continent. The arid belts around 30° latitude are the result of descending air in the atmospheric circulation at that latitude (see Figure 7-3). The modification of this basic pattern by prevailing winds and distance from oceans is illustrated in Figure 8-10.

EFFECT OF LARGE BODIES OF WATER ON CLIMATE. Large bodies of water serve to modify the latitudinal climate patterns. If an area is near the ocean or a large lake, its temperatures will be moderated by the slow heating up and cooling off of the water body. An area with these moderated temperatures is said to have a **marine climate.** Marine climates have cooler summers and warmer winters, thus a small annual range of temperatures compared to inland areas at the same latitude. Inland areas away from large bodies of water have cooler winters and warmer summers and a large annual range of temperatures. Such areas are said to have a **continental climate.**

EFFECT OF LARGE LANDMASSES ON CLIMATE. As explained on page 67, bodies of land heat up and cool off more rapidly than bodies of water. As a result, the temperatures over a continent in the mid-latitudes are higher than the adjacent oceans in summer and lower in winter. These temperature differences produce convection currents that modify the planetary wind patterns and thus modify the latitudinal climate patterns. The general effect on the basic climate patterns of a continent is illustrated in Figure 8-10.

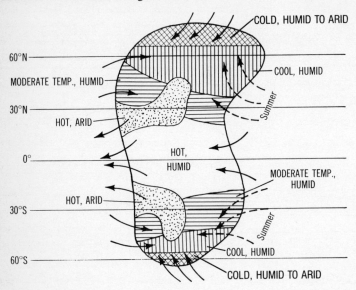

Figure 8-10. Modification of basic climate patterns by prevailing winds.

Note that the arid belt around 30° latitude does not extend across the eastern portion of the continent. The reason for this is that in the summer months the land temperatures are higher than the ocean temperatures, causing air to rise over the land and resulting in prevailing winds carrying moisture inland from the oceans on the east. The eastern regions of the continent therefore have much more precipitation than they would have if the planetary wind pattern remained unchanged.

A second effect is the arid region in the central portion of the continent at the mid-latitudes (40° to 50°). The reason for this is that the prevailing winds from the western oceans lose their moisture by precipitation and become increasingly dry as they blow inland.

STORM TRACKS AND CLIMATE. In the mid-latitudes, such as the continental United States, temperature and moisture are greatly affected by a succession of low-pressure systems. Major tracks of low-pressure storm systems are shown in Figure 8-11.

OCEAN CURRENTS AND CLIMATE. Coastal climate patterns are modified by ocean currents. Currents flowing away from the equator carry warm water to higher latitudes, while currents flowing toward the

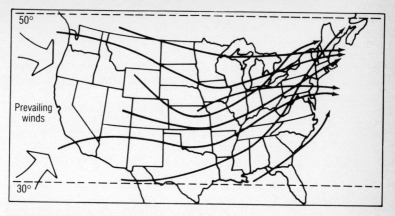

Figure 8-11. The usual paths followed by low-pressure storm centers as they pass across the United States.

equator carry cold water to lower latitudes. A cold ocean current will cause a coastal area to have cooler temperatures and less precipitation. One reason there is low precipitation is that cold water results in cold air, which has a low saturation vapor pressure and thus cannot hold much water vapor.

ELEVATION AND CLIMATE. The elevation of an area above sea level modifies the latitudinal climate pattern, because as air rises, it expands and cools (at the rate of 10°C/kilometer). Thus the higher the altitude at any given latitude, the cooler it is. Elevation also affects precipitation. As the elevation increases, the temperature and saturation vapor pressure decrease; the air thus approaches the dew point. Therefore, areas at higher altitudes generally have more precipitation than lower areas.

MOUNTAINS AND CLIMATE—OROGRAPHIC EFFECT. Mountains that intersect prevailing winds, such as those associated with the planetary wind belts, can modify the latitudinal climate pattern in the following manner. Figure 8-12 on page 118 shows a cross section of a mountain against which the prevailing winds blow from the left. This side is called the *windward side.* As the wind strikes the windward side of the mountain, the air is forced to rise. As it does so, it cools adiabatically. As long as the air temperature is above the dew point, the adiabatic cooling rate is about 10°C per kilometer. If the cooling continues until the dew point is reached, condensation will occur above this altitude. Since large amounts of latent heat are released during condensation, the temperature of the rising air does not drop as rapidly as before. The adiabatic cooling rate during condensation is only 6°C per kilometer.

On the opposite side of the mountain, called the *leeward side,* the air begins to descend. It therefore begins to warm adiabatically. Since condensation immediately stops, the warming rate is constant at the dry rate of 10°C per kilometer all the way down. As a result, the leeward side is warmer than the windward side at any given altitude. The leeward side also has much less precipitation, because the air has lost much of its moisture on the windward side, and its saturation vapor pressure rises as its temperature increases. Both of these factors make condensation and precipitation unlikely.

Another way that mountains modify climate is by acting as barriers to moving air masses, preventing cold air or warm air from crossing the mountain to the other side. As a result, opposite sides of a mountain can have different temperature patterns.

The effects of mountains on climate are called the **orographic effect.**

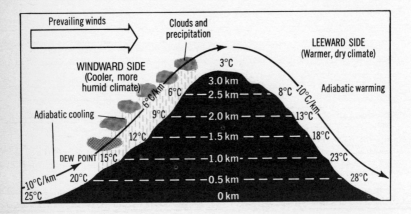

Figure 8-12. Orographic climate effect of mountains that intersect prevailing moist winds (such as those on the northwest coast of the United States). Compare the temperature at the same altitude on the two sides of the mountain. (See text for detailed explanation.)

CLIMATIC CLASSIFICATION BASED ON PRECIPITATION AND POTENTIAL EVAPOTRANSPIRATION. Climatic regions or zones can be distinguished qualitatively based on either P/E_p (precipitation divided by potential evapotranspiration) or $P - E_p$ (precipitation minus potential evapotranspiration). The classification can be based on a system like the one in the table below.

Climate Type	P/E_p	$P - E_p$ in cm
Humid	1.2 or greater	26.7 or greater
Sub-humid	1.2 to 0.8	26.7 to 0.0
Semi-arid	0.8 to 0.4	0.0 to −26.7
Arid	0.4 or lower	−26.7 or lower

VOCABULARY

water cycle	local water budget
infiltration	precipitation (P)
subsurface water	potential evapotranspiration (E_p)
runoff	change in soil storage (ΔSt)
zone of saturation	recharge $(+\Delta St)$
zone of aeration	usage $(-\Delta St)$
water table	soil storage (St)
ground water	actual evapotranspiration (E_a)
porosity	deficit (D)
sorted and unsorted particles	surplus (S)
permeability	climate
permeability rate	arid climate
capillarity	humid climate
capillary water	desert
capillary migration	latitudinal climate pattern
stream discharge	marine climate
aerobic bacteria	continental climate
anaerobic bacteria	orographic effect

QUESTIONS ON TOPIC VIII—WATER, ENERGY, AND CLIMATE

Questions in Recent Regents Exams (end of book)

June 1984:   18, 20, 22, 23, 24, 52, 68
June 1985:   24, 25, 26, 27, 76, 77, 78, 79, 80
June 1986:   25, 26, 27, 31
June 1987:   4, 22, 23, 25, 55, 75–80

Questions from Earlier Regents Exams

1. Although New York City is at approximately the same latitude as Omaha, Nebraska, its winter months are warmer and its summer months cooler. Which statement best explains why this is so?   (1) the sun's rays are more direct on New York City in the winter   (2) Nebraska is nearer the Rocky Mountains   (3) the water around New York City has a moderating effect on the temperature   (4) the prevailing westerlies have a greater effect on Omaha than on New York City

2. During a given month in a certain locality, the potential evapotranspiration exceeded the actual evapotranspiration. Which probably occurred?   (1) a water deficit   (2) a water surplus   (3) a higher potential evapotranspiration than usual   (4) low temperatures and high humidity

3. As the number of degrees of latitude from the equator increases, the yearly average temperature generally   (1) decreases   (2) increases   (3) remains the same

Base your answers to questions 4 through 8 on the water budget diagram for Rockford, Illinois, below, and on your knowledge of earth science.

Water Budget Diagram for Rockford, Illinois

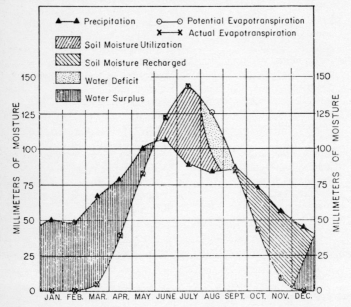

4. A water deficit occurred in Rockford, Illinois, during   (1) February   (2) June   (3) August   (4) December

5. During how many months of the year did Rockford have a water surplus?   (1) ten   (2) eight   (3) six   (4) four

6. During which of these months did the potential evapotranspiration equal the precipitation in Rockford?   (1) March   (2) January   (3) September   (4) November

7. During which month was the soil moisture recharge the greatest?   (1) December   (2) November   (3) October   (4) August

8. If the storage capacity of Rockford were increased from 100 to 150 mm, which would not change?   (1) actual evapotranspiration   (2) potential evapotranspiration   (3) deficit   (4) surplus

9. An area of high precipitation and low potential evapotranspiration is most likely to have   (1) a large water deficit   (2) low root zone storage   (3) streams of low velocity   (4) streams of large volume

10. Surface runoff of precipitation occurs when   (1) porosity is exceeded by permeability   (2) the infiltration rate is greater than the precipitation rate   (3) the precipitation rate is greater than the infiltration rate   (4) there is no demand for evapotranspiration

11. For the earth as a whole, what happens to most of the precipitation? (1) it recharges the soil moisture deficit (2) it becomes runoff and moves to the oceans (3) it is stored in the soil as capillary water (4) it is returned to the atmosphere through evapotranspiration

12. Which would cause the potential evapotranspiration to decrease in a given month? (1) below-normal precipitation (2) drilling of a large well (3) a month-long cold spell (4) a high actual evapotranspiration

13. Which area of New York State would probably have the lowest annual temperature range? (1) Long Island (2) the Catskills (3) the Adirondack peaks (4) the Mohawk Valley

14. As the amount of precipitation on land increases, the depth from the surface of the earth to the water table will probably (1) decrease (2) increase (3) remain the same

15. The ground just below the water table is (1) below sea level (2) drier than the ground above the water table (3) impermeable to water (4) saturated with water

16. Which generally has the greatest effect in determining the climate of an area? (1) degrees of longitude (2) extent of vegetation cover (3) distance from equator (4) month of the year

17. On one of the Hawaiian Islands the annual rainfall is 200 inches per year on one side of the island and less than 20 inches per year on the opposite side of the same island. This difference is most likely caused by (1) doldrums (2) hurricanes or typhoons (3) monsoons (4) prevailing winds and mountains

Base your answers to questions 18 through 22 on the statement below and your knowledge of earth science.

The diagram below represents two identical barrels each filled to the same level, one with BB's and the other with marbles.

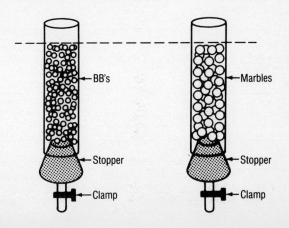

Note that questions 18 through 22 have only three choices.

18. If water were added to each barrel to the height of the dotted line and then the clamps opened, which graph best illustrates how fast the water would run through each barrel?

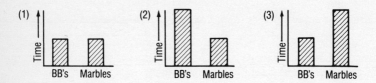

19. After the water has been allowed to pass freely through the barrels, which graph best illustrates the amount of water retained by each barrel?

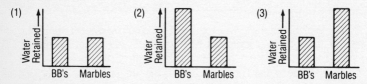

20. If the barrels and their contents were dried of all water and then arranged in such a way as to show capillary action, which graph best illustrates the height water would rise in each tube?

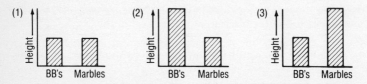

21. How does the total amount of pore space in the barrel with the BB's compare with the total amount of pore space in the barrel with the marbles? (1) It is much more. (2) It is much less. (3) It is approximately the same.

22. If an identical third barrel were filled with a mixture of BB's and marbles to the same level as the other two barrels, how would the total amount of the pore spaces in this barrel compare with the total amount of the pore spaces in the barrel of marbles? (1) It would be less. (2) It would be greater. (3) It would be the same.

Base your answers to questions 23-27 on your knowledge of earth science and on the diagram. The diagram represents an imaginary continent on the earth surrounded by water. The arrows indicate the direction of the prevailing winds. Two large mountain regions are also indicated. Points

A, B, E, and *H* are located at sea level; *C, D,* and *F* are in the foothills of the mountains; *G* is high in the mountains.

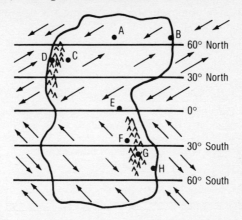

23. Which graph best represents the average monthly temperatures that would be recorded during one year at location *E?*

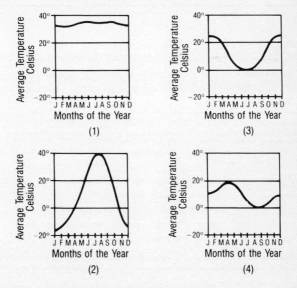

24. Which physical characteristic would cause location *G* to have a colder yearly climate than any other location?   (1) the nearness of location *G* to a large ocean   (2) the location of *G* with respect to the prevailing winds   (3) the elevation of location *G* above sea level   (4) the distance of location *G* from the Equator

25. Which location probably has the greatest annual rainfall? (1) *A*   (2) *F*   (3) *C*   (4) *D*

26. Which location probably has the greatest range in temperature during the year?   (1) *A*   (2) *B*   (3) *H*   (4) *D*

27. Which location will probably record its highest potential evapotranspiration values for the year during January?   (1) *A*   (2) *F* (3) *C*   (4) *D*

Additional Questions

Refer to the four graphs below to answer questions 1 through 18. The first variable listed in each question corresponds to the *y* axis and the second variable corresponds to the *x* axis. For each of the questions choose the number of the graph that best matches the statement.

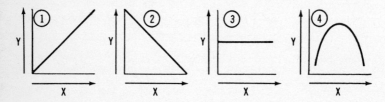

1. Height of capillary water above the water table versus grain size of loose, sorted particles.

2. Porosity versus the size of sorted, loose particles.

3. Porosity versus the degree of packing of particles.

4. Permeability to water versus particle sizes of loose particles.

5. Height of the water table versus the amount of infiltration.

6. Amount of anaerobic bacteria versus amount of oxygen in lake water.

7. Amount of water pollution in lakes and ground water versus population density.

8. Temperature of lake water versus amount of oxygen in lake water.

9. Potential evapotranspiration versus precipitation.

10. Recharge after a deficit versus positive differences between precipitation and potential evapotranspiration.

11. Temperature range during the year versus the distance of an area from a large body of water.

12. Average temperature versus latitude from 90°S to 90°N at an equinox.

13. Amount of infiltration versus slope of the land.

14. The rate of infiltration versus permeability of the earth's surface.

15. Amount of surface runoff versus slope of the land.

16. Potential evapotranspiration versus amount of insolation in an area.

17. Potential evapotranspiration versus amount of evaporation surface in an area.

18. Potential evapotranspiration versus latitude from 90°N to 90°S.

19. The purification of water for human use is   (1) simple and cheap   (2) simple and costly   (3) complex and cheap   (4) complex and costly

Refer to the diagram below to answer questions 20 through 23.

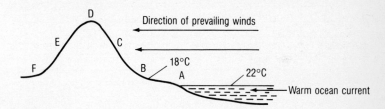

20. Which location would have the coolest average temperature? (1) A   (2) C   (3) D   (4) F

21. Which location would have the most condensation in the atmosphere above it during the year?   (1) B   (2) C   (3) E   (4) F

22. Which place would have the largest negative value for $P - Ep_p$ (precipitation minus potential evapotranspiration) during the year? (1) A   (2) B   (3) D   (4) F

23. How is the potential evapotranspiration of area A-B affected by the ocean current?   (1) it is reduced   (2) it is increased   (3) it is unchanged

24. A surplus exists in the local water budget when   (1) the soil is saturated   (2) the soil is saturated and precipitation is less than potential evapotranspiration   (3) the soil is unsaturated and precipitation is less than potential evapotranspiration   (4) the soil is saturated and precipitation is greater than potential evapotranspiration

25. After a drought, if precipitation is greater than potential evapotranspiration,   (1) soil moisture is recharged   (2) available moisture is taken from the soil   (3) surface runoff decreases   (4) porosity increases

26. If precipitation is greater than potential evapotranspiration and soil moisture is maximum,   (1) soil water usage occurs   (2) soil moisture is recharged   (3) a moisture surplus exists   (4) the rate of infiltration increases

27. In the United States generally, the higher the elevation is, (1) the higher the temperature and the lower the precipitation   (2) the higher the temperature and the higher the precipitation   (3) the lower the temperature and the lower the precipitation   (4) the lower the temperature and the higher the precipitation

28. A rock with a high percentage of open space has to have a large   (1) permeability   (2) porosity   (3) capillarity   (4) compaction

Complete the water budget for Fairbanks, Alaska, given below to answer questions 29 through 32.

	J	F	M	A	M	J	J	A	S	O	N	D
P	27	13	10	6	18	36	48	60	28	22	15	13
Ep	0	0	0	0	71	114	115	86	48	0	0	0
P–Ep	27	13	10	6	−53	−78	−67			22	15	13
△ St	27	13	10							22	15	13
St	77	90	100							22	37	50
Ea	0	0	0							0	0	0
D	0	0	0							0	0	0
S	0	0	0							0	0	0

Values in millimeters of water   Maximum storage: 100 mm

29. Stream flow discharge would be the greatest in the month of (1) February   (2) April   (3) October   (4) December

30. How would you classify the climate of Fairbanks from June to September?   (1) rain forest   (2) low-latitude   (3) arid   (4) moist

31. If streams are flowing in May in Fairbanks, the water in the streams would most likely come from   (1) precipitation   (2) surplus (3) soil storage   (4) actual evapotranspiration

32. If the porosity of the soil in this area increases, which of the following would change the most?   (1) precipitation   (2) potential evapotranspiration   (3) soil storage   (4) precipitation minus potential evapotranspiration

33. An area has a water deficit when   (1) potential evapotranspiration is greater than precipitation   (2) potential evapotranspiration is greater than precipitation plus surplus   (3) potential evapotranspiration is greater than precipitation plus soil storage   (4) actual evapotranspiration is greater than potential evapotranspiration

34. During a dry summer, stream discharge is primarily controlled by the   (1) supply of ground water in the area of the stream   (2) loss of capillary water through evapotranspiration   (3) shape of the stream channel   (4) amount of vegetation on the banks of the stream

TOPIC IX — Weathering and Erosion

WEATHERING

Weathering is the breakdown of rocks into particles called **sediment.** Rocks weather because they are adjusting to a new environment different from the one in which they were formed. Weathering occurs when rocks are exposed to the air, water, and living things at or near the earth's surface.

TYPES OF WEATHERING. There are two general types of weathering—*physical* and *chemical.*

Physical weathering is the breakdown of rock into smaller pieces (sediment) without chemical change. Physical weathering includes *frost action,* which breaks up rocks when water in the rocks freezes and expands.

Chemical weathering is the breakdown of rock by chemical action and results in a change in the mineral composition. Chemical weathering includes the uniting of minerals with oxygen *(oxidation)* or with water *(hydration),* and the dissolving of minerals by acids.

FACTORS AFFECTING THE RATE AND TYPE OF WEATHERING. Many variables determine the rate and type of weathering that will occur:

1. *Exposure.* The more exposed the rocks are to the air, water, and living things near the earth's surface, the faster the weathering.

2. *Particle size.* The smaller the particle size, the greater the total surface area per unit volume exposed to weathering and the greater the rate of weathering (see Figure 9-1).

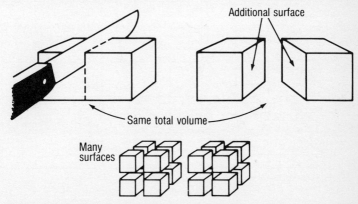

Figure 9-1. Explaining why surface area increases as particle size decreases. A single division of the block at the left exposes two new surface areas. If the two blocks at the bottom are divided again and again into smaller and smaller pieces, the total surface area will increase rapidly, although the total mass of material will remain the same.

3. *Mineral composition.* A rock's mineral composition determines the rate of weathering because different minerals have different resistances to weathering.

4. *Climate.* Climate greatly influences the rate and type of weathering (see Figure 9-2). Chemical weathering is most pronounced in warm, moist climates. The higher the average temperatures and the more humid the climate, the more intense the chemical weathering becomes. In cold climates, frost action (a type of physical weathering) is the most common and most effective form of weathering. It is especially intense where the climate is moist and the temperature variations lead to much alternate freezing and thawing.

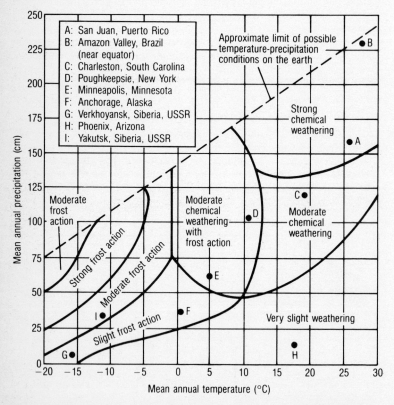

Figure 9-2. Dominant type of weathering for various climatic conditions. For example, if the mean annual temperature is 15°C and the mean annual precipitation is 100 cm, moderate chemical weathering is the main agent of weathering. The blank region of the chart in the upper left represents conditions that almost never occur on the earth.

PRODUCTS OF WEATHERING.   Weathering results in the formation of three different types of sediment: (1) solid sediments such as sand and pebbles; (2) very small solid sediments called *colloids* (or clay-sized particles); and (3) dissolved ionic minerals, which are a major end product of much weathering. Dissolved minerals are what cause the "hardness" in all surface and ground water and what make the oceans "salty."

SOIL

One product of weathering is **soil,** which is the part of the regolith that will support rooted plants.

TYPES OF SOIL.   Soil can be divided into two general types—*residual* and *transported.* A **residual soil** is a soil that formed from the rocks or regolith under the soil. A **transported soil** is one that has been moved into an area from another place by erosion.

SOIL FORMATION.   The composition of soil varies with depth. This is indicated by horizontal layers or zones called **soil horizons,** which develop as a result of weathering processes. Soil and soil horizon development starts at the earth's surface and progresses downward with time, as illustrated in Figure 9-3.

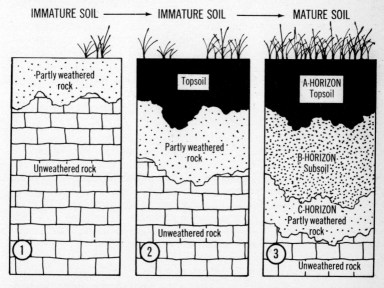

Figure 9-3. Profile development of horizons in a residual soil. Originally, there is unweathered bedrock at the surface. Weathering gradually proceeds downward to deeper levels. Meanwhile, infiltration, capillary migration, the addition of plant material, and the movement of sediment by organisms in the developing soil produce horizons with characteristic features.

Living things play a significant part in soil formation. For example, plant roots break up rock by widening cracks; accumulation of organic matter is an important part of soil; decay of organic matter forms acids that dissolve rock; earthworms, ants, and burrowing animals expose fresh rock material to weathering.

EROSION

Weathering is a process that produces most sediments; **erosion** is the process by which sediments are obtained and transported. Erosion is also the process by which the earth's surface is worn away, sculpted, and lowered.

EROSION THROUGH TRANSPORTING SYSTEMS.   Erosion of sediments is accomplished by means of *transporting systems*. A **transporting system** includes (1) the transporting agent (agent of erosion), such as running water (streams), glaciers, waves, density currents in water, wind, and people; (2) the "driving" force, which consists of gravity and the energy transfer from potential to kinetic energy; and (3) the material being transported, called sediment.

GRAVITY AND EROSION.   Gravity plays a two-fold role in the erosional process:

1. Gravity is the primary driving force behind all transporting systems, causing sediment to move downslope. For example, glaciers and streams move and erode sediments downhill because of the pull of gravity.

2. Gravity may act alone (that is, without the transporting agents mentioned above) in transporting earth materials. Loose sediment on steep slopes may break away and move downhill under the direct influence of gravity, such as in a landslide.

EVIDENCE OF EROSION.   Sediments displaced from their source are evidence of erosion. Such sediments can be seen in muddy streams, rock fields near glaciers, the assortment of rocks at shorelines, shifting sands, and earth moved by people in construction.

Weathered rock that is transported from its place of origin to its present location is called **transported sediment.** Weathered rock that remains in its place of origin is called **residual sediment.** Transported sediment is far more common than residual sediment.

STREAM, OR RUNNING WATER, EROSION.   Running water is the dominant agent of erosion in terms of the amount of sediment moved, even in many arid climates. Streams obtain sediments by (1) the direct lifting of particles from the stream bottom, or **stream bed;** (2) by collisions between carried sediments and the stream bed (abrasion); and (3) by receiving dissolved minerals, produced by weathering, from ground water flow or by directly dissolving the stream bed.

Streams carry sediments in three major ways: (1) dissolved minerals are carried in solution; (2) solid sediments of small size, including colloids, are carried by suspension; and (3) larger solid sediments are carried by rolling and bouncing along the bed (see Figure 9-4).

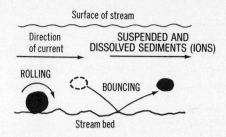

Figure 9-4. Transport of sediments by a stream.

STREAM VELOCITY. The two most important factors that determine the average velocity of a stream are the *slope,* or *gradient,* of the stream and the *discharge,* or volume of water. Generally, as either the slope or the discharge of a stream increases, the velocity will increase. When a stream changes direction, the region of maximum velocity shifts as shown in Figure 9-5.

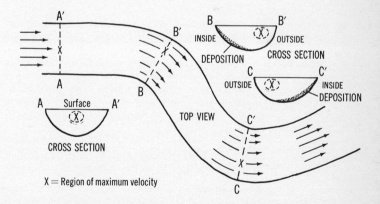

Figure 9-5. Variations in stream velocity in the cross section of an idealized stream. Where the stream course is straight (as at A), the location of maximum velocity is at the center of the cross section. Where the stream course changes direction (as at B and C), the location of maximum velocity moves toward the outside of the curve, or meander. Low velocity at the inside of curves results in deposition of the larger and denser sediments. Velocity also varies with depth. It is greatest just below the surface and least near the stream bed. At the air-water interface and at the stream bed velocity is reduced by friction.

SEDIMENT SIZE AND STREAM VELOCITY. The sediments being transported by a stream generally flow much slower than the stream. The greater the velocity of a stream, the larger the sediment particles it can carry (see Figure 9-6). For any given stream, the greater its velocity the more total sediment it can carry.

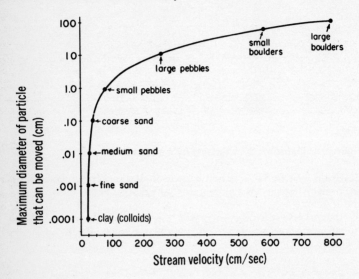

Figure 9-6. Relationship between stream velocity and maximum size of particle that can be moved. (Also see *Earth Science Reference Tables,* page 249.)

EROSION BY WIND AND GLACIERS. Many of the factors that affect stream erosion are found also in glacial and wind erosion. The greater the slope of a glacier, the faster it generally moves. The positions of maximum velocity in a glacier are similar to those of a stream shown in Figure 9-5. The greater the velocity of the wind, the larger the size of sediment particles it can carry.

SEDIMENT FEATURES AND EROSIONAL AGENT. Each agent of erosion produces distinctive characteristics in the sediment it transports.

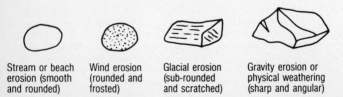

Figure 9-7. Sediment features reflect the erosional or weathering agents that produced or transported them.

A solid sediment in wind or stream erosion will become rounded and smooth. The longer the time the sediment is eroded, the more smooth and rounded it becomes. Wind-blown sediments are often more frosted (pitted) than stream sediments. Glacial sediments are only partly rounded and often have scratches of various sizes. Sediments produced by physical weathering or moved by gravity are often very angular in shape.

PEOPLE AND EROSION. People greatly increase the erosion of land by their activities. The burning and cutting down of forests, poor farming methods, road and building construction, and mining expose loose soil and regolith to the agents of erosion and thereby increase erosion rates. The removal and lowering of the soil, regolith, and vegetation at the earth's surface is an aspect of erosion called **denudation.** Denudation has been greatly increased in the last few hundred years by the activities of people.

VOCABULARY

weathering	soil horizon
sediment	erosion
physical weathering	transporting system
chemical weathering	transported sediment
soil	residual sediment
residual soil	stream bed
transported soil	denudation

QUESTIONS ON TOPIC IX—WEATHERING AND EROSION

Questions in Recent Regents Exams (end of book)

June 1984: 25, 26, 27, 43, 59
June 1985: 28, 29, 55, 83
June 1986: 28, 29, 34, 51, 63, 77, 86–89
June 1987: 26–28, 81–85, 87

Questions from Earlier Regents Exams

1. Which material could best be carried in solution by a stream? (1) clay (2) salt (3) silt (4) sand

2. Rounded-bottom valleys with almost vertical sides, small hills and ridges composed of unsorted sediments, and exposed bedrock with small, parallel grooves and scratches are observed. Which events probably produced these features? (1) extensive glaciation (2) widespread earthquakes and associated faulting (3) a period of volcanoes and lava flows (4) extensive flooding followed by periods of wind erosion

3. As the kinetic energy of a stream increases, the size of the particle that can be moved (1) decreases (2) increases (3) remains the same

4. Which has the greatest effect on the speed of a river? (1) width (2) depth (3) length (4) gradient

5. Which is indicated by a deep residual soil? (1) resistant bedrock (2) a large amount of glaciation (3) a long period of weathering (4) a youthful stage of erosion

6. Which agent probably contributes most to the general wearing down of the earth's surface? (1) wind (2) glaciers (3) running water (4) ocean waves

7. The increase of dissolved materials in the ocean is primarily the result of the (1) abrasion of the ocean floor (2) transporting of material by rivers (3) melting of continental glaciers (4) deposition of materials by ground water

8. Which property of water makes frost action a common and effective form of weathering? (1) Water dissolves many earth materials. (2) Water expands when it freezes. (3) Water cools the surroundings when it evaporates. (4) Water loses 80 calories of heat per gram when it freezes.

9. Based on the diagrams of rock fragments below, which shows the *least* evidence of erosion?

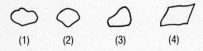

(1)   (2)   (3)   (4)

10. According to the *Earth Science Reference Tables*, which is the largest sediment that could be carried by a stream flowing at a velocity of 75 centimeters per second? (1) silt (2) sand (3) pebbles (4) cobbles

11. Most of the surface materials in New York State can be classified as (1) igneous rocks (2) metamorphic rocks (3) coastal plain deposits (4) transported soils

12. Which landscape characteristic best indicates the action of glaciers? (1) few lakes (2) deposits of well-sorted sediments (3) residual soil covering large areas (4) polished and scratched surface bedrock

13. Which graph best represents the relationship between the maximum particle size that can be carried by a stream and the velocity of the stream?

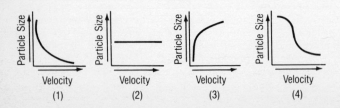

(1)   (2)   (3)   (4)

14. The chemical composition of a residual soil in a certain area is determined by the (1) method by which the soil was transported to the area (2) slope of the land and the particle size of the soil (3) length of time since the last crustal movement in the area occurred (4) minerals in the bedrock beneath the soil and the climate of the area

15. The diagram below represents a geologic cross section with sedimentary rock layers *A, B, C,* and *D* exposed to the atmosphere. Which rock layer in the diagram is most resistant to weathering and erosion?

(1) *A*
(2) *B*
(3) *C*
(4) *D*

16. Which is the best evidence that erosion has occurred? (1) a soil rich in lime on top of a limestone bedrock (2) a layer of basalt found on the floor of the ocean (3) sediments found in a sandbar of a river (4) a large number of fossils embedded in limestone

17. A pebble is being transported in a stream by rolling. How does the velocity of the pebble compare to the velocity of the stream? (1) The pebble is moving slower than the stream. (2) The pebble is moving faster than the stream. (3) The pebble is moving at the same velocity as the stream.

18. Which rock material most likely has been transported by wind? (1) large boulders with sets of parallel scratches (2) jagged cobbles consisting of intergrown crystals (3) irregularly shaped pebbles which contain fossils (4) rounded sand grains which have a frosted appearance

19. The primary force responsible for most of the transportation of rock material on the surface of the earth is (1) gravity (2) wind (3) running water (4) glaciers

20. While studying the movement of valley glaciers that are advancing from the north, geologists placed metal stakes extending in a straight line from one valley wall to the other. Which sketch would best illustrate the position of the stakes one year later?

Base your answers to questions 21 through 25 on your knowledge of earth science, the *Earth Science Reference Tables,* and the diagrams at the top of the next page. Diagram I shows the paths of two streams over the earth's surface. Diagram II shows the longitudinal profile of the major stream.

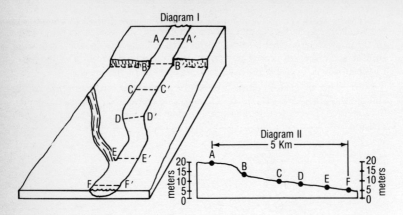

Diagram I

Diagram II
5 Km

21. At which location would the water in the stream have the greatest potential energy?   (1) *A*   (2) *B*   (3) *C*   (4) *E*

22. What is the approximate average gradient of this stream between points *A* and *F*?   (1) 1 m/km   (2) 15 m/km   (3) 3 m/km   (4) 20 m/km

23. The greatest volume of water would most likely be moving past which location?   (1) *F—F'*   (2) *B—B'*   (3) *C—C'*   (4) *D—D'*

24. Which cross section best represents the shape of the stream at *D—D'*?

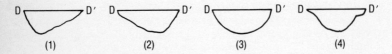

(1)   (2)   (3)   (4)

25. The diagram at the right shows the cross section of the stream at *C—C'*. At which position in the stream channel would the velocity of the water be greatest?
(1) 1   (2) 2   (3) 3   (4) 4

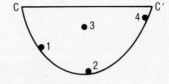

Additional Questions

1. The formation of residual soil is most related to   (1) the activities of animals and plants   (2) the height of the water table   (3) the amount of stream deposition   (4) the direction of prevailing winds

2. Why does rock weather faster when it is broken up?   (1) there is a decrease in mass   (2) there is a decrease in volume   (3) there is an increase in density   (4) there is an increase in surface area

3. What is the main difference between chemical and physical weathering?   (1) chemical weathering alters the composition of minerals, and physical weathering does not   (2) chemical weathering increases the surface area of minerals, and physical weathering does not (3) physical weathering alters the composition of minerals, and chemical weathering does not   (4) physical weathering increases the surface area of minerals, and chemical weathering does not

4. What condition must occur in order for rocks to weather? (1) the rocks must be composed of silicate minerals   (2) the rocks must be exposed to air or water   (3) the rocks must be moved by erosion (4) the rocks must be deeply buried in the earth

5. Large solid sediments such as pebbles are most often carried in streams   (1) in solution   (2) by rolling   (3) in suspension   (4) by floating

6. Very small solid sediments (colloids) are carried by a stream (1) by flotation   (2) in suspension   (3) in solution   (4) by rolling

7. Which would have the *least* effect on the amount of weathering of a rock?   (1) mineral composition   (2) porosity and permeability of the rock   (3) amount of wind in the area   (4) amount of precipitation in the area

8. Soil forms layers called   (1) beds   (2) stratifications   (3) horizons   (4) zones

9. Ground water is often hard because it contains minerals dissolved in the process of   (1) physical weathering   (2) chemical weathering   (3) precipitation   (4) deposition

10. Most of the earth's surface is covered by   (1) barren rock (2) residual sediment   (3) transported sediment   (4) deposits caused by gravity alone

11. Angular rock fragments at the bottom of a cliff were probably transported by   (1) wind   (2) streams   (3) gravity   (4) glaciers

12. The total amount of erosion by a glacier at any one location depends mainly upon its cutting tools and its   (1) altitude (2) temperature   (3) volume of ice   (4) direction of flow

13. Which is an example of physical weathering?   (1) combining of iron with oxygen   (2) breaking of rock due to rapid heating and cooling   (3) changing the mineral feldspar to a clay mineral (4) dissolving of rock by organic acids

14. Which pair of temperature and rainfall conditions would tend to promote the most intense chemical weathering of a rock?   (1) low temperature and low rainfall   (2) low temperature and high rainfall (3) high temperature and low rainfall   (4) high temperature and high rainfall

15. Sharp, angular rock sediments were most probably deposited by   (1) waves   (2) wind   (3) gravity   (4) streams

16. According to the *Earth Science Reference Tables,* which is the *slowest* stream velocity needed to maintain 1 cm particles moving downstream?   (1) 50 cm/sec   (2) 75 cm/sec   (3) 100 cm/sec   (4) 125 cm/ sec

TOPIC X Deposition

Deposition, also called *sedimentation,* is the process by which sediments are released, settled from, or dropped from an erosional system. Deposition includes the releasing of solid sediments and the process of *precipitation,* which is the releasing of dissolved ionic minerals from a water solution. Most final deposition occurs in large water bodies, because running water is the dominant erosional system.

FACTORS CAUSING DEPOSITION

Deposition usually occurs when the velocity of the stream, wind, or other erosional system decreases. Some of the factors that determine which sediments are deposited, and their rates of settling, are described below.

1. Size. All other factors being equal, when wind or running water slows down, the larger sediments settle out first. This occurs because the larger sediment particles are heavier and therefore sink faster. Very small particles (less than 0.0004 cm in diameter), called **colloids** (or clay), may remain suspended in water almost indefinitely.

2. Shape. The shape of a particle helps determine how fast it will be deposited from wind or running water. All other factors being equal, the more spherical a sediment, the faster it will settle out, and the more flattened it is, the greater its resistance to deposition.

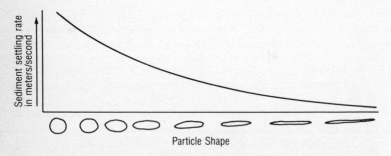

Figure 10-1. Settling rates of sediments of various shapes. As sediments of equal volume and density become less spherical (or rounded) and more flattened it takes more time for them to settle, so settling rate decreases (gets slower).

3. Density. All other factors being the same, the higher the density of a sediment, the faster it will settle out of air or water. The reason for this is that if two particles have the same size and shape, the denser one will be heavier.

SORTING OF SEDIMENTS AND DEPOSITION

Sorting of sediments is the degree of similarity of sediment size in a given deposit. The greater the similarity of size, the more sorted the sediments are said to be.

GRADED BEDDING.   When a mixture of sediment sizes in water settles out rapidly, a horizontal layer *(bed)* develops with sediment size decreasing toward the top of the bed. Such an arrangement in a sediment layer is called **graded bedding** (see Figure 10-2). Graded bedding is most often associated with sediment-laden density currents, called *turbidity currents.* These turbidity currents are most common on the sloped ocean bottoms off the coasts of continents, and produce graded bedding on the flatter ocean bottom further offshore *(abyssal areas)*. Graded bedding can also form in lakes fed by streams.

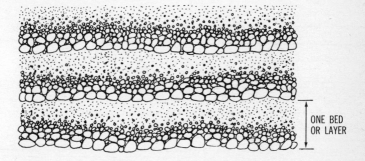

Figure 10-2. Layers of sediment with graded bedding. In each bed or layer, sediment sizes decrease from bottom to top. Graded bedding results from rapid deposition in an erosional system, as by a turbidity current (see text). Each bed is the result of a single turbidity flow.

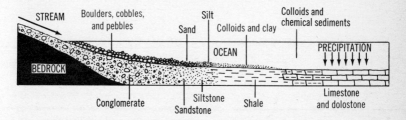

Figure 10-3. Horizontal sorting where a stream enters the ocean. The larger sediments settle first (nearer the shore). Sediments become smaller as distance from shore increases. Where solid sediments are rare, chemical precipitation is the dominant type of deposition. Precipitation nearer the shore may provide the cement for the formation of the types of sedimentary rocks indicated. Limestone and dolostone are common evaporite sedimentary rocks formed largely by precipitation.

HORIZONTAL SORTING. When the velocity of a wind or water erosional system gradually decreases (such as when a stream flows into the ocean at a delta), the larger, denser, and more spherical sediments settle out first. This results in layers with **horizontal sorting,** in which the sediment size, sphericalness, and density generally decrease in the direction the erosional system was moving (see Figure 10-3).

UNSORTED GLACIAL DEPOSITS. In a solid erosional system such as a glacier, sediments of all sizes, shapes, and densities are deposited together. This results in the unsorted deposits characteristic of direct glacial deposits (see Figure 10-4).

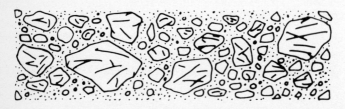

Figure 10-4. Unsorted glacial deposits. In glacial deposition there is no fluid medium in which sediments can become sorted. Thus, glacial deposits are characterized by a random distribution of sediment sizes and no bedding or layering. Note glacial scratches on sediments.

CHARACTERISTICS OF AN EROSIONAL-DEPOSITIONAL SYSTEM

MODEL OF AN EROSIONAL-DEPOSITIONAL SYSTEM. Figure 10-5 shows a side view and a top view of an imaginary stream used as a model of an erosional-depositional system. In this simple model it is assumed that the volume of flow (discharge) is the same throughout the length of the stream.

ENERGY TRANSFORMATIONS IN THE MODEL SYSTEM. At the beginning, or *source,* of the stream (A), the system has a maximum of potential energy. As the stream flows toward its end, or *mouth* (D), potential energy is continuously being transformed into kinetic energy. This kinetic energy is at the same time being lost to the environment in the form of heat produced by friction. Where the slope of the stream is steep, the transformation of energy occurs most rapidly, the stream has its greatest velocity, and the system has its greatest kinetic energy. Where the slope is small, the rate of energy transformation decreases, the stream slows down, and the kinetic energy of the system decreases. At the mouth of the stream, the velocity drops to zero, and the system has zero kinetic energy. Since the system has less potential energy because of its lower elevation, there has been a net loss of energy between the source and the mouth.

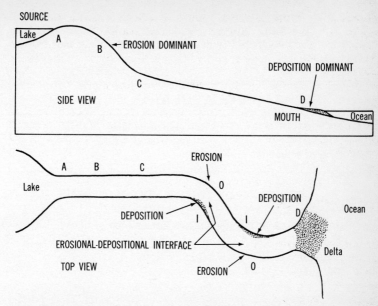

Figure 10-5. Model of a stream representing an erosional-depositional system. "O" indicates the outside of a curve and "I" indicates the inside. Some deposition may occur at **C**, where the slope and velocity decrease. Erosional-depositional interfaces will then exist between **B** and **C** and between **C** and **D**.

EROSION AND DEPOSITION IN RELATION TO ENERGY CHANGES. Wherever the kinetic energy of the system is large, erosion is the dominant process. Where the kinetic energy is small, deposition is the dominant process. Thus, erosion occurs in regions of steep slope, and deposition occurs in regions of gentle slope. Deposition is particularly rapid at the mouth of the stream, where the kinetic energy becomes zero. Stream velocity is also larger at the outside of curves and smaller at the inside. Therefore, erosion usually occurs at the outside of curves and deposition occurs at the inside.

EROSIONAL-DEPOSITIONAL INTERFACES. Since there are regions of erosion and regions of deposition along the length of the stream, an interface between an erosional and a depositional state can often be located in the system. Interfaces between erosion and deposition exist at the curves in the model stream, and near the mouth of the stream. They may also be found where changes in slope occur, as between B and C in Figure 10-5.

DYNAMIC EQUILIBRIUM OF THE SYSTEM. Since all sediments picked up by the stream during erosion must eventually be deposited, the system is in a state of *dynamic equilibrium*. Although erosion and deposition are occurring continuously, the rate of erosion equals the rate of deposition by the system as a whole. If a flood occurs, a stream will erode (pick up and transport) more sediment, but it will also deposit an equally increased volume of sediment, thus establishing a new balance or equilibrium.

VOCABULARY

deposition	graded bedding
colloid (clay)	horizontal sorting
sorting of sediments	

QUESTIONS ON TOPIC X—DEPOSITION

Questions in Recent Regents Exams (end of book)

June 1984: 28, 29
June 1985: 30, 31, 81, 82, 83, 84, 85
June 1986: 30, 35, 54, 90
June 1987: 29, 30, 52, 86, 88, 90

Questions from Earlier Regents Exams

1. A low hill is composed of unsorted sediments that have mixed grain sizes. This hill was probably deposited by ● a glacier (2) the wind (3) running water (4) wave action

2. The rate at which particles are deposited by a stream is *least* affected by the (1) size and shape of the particles (2) velocity of the stream ● stream's elevation above sea level (4) density of the particles

3. Which is the most probable description of the energy of a particle in an erosional-depositional system? ● Particles gain kinetic energy during erosion and lose kinetic energy during deposition. (2) Particles lose kinetic energy during erosion and lose kinetic energy during deposition. (3) Particles gain potential energy during erosion and gain potential energy during deposition. (4) Particles lose potential energy during erosion and gain potential energy during deposition.

4. Clay, silt, and sand are added to a jar of water. The jar is shaken and then allowed to stand quietly for a number of hours. The result of this demonstration, which is shown at the right, could be best used as a model to show that (1) particles with the lowest density settle the fastest ● particles with the largest diameter settle the fastest (3) water has a higher specific gravity than clay, silt, and sand (4) the bottom layer of a series of sediments is the youngest

Base your answers to questions 5 through 8 on the diagram below, which represents a stream profile.

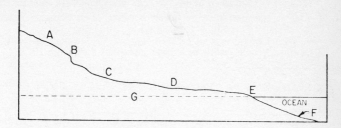

5. The most deposition will take place at   (1) A   (2) B   (3) C   ⬤ E

6. The rate of stream erosion is probably greatest between   ⬤ A and C   (2) C and D   (3) D and E   (4) E and F

7. The position where the stream's potential energy is greatest is at   ⬤ A   (2) B   (3) C   (4) D

8. Line G generally represents the limit of   (1) highest tide   ⬤ stream erosion   (3) deposition   (4) local water table

Additional Questions

1. Glacial deposits are different from stream deposits because the glacial deposits are   (1) more sorted   ⬤ more mixed, or unsorted   (3) more rounded   (4) more chemically weathered

To answer questions 2 through 6, refer to the diagrams below, which show cross sections of deposited sediments.

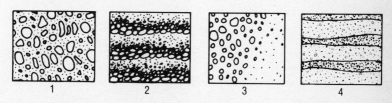

2. Which deposit represents a direct glacial deposit?   ⬤ 1   (2) 2   (3) 3   (4) 4

3. Which deposit would most likely have been deposited by wind?   (1) 1   (2) 2   (3) 3   ⬤ 4

4. Which deposit would most likely have been made by density currents on the ocean bottom?   (1) 1   ⬤ 2   (3) 3   (4) 4

5. Which deposit was formed by continuous deposition by a stream whose velocity decreased as it entered the ocean?   (1) 1   (2) 2   ⬤ 3   (4) 4

6. Which deposit can be best explained by the velocity of water rapidly decreasing during deposition?   (1) 1   ● 2   (3) 3   (4) 4

7. Which of these sediments would you expect to find in the greatest quantity far out into the ocean because of suspension of sediment?   (1) sand   (2) pebbles   ● colloids   (4) boulders

Refer to the four graphs below to answer questions 8 through 10.

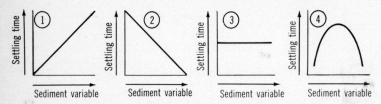

8. Which graph shows the relationship between settling time and the change in sediment from spheroids to flat thin sheets?   ● 1 (2) 2   (3) 3   (4) 4

9. Which graph shows the relationship between settling time and increasing density of sediments?   (1) 1   ● 2   (3) 3   (4) 4

10. Which graph shows the relationship between settling time and increasing sediment size?   (1) 1   ● 2   (3) 3   (4) 4

To answer questions 11 through 18 refer to the diagram below, which shows the top and side views of a stream. Consider the volume of water in the stream to be everywhere the same.

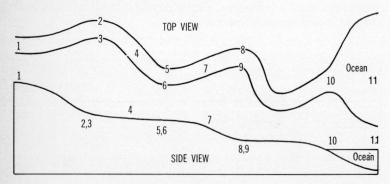

11. At which place in the stream would there be the most clear interface between erosion and deposition?   (1) 1   ● 2–3   (3) 3–4 (4) 7

12. What is true about the total amount of energy of this stream as it flows from 1 to 10?   (1) it steadily increases   ● it steadily decreases   (3) it increases and decreases   (4) it remains the same

13. Between what two points would the most potential energy be converted to kinetic energy?   ● 1–2   ● 2–5   (3) 5–8   (4) 8–10

14. At which location would the most deposition occur because of loss of energy?   (1) 4   (2) 6   (3) 9   ● 10

15. At which location would the stream be doing the most eroding of its side and banks?   (1) 1   (2) 3   (3) 5   ● 8

16. If the stream is eroding as much as it is depositing between 8 and 10, the stream at this location can be said to   (1) be an interface   ● have dynamic equilibrium   (3) be sorted   (4) have equal amounts of kinetic and potential energy

17. Which characteristic would usually decrease the most between locations 10 and 11?   (1) the amount of salt in solution   ● the size of the sediments   (3) the density of the water   (4) the depth of the water

18. As the water of the stream flows from 1 to 10, the total potential energy of the stream will   (1) increase   ● decrease   (3) remain the same

Rocks are any naturally formed solid matter that makes up a part of the solid earth. Rocks are usually composed of a mixture of minerals.

ROCK TYPES.   Rocks are classified according to type of origin into three groups: *sedimentary, metamorphic,* and *igneous.* The igneous and metamorphic rocks may be grouped together as *nonsedimentary rocks,* so that rocks may also be classified as sedimentary and nonsedimentary.

SEDIMENTARY ROCKS

Sedimentary rocks are rocks that form from an accumulation of sediments derived from preexisting rocks and/or organic material.

FORMATION OF SEDIMENTARY ROCKS.   Most sedimentary rocks are made up of solid sediments weathered from other rocks. The sediments are then transported and deposited by water, wind, or glaciers to new locations in water or on land. Most sedimentary rocks form under bodies of water such as lakes and oceans. Sedimentary rocks are formed in the following ways:

   1. Cementation. Larger solid sediments, such as sand and pebbles, form rocks when the sediments are cemented together by minerals that are precipitated out of solution (see Figure 11-1, A and B).

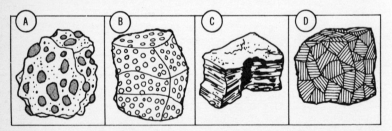

Figure 11-1. Some characteristics of sedimentary rocks. (A) Conglomerate. Particles of unsorted sizes cemented together. **(B)** Sandstone. Particles of fairly uniform (sorted) size cemented together. **(C)** Shale. Rock formed by compression of very small (colloidal) sediments, possibly cemented as well. **(D)** Evaporite. Monomineralic crystalline rock (composed of intergrown mineral crystals) formed by precipitation.

   2. Compression. When very small solid sediments (colloids) are compressed by the pressure of overlying water and sediments, they form rocks like the one in Figure 11-1C. Sedimentary rocks may also be formed by a combination of compression and cementation.

   3. Chemical action. Ionic minerals dissolved in water may **precipitate** out as the result of chemical processes or of evaporation of the water.

A rock formed in this manner is a **monomineralic** rock, that is, it consists of **crystals,** or grains, of a single mineral (see Figure 11-1D). Rocks formed by these chemical processes are called **evaporites.** Limestone and salt are evaporites.

4. Biologic processes. Some sedimentary rocks form as a result of biologic processes. Many forms of life that live in water, such as clams and corals, extract dissolved minerals from the water to form their hard parts. When the organisms die, these hard parts accumulate to form rocks such as limestone. Coal is a rock formed when dead plant matter is deposited in water and compressed.

CHARACTERISTICS OF SEDIMENTARY ROCKS.

1. Most sedimentary rocks are composed of fragments or particles which strongly resemble sediments.

2. Some sedimentary rocks have a range of particle or sediment sizes (see Figure 11-1A).

3. Other sedimentary rocks consist mainly of one sediment size because of the sorting of sediments in deposition (see Figures 11-1B and 11-1C).

4. Some sedimentary rocks are of **organic** origin; that is, they are composed of plant and animal products or remains.

5. Sedimentary rocks often have discrete (separate and distinct) parallel layers, as shown in Figure 11-2. Such layers are also called **beds** or **strata.**

6. Sedimentary rocks often contain *fossils*.

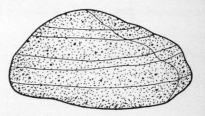

Figure 11-2. Layers in a sedimentary rock. Layers may result from changes in the type of sediment during the period of deposition.

IDENTIFYING SEDIMENTARY ROCKS.   Refer to the chart *Common Sedimentary Rocks* on page 249 of the *Earth Science Reference Tables.* As can be inferred from the chart, sedimentary rocks are classified and identified largely on the basis of size of solid sediments (particle diameter) and/or mineral composition of the rock. Monomineralic rocks, such as limestone and dolostone, and the evaporites are identified primarily based on the one mineral they contain. For example, the rock gypsum is composed of the mineral gypsum, and dolostone is composed of dolomite.

The vast majority of sedimentary rocks are composed of solid sediments (boulders to clay in the chart) that have been cemented and/or compacted together. These sedimentary rocks are most commonly identified according to the size of the majority of the sediments they contain, regardless of their mineral composition. For example, if a rock is composed largely of solid sediments of 0.01 cm in diameter (sand size), the rock would be called a sandstone.

NONSEDIMENTARY ROCKS

Nonsedimentary rocks are those rocks that do not form from sediments. There are two groups of nonsedimentary rocks—the *igneous* and the *metamorphic* rocks.

IGNEOUS NONSEDIMENTARY ROCKS.   **Igneous rocks** are those rocks that form from the cooling and **solidification,** or **crystallization,** of liquid rock. (Liquid rock beneath the earth's surface is known as *magma.* When liquid rock reaches the earth's surface, it is called *lava.*) When liquid rock cools, it forms a solid, usually by the growth of various mineral crystals in a process called crystallization. This results in a **crystalline** texture, consisting of intergrown mineral crystals of different sizes, shapes, and chemical composition, as shown in Figure 11-3. Such a rock is called **polymineralic,** because it contains two or more different minerals. Solidification includes the change from liquid rock to a noncrystalline igneous rock (as shown in Figure 11-3C) and it includes the process of crystallization.

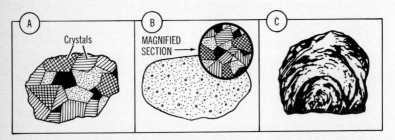

Figure 11-3. Cross sections showing three types of texture in igneous nonsedimentary rocks. (A) Slow cooling of the liquid rock results in large crystals visible to the unaided eye. **(B)** If cooling is more rapid, the crystals are too small to be seen without magnification. A magnified section resembles the texture in **A. (C)** If cooling is very rapid, the solid rock has a glassy texture without mineral crystals.

    1. Size of crystals. The size of the crystals in an igneous nonsedimentary rock depends on the conditions of the environment in which the rock formed. The immediate cause of the difference in the size of the crystals is the amount of time in which the cooling takes place. The longer the time of cooling, the larger the crystals become. However, the cooling time itself depends on the temperature and pressure of the environment. The pressure and temperature deep within the earth are very high, and therefore liquid rock cools slowly (possibly for thousands of years). The result is rocks with large crystals. (A body of rock formed by solidification below the earth's surface is called an **intrusion,** and the igneous rocks that form are called **intrusive.)**

The temperature and pressure at or near the earth's surface are much lower, and liquid rock cools there much more quickly than at great depths. This produces rocks with much smaller crystals. (A body of rock formed by solidification at the earth's surface is called an **extrusion,** and the igneous rocks that form are called **extrusive.)**

2. Texture of igneous rocks. The **texture** of igneous rocks depends on the size of the crystals, as well as on their shape and arrangement within the rock. Rocks with large crystals have a coarse texture (see Figure 11-3A). Those with crystals that are too small to be seen clearly with the unaided eye have a fine texture. Igneous rocks that cool very rapidly at the earth's surface have no crystals at all, and have a glassy texture.

IDENTIFYING IGNEOUS ROCKS. Refer to the diagram *Scheme for Igneous Rock Classification* on page 250 of the *Earth Science Reference Tables.* The diagram shows a common method of classifying and identifying igneous rocks. Igneous rocks are identified largely on the basis of texture (mostly size of the mineral crystals—coarse or fine) and percent mineral composition. The majority of the mineral crystals in a coarse-grained rock are easily visible to the unaided eye (2 mm or larger), while the majority of the mineral crystals in a fine-grained rock are *not* easily seen by the unaided eye.

Percent mineral composition divides igneous rocks on the diagram into vertical columns (igneous rock families), labeled zones A–F. Within a lettered family (zone), rocks have similar mineral compositions.

Other information indicated by the *Scheme for Igneous Rock Identification* includes:

1. As rocks appear farther to the right on the diagram, they become more mafic (high in magnesium and iron) and less felsic or granitic (high in silicon and aluminum).

2. As rocks appear farther to the right on the diagram, their density increases.

3. As rocks appear farther to the right on the diagram, their overall color becomes darker.

METAMORPHIC NONSEDIMENTARY ROCKS. Metamorphic rocks are those rocks that are formed from other rocks (igneous, sedimentary, or other metamorphic rocks) within the earth's crust. The formation of metamorphic rocks occurs in response to conditions of heat, pressure, and/or chemical change. Such conditions are often associated with the pressure and deep burial that result from mountain building processes; therefore, metamorphic rocks are often found in mountainous regions where weathering and erosion have exposed rock that was once deeply buried. Under conditions of high temperature and pressure, many metamorphic rocks form by the process of **recrystallization,** which is a growth of mineral crystals at the expense of surrounding sediments or other crystals of the original rock (see Figure 11-4). Recrystallization occurs without true melting.

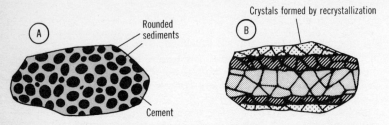

Figure 11-4. **Metamorphic nonsedimentary rock formed by recrystallization.** Under the influence of heat and pressure, similar minerals in the sediments or cement of a sedimentary rock combine to form mineral crystals, producing a crystalline texture. However, recrystallization occurs without melting of the rock.

Metamorphic nonsedimentary rocks often have certain textural and structural characteristics that result from the environment of formation:

1. Banding is a layered arrangement in a metamorphic rock in which firmly joined crystals of like minerals are aligned in layers, or bands (see Figure 11-4B). The layers are formed when the rock is subjected to extreme environmental pressure and high temperatures. Usually, the greater the pressure and temperature, the thicker the bands (see Figure 11-5).

Figure 11-5. **Banding in metamorphic nonsedimentary rocks.**

2. Distorted structure is the curving and folding of the bands in metamorphic rocks (see Figure 11-6). These distortions of the once-horizontal layers are caused by great environmental pressures exerted on the rock from different directions.

ENVIRONMENT OF ROCK FORMATION

The type of environment in which a rock formed is inferred from its composition, structure, and texture. The following are examples of such inferences.

1. Composition. If the composition of a sedimentary rock is salt, the rock probably formed by means of evaporation and precipitation in a body of salt water. The presence of fossils indicates formation at or near the earth's surface.

2. Structure. The distorted structure of the metamorphic rock shown in Figure 11-6 was caused by an environment of great pressure.

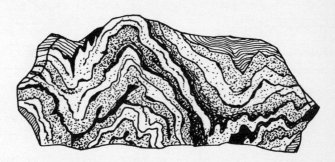

Figure 11-6. Distorted structure in a metamorphic nonsedimentary rock.

3. Texture. The texture of a rock results from the size, shape, and arrangement of its mineral crystals or sediments. If the sediments found in a sedimentary rock are angular in shape, it may be inferred that the rock was formed near the source of the sediments.

DISTRIBUTION OF ROCK TYPES.   Sedimentary rocks are usually found as a *veneer* (relatively thin coating) over large areas of continents. The nonsedimentary rocks that occur at or near the surface are most often found in regions of volcanoes and mountains (see Figure 11-7). The nonsedimentary rocks in mountain regions are exposed on the surface after millions of years of weathering and erosion have removed the veneer of sedimentary rocks.

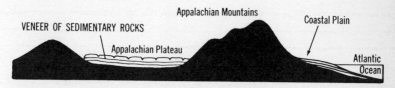

Figure 11-7. Veneer of sedimentary rocks in the Appalachian Plateau in the eastern United States. The solid black indicates nonsedimentary rock.

THE ROCK CYCLE.   The **rock cycle** is a model used to show how the rock types (sedimentary, igneous nonsedimentary, and metamorphic nonsedimentary) are interrelated, and the processes that produce each rock type. Figure 11-8 on page 152 is a diagram of the rock cycle.

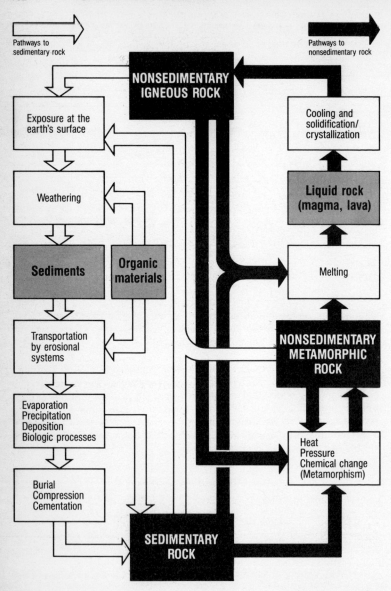

Figure 11-8. The rock cycle. Some of the processes by which one type of rock can be changed to another.

Some of the major concepts of the rock cycle are:

1. *Any one rock type can change into any other rock type.* Thus a specimen of any one type can have materials in it that were once part of any other type.

2. *There is no preferred direction of movement of materials in the rock cycle for any one mass of material.* Any one piece of material can stay in any one place for any length of time, or it can follow any of the arrows indicated on the diagram.

3. *There is no exact point of separation between the rock types.* For example, where local rock has been in contact with an intrusion of molten rock, or with a lava flow (extrusion), there is a **transition zone (contact metamorphic zone)** between the original local rock and the intrusion or the lava flow. In this transition zone there is a blending of the rock types and often no exact boundary (see Figure 11-9).

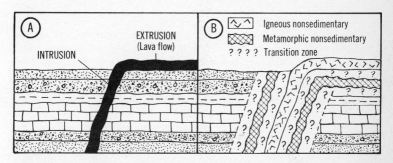

Figure 11-9. Formation of transition zones between rock types by a flow of molten rock. In **A,** molten rock has flowed up through a crack in sedimentary rock to the surface, forming an intrusion below the surface and an extrusion (lava flow) on the surface. In the contact zone between the original local rock and the intrusion or extrusion, there is a blending of rock types from sedimentary, through metamorphic nonsedimentary, to igneous nonsedimentary.

4. *Sedimentary rocks often contain sediments (fragments) which have varied origins.* This occurs because (a) sedimentary rocks form from the weathered products of any type of rock and/or organic materials, and (b) in any one depositional basin where sedimentary rocks form, the sediments can be brought from many different areas and by various methods of transport.

5. *The composition of some rocks suggests that the materials (sediments or minerals) in the rock have undergone multiple transformations (changes) within the rock cycle.* This is so because of the many possible paths within the rock cycle that can produce any one rock. For example, a sedimentary rock may contain fragments, or sediments, that were once part of a metamorphic rock that formed deep within the earth. However, that metamorphic rock itself may have been transformed from a sedimentary rock that formed near the earth's surface. A sedimentary rock may also contain sediments from previous sedimentary rocks and fragments which were once part of an intrusive igneous rock. The cement holding the rock together may once have been part of an igneous rock that was uplifted to the earth's surface and chemically weathered to form dissolved minerals; the minerals were then transported by water and later precipitated to become the cement.

MINERALS

A **mineral** is a naturally occurring, crystalline, inorganic substance with characteristic physical and chemical properties. That is, a mineral is a natural substance, a solid with a specific arrangement of constituent units, and either a chemical element or compound, which is not derived from parts of organisms (forms of life) or their products.

RELATION OF MINERALS TO ROCKS.   Nearly all rocks are composed of minerals. (A few rocks, such as coal, are composed of organic substances not considered to be minerals.) Most rocks, such as those shown in Figure 11-5, are **polymineralic,** that is, they consist of more than one mineral. Some rocks are **monomineralic,** that is, they consist entirely of one mineral. Many sedimentary rocks and the metamorphic nonsedimentary rocks that form from those sedimentary rocks are monomineralic.

Only a limited number of the approximately 2,500 minerals are commonly found in most rocks. These are called the **rock-forming minerals.**

MINERAL COMPOSITION.   Minerals are composed of *elements*. A few minerals, such as copper, sulfur, and graphite, are each composed of only one element. Most minerals are composed of two or more elements in chemical combination and are called *compounds.*

The circle graph and the table in Figure 11-10 illustrate the following points:

1. Most of the earth's crust and thus most minerals are made up of only a few elements.

2. Oxygen is the most abundant element by weight and volume.

3. Silicon is the second most abundant element by weight.

MINERAL PROPERTIES.   Minerals have characteristic physical and chemical properties. Some of these properties are color, hardness, luster, streak, how the mineral breaks (cleavage and fracture), and density. Many of the physical properties of minerals are related to the structural arrangement of the mineral's **constituent units** (atoms or ions). A good example of this is the way the mineral halite (common salt) breaks into cubes because of a cubic arrangement of the constituent units (ions), as shown in Figure 11-11. Another example is the characteristic external crystal shape of minerals.

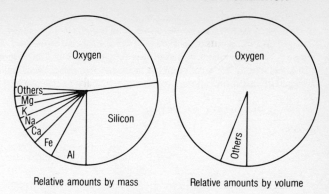

Figure 11-10. Percentages of the chief elements in the earth's crust by mass and by volume. "Volume" in this case means the amount of space occupied by the atoms of each element in the solid substances of the crust. Also see *Average Chemical Composition of Crust, Hydrosphere, and Troposphere* in the *Earth Science Reference Tables*

Composition of the Earth's Crust			
Element	Sym-bol	Percent by mass	Percent by volume
Oxygen	O	46.6	93.8
Silicon	Si	27.7	0.9
Aluminum	Al	8.1	0.5
Iron	Fe	5.0	0.4
Calcium	Ca	3.6	1.0
Sodium	Na	2.8	1.3
Potassium	K	2.6	1.8
Magnesium	Mg	2.1	0.3
All others	—	1.5	—

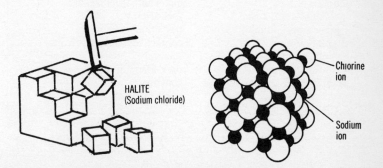

Figure 11-11. Cleavage of the mineral halite. When a piece of halite is broken, it tends to break into roughly cubic pieces. This is the result of a cubic arrangement of the constituent units (sodium and chlorine ions) in the halite crystal.

MINERAL STRUCTURE.   In many minerals the constituent unit is in the form of a *tetrahedron* composed of silicon and oxygen (see Figure 11-12). This **silicon-oxygen tetrahedron** can combine with itself and with other elements to form different structures (such as chains and sheets). These different structural arrangements account for differences in the physical properties of minerals.

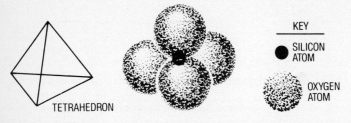

TETRAHEDRON

KEY

● SILICON
   ATOM

OXYGEN
ATOM

Figure 11-12. The silicon-oxygen tetrahedron. A tetrahedron is a geometric figure having four faces, all of which are equilateral triangles of the same size. In silicates, there are oxygen atoms at the four corners of a tetrahedron, with a silicon atom at the center.

VOCABULARY

sedimentary rock	intrusive igneous rock
cementation	extrusion
compression	extrusive igneous rock
precipitation	texture
monomineralic	metamorphic nonsedimentary
crystal	rock
evaporite	recrystallization
organic	banding
beds/strata	distorted structure
nonsedimentary rock	rock cycle
igneous nonsedimentary rock	transition zone
solidification	contact metamorphic zone
crystallization	mineral
crystalline	rock-forming mineral
polymineralic	constituent unit
intrusion	silicon-oxygen tetrahedron

QUESTIONS ON TOPIC XI—ROCK FORMATION

Questions in Recent Regents Exams (end of book)

June 1984:   30, 31, 32, 33, 42, 48, 53, 88
June 1985:   32, 33, 34, 35, 36, 53, 84, 90
June 1986:   3, 32, 33, 36, 37, 38, 61, 98
June 1987:   31–35, 89, 100

Questions from Earlier Regents Exams

1. Which statement concerning a large outcrop of granite (coarse-grained igneous nonsedimentary rock) is most likely correct?   (1) a number of volcanoes are nearby   (2) the granite is the probable result of a lava flow   (3) the rock was never under water   (4) a great deal of erosion has taken place at this location

2. A certain igneous (nonsedimentary) rock is composed of large mineral grains. This suggests that the rock formed   (1) on the surface, under high pressure, and at a rapid rate of cooling   (2) on the surface, at high temperature, and at a slow rate of cooling   (3) under high pressure, at high temperature, and at a rapid rate of cooling   (4) under high pressure, at high temperature, and at a slow rate of cooling

To answer questions 3 through 6 refer to the sketches below, which show four specimens of rocks.

3. Which sketch best represents a sedimentary rock?   (1) 1   (2) 2   (3) 3   (4) 4

4. Which sketch best represents a metamorphic rock?   (1) 1   (2) 2   (3) 3   (4) 4

5. Which sketch best represents a rock formed at great depth directly from molten rock?   (1) 1   (2) 2   (3) 3   (4) 4

6. Which sketch represents a rock originating in a lava flow (thus cooling in a short period of time)?   (1) 1   (2) 2   (3) 3   (4) 4

7. By both volume and weight, oxygen is the most abundant element in the   (1) atmosphere   (2) biosphere   (3) hydrosphere   (4) lithosphere

8. According to the *Earth Science Reference Tables,* generally, as the percentage of felsic minerals in a rock increases, the rock's color will become   (1) darker and its density will decrease   (2) lighter and its density will increase   (3) darker and its density will increase   (4) lighter and its density will decrease

9. In which rock type are fossils usually found?   (1) igneous   (2) volcanic   (3) sedimentary   (4) metamorphic

10. Which would most likely occur during the formation of igneous rock?   (1) compression and cementation of sediments   (2) recrystallization of unmelted material   (3) solidification of molten materials   (4) evaporation and precipitation of sediments

11. As the depth within the earth's crust increases, the amount of sedimentary rock, compared to the amount of nonsedimentary rock, will generally   (1) decrease   ● increase   (3) remain the same

12. The cubic shape of a crystal is most likely the result of that crystal's   (1) hardness   (2) density distribution   ● internal arrangement of atoms   (4) intensity of radioactive decay

13. Which object is the best model of the shape of a silicon-oxygen structural unit?

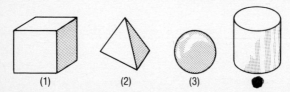

(1)   (2)   (3)   ●

14. What is the main difference between metamorphic rocks and most other rocks?   (1) Many metamorphic rocks contain only one mineral.   (2) Many metamorphic rocks have an organic composition.   ● Many metamorphic rocks exhibit banding and distortion of structure.   (4) Many metamorphic rocks contain a high amount of oxygen-silicon tetrahedra.

15. According to the *Earth Science Reference Tables*, compaction and cementation of pebble-size particles would form the sedimentary rock known as   (1) shale   ● conglomerate   (3) sandstone   (4) siltstone

16. When dilute hydrochloric acid is placed on the sedimentary rock limestone and the nonsedimentary rock marble, a bubbling reaction occurs with both. What would this indicate?   ● The minerals of these two rocks have similar chemical compositions.   (2) The molecular structures of these two rocks have been changed by heat and pressure.   (3) The physical properties of these two rocks are identical.   (4) The two rocks originated at the same location.

17. According to the *Earth Science Reference Tables*, which is a sedimentary rock that forms as a result of precipitation from seawater?   (1) conglomerate   ● gypsum   (3) basalt   (4) shale

18. An igneous rock which has crystallized deep below the earth's surface has the following approximate composition: 70% pyroxene, 15% plagioclase, and 15% olivine. According to the *Earth Science Reference Tables*, what is the name of this igneous rock?   (1) granite   (2) rhyolite   ● gabbro   (4) basalt

19. Which graph best shows the relationship between the size of the crystals in an igneous rock and the length of time it has taken the rock to solidify?

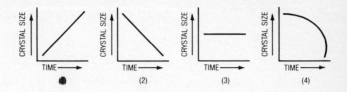

(2)   (3)   (4)

Additional Questions

1. Diamond and graphite are two minerals composed totally of carbon. Why are diamond and graphite so different in physical properties?   (1) the atoms of carbon are different   (2) graphite and diamond formed at different ages of the earth   (3) the arrangement of carbon atoms in graphite is different from the arrangement of carbon atoms in diamond   (4) graphite is organic and diamond is not

2. Of the ninety or so elements found in the earth's crust,   (1) many are found in abundance in most minerals   (2) only a few are found in abundance in most minerals   (3) most are not found in any mineral   (4) silicon is second most abundant by volume

To answer questions 3 through 6 refer to the diagrams below, which represent six rock samples. The shadings indicate different minerals, sediments, or fossils.

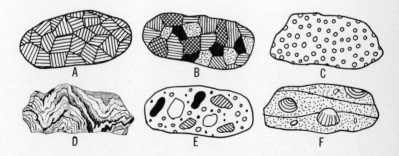

3. Which rock would be considered monomineralic?   (1) A   (2) B   (3) D   (4) E

4. Which rock formed partly as the result of biologic processes?   (1) B   (2) C   (3) D   (4) F

5. Which sample is nonsedimentary?   (1) B   (2) C   (3) E   (4) F

6. Which sample has distorted structure and banding?   (1) A   (2) B   (3) C   (4) D

To answer questions 7 through 11 refer to the diagram below, which represents a portion of the earth's crust.

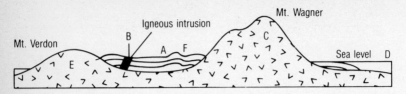

7. At which location would contact metamorphic rock most likely be found?   (1) B   (2) F   (3) C   (4) D

8. At which location would you find a veneer of sedimentary rocks?   (1) A   (2) B   (3) C   (4) E

9. At which location would you find the largest mass of nonsedimentary rocks above sea level?   (1) A   (2) B   (3) C   (4) D

10. At which location would you find a transition zone between once molten rock and local rock?   (1) A   (2) B   (3) D   (4) F

11. At which location could rock be forming by the process of precipitation?   (1) A   (2) B   (3) C   (4) D

12. Which rock would most likely be monomineralic (contains only one mineral)?   (1) granite   (2) rhyolite   (3) basalt   (4) rock salt

The Dynamic Crust (Lithosphere) and the Earth's Interior

There is much evidence indicating that the crust is constantly undergoing change, and that parts (if not all) of it move to new locations, thereby changing the surface of the earth. In some cases we know the crust moves because its movement has been observed directly during earthquakes or the sudden birth of volcanoes. Evidence of past crustal movements must be indirect. Much of that indirect evidence is based on the concept of **original horizontality,** which assumes (on the basis of geologic evidence) that sedimentary rocks and some extrusive igneous rocks form in generally horizontal layers, or **strata.** Therefore, most strata found in other than horizontal positions are believed to have been deformed by crustal movement. Note: In this topic whatever is stated about the crust also applies to the lithosphere, except when the terms "granitic crust" or "basaltic crust" are used.

EVIDENCE OF MINOR CRUSTAL CHANGES

DEFORMED STRATA. Rock strata that no longer show their original horizontality are called *deformed strata.* Some of the types of deformed strata are **folded strata, tilted strata,** and **faults** (see Figure 12-1). All such deformed strata are considered evidence of past crustal movements. A **fault** is a crack in a mass of rock along which there has been *displacement,* or movement, of the rock layers. Movement along a fault results in a shaking of the earth called an earthquake.

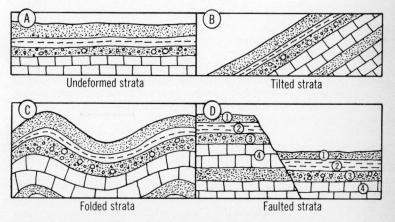

Undeformed strata   Tilted strata

Folded strata   Faulted strata

Figure 12-1. Three types of deformed horizontal strata. The numbers in Diagram D mark strata that were originally continuous.

MOVEMENTS DURING EARTHQUAKES.   It is sometimes possible to observe the actual movement of the crust or immediate effects of that movement during an earthquake. This occurs when the movement along a fault results in obvious changes in the positions of surface features, sometimes forming cliffs (see Figure 12-2).

Figure 12-2. Displacement of surface features as the result of movement of strata along a fault. The portions of the power line, road, orchard, and fields in the foreground have moved down and to the right relative to their continuations at the top of the cliff. Displacements during a single fault movement seldom exceed a few meters. However, successive movements over millions of years may produce accumulated displacements of 1,000 meters or more.

DISPLACED FOSSILS.   Marine (meaning ocean) fossils, such as corals and clams, found in sedimentary rock high (sometimes thousands of feet) above sea level indicate that the land has been uplifted to its present location. A lowering of the level of the sea could not have changed the location of the fossils so much because it is believed that sea level can vary only a few hundred feet. On the other hand, shallow water marine fossils found in deep ocean areas may indicate **subsidence,** or a sinking of part of the earth's crust.

VERTICAL MOVEMENTS.   Along many shorelines there are raised beaches and other coastline features that normally occur at sea level (see Figure 12-3). These features are often associated with tilted rocks. Changes in elevation have also been observed directly in many locations by means of *bench marks*. A **bench mark** is a permanent marker set into the ground and labeled with its exact elevation at the time of placement. Later measurements often show changes in elevation. All these changes indicate that vertical movements of the earth's crust have taken place. Vertical movements often affect large portions of the earth's crust.

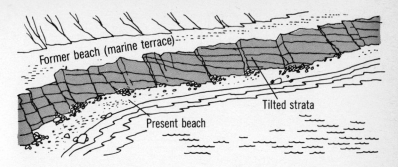

Figure 12-3. Evidence of vertical movement of the crust along a shoreline.
The flat marine terrace can be recognized as having once been a beach. The
beach was raised by crustal movement. When movement stopped, the ocean
once again began to cut a level beach into the new shore.

EVIDENCE OF MAJOR CRUSTAL CHANGES

GEOSYNCLINES AND MOUNTAINS.   Large thicknesses of sedimentary rock have been found in parts of various mountain systems. These
rocks contain fossils and other evidence which indicate that they formed
in shallow marine (ocean) water. For this reason, many geologists believe
that the continental mountain systems formed from *geosynclines*. A
geosyncline is a large shallow ocean basin, located near the margin of a
continent, that subsides, or sinks, as sediments are added to it. This
subsidence would explain how the great thicknesses of sediments needed
to form mountains can be deposited in a relatively shallow geosyncline
without filling it. In this way, the geosyncline can remain a shallow-water
area for millions of years. Later, the sedimentary rock strata of the
geosyncline are believed to be deformed and uplifted to form mountains
and enlarge the continent.

Figure 12-4 on page 164 indicates some possible geosynclines, that
is, large shallow basins where sedimentation and possibly subsidence are
presently occurring. Note that many of these basins are located near
areas of other major crustal activities.

ISOSTASY AND GEOSYNCLINES.   The principle of **isostasy** has been
used to explain part, but not all, of the sinking of geosynclines. The
principle states that the crust of the earth is in a state of equilibrium,
and that any change in mass of one part of the crust will be offset by a
change in mass of another part to maintain the equilibrium. Think of
the crust as floating on the denser rock of the mantle as an ice cube
floats in water. If erosion causes the continental crust to lose sediments
to a geosyncline, the continental crust will slowly rise and the geosyncline
will slowly sink. This occurs because the continent has lost mass and
therefore floats higher, while the geosyncline has gained mass and therefore floats lower (see Figure 12-5 on page 165). Isostasy is probably due
partly to the plasticlike properties of the upper mantle layer called the
asthenosphere.

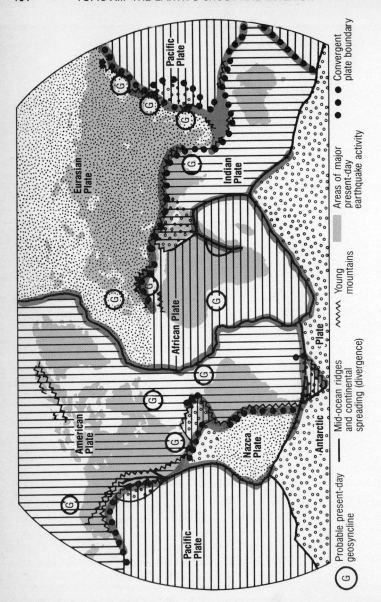

Figure 12-4. Regions of the earth's major plates and zones of current crustal activity. Note that the borders of the plates are the locations of most current crustal activity, which includes volcanic eruptions. Most of the world's active volcanoes are located where mid-ocean ridges or young mountains are indicated on the map.

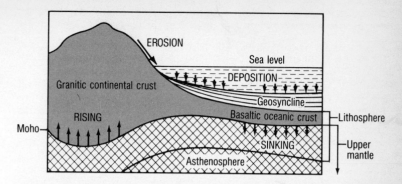

Figure 12-5. The theory of isostasy. As the geosyncline becomes heavier because of the accumulation of sediments, the oceanic crust sinks lower into the mantle. At the same time, the continental crust becomes lighter because of the erosion of material, and it rises higher. Note that where elevations are highest the crust is thickest.

ZONES OF CRUSTAL ACTIVITY.   Zones of frequent crustal activity can be located on the earth's surface. Earthquakes, volcanoes, geosynclines, mid-ocean ridges (mountain ranges in the ocean), and young continental mountains occur in these zones, or belts, as shown in Figure 12-4. The fact that these features are found together indicates that they are closely related.

CONTINENTAL DRIFT.   In recent years much evidence has been presented to support the idea that the continents have been moving around on the earth's surface. This concept is called **continental drift.** Some of the evidence for continental drift is given below:

1. The outlines of the continents appear to fit together almost like a jigsaw puzzle. It is believed that at least twice in the geologic past all the continents were connected, and that for the last 200,000,000 years the continents have mainly moved apart. (See Figure 12-6 on page 166 and *Inferred Position of Earth Landmasses* in the *Earth Science Reference Tables*, page 243.)

2. The present orientations of rock crystals with magnetic properties also give evidence of crustal shifts. When a rock crystallizes from the molten state, any of its minerals that are magnetic will align themselves, like tiny bar magnets, with the earth's magnetic field. By studying the alignment of these crystals, we can tell the relative direction of the earth's magnetic poles at the time the rock formed. When rocks of different geological times are studied in this way, it is found that the earth's magnetic poles *seem* to have wandered around the earth. However, it is more likely that the magnetic poles have remained approximately where they are, and that it was the gradual shifting of the crust

during geologic time that caused these crystals to change direction, the change being greater the greater the age of the rock. (See Figure 12-6.)

3. At places where the continents may have fitted together, the similarity of the minerals, fossils, and rock types indicates that these rocks of the different continents are similar in age and origin. The northern Appalachian Highlands (see Figure 14-2, page 205) contain many rock types, structures, and fossils similar to those in parts of western Europe. This suggests that the continents were together when the rocks were formed.

4. Today the continents are separated and their respective life forms are greatly different. However, fossil evidence shows that at times in the past many land (terrestrial) plants and animals were the same throughout the world. Similar dinosaurs lived on most land areas during the Triassic Period, but not during the Cretaceous Period (see the *Geologic Time Scale* and *Inferred Positions of Earth Landmasses* in the *Earth Science Reference Tables*, page 243. Such a wide distribution of the same plants and animals probably could not have occurred unless the continents were connected.

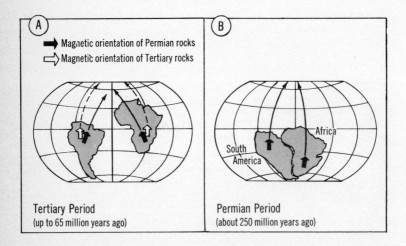

Figure 12-6. Evidence of continental drift. The present continents have shapes that suggest that they once were parts of larger landmasses, which have drifted apart by crustal movement. Magnetic orientation of rock crystals supports this hypothesis. Diagram A shows the magnetic orientation of rocks of different ages in South America and Africa. Crystals in rocks of relatively recent formations are magnetically oriented toward the earth's magnetic poles. Older rocks are oriented in different directions. If, however, it is assumed that South America and Africa were parts of a single landmass when these older rocks were forming, as shown in Diagram B, then the magnetic orientation of these older formations is found to agree reasonably well.

OCEAN-FLOOR SPREADING. Much evidence indicates that the sea floor has spread out from the **mid-ocean ridge** systems (mountain ranges in the ocean). This concept is called **ocean-floor spreading** or sea-floor spreading. The location of mid-ocean ridges is shown in Figure 12-4 on page 164. Here is some of the evidence for ocean-floor spreading:

1. Molten rock rises and crystallizes into basaltic igneous rock in the mid-ocean ridges, as shown by high heat flows and observed volcanic activity. Samples of this basaltic rock taken from the ocean floor show that the age of the rock increases with distance from the center of the mid-ocean ridge. Heat flow also decreases with distance from the mid-ocean ridges in oceanic crust. This indicates that the basaltic rock formed at the ridges and spread outward (see Figure 12-7A, page 168).

2. The spreading of the oceanic crust is also shown by the magnetism in the basaltic rocks. The earth's magnetic poles flip-flop in polarity (north changes to south or south to north) in periods of thousands of years in a process called **reversal of earth's magnetic polarity.** The earth's magnetic fields have reversed polarity thousands of times since its origin. When the basaltic rock crystallizes at the mid-ocean ridges, its magnetic minerals are aligned so that they record the particular polarity of the earth at the time of crystallization. It has been found that there are corresponding parallel strips of basaltic rock on either side of the mid-ocean ridges. Some strips show normal polarity (poles as they are today) and others show reverse polarity. This evidence suggests that the corresponding strips were formed at similar times and that ocean-floor spreading has separated them.

PLATE TECTONICS AND CRUSTAL CHANGE. Since the total mass and volume of the earth are fixed, the creation of new areas of oceanic crust by ocean-floor spreading requires that the crust be destroyed elsewhere at the same rate. As part of a major revolution in scientific thought about the earth's structure, geologists are attempting to explain crustal changes in terms of the creation, motion, and destruction of large sections of the lithosphere called *plates*. This revolutionary idea is called the **plate tectonic theory.** It includes the concepts of continental drift and ocean-floor spreading. (*Tectonics* is a term that applies to changes in the earth's crust and the forces that cause them.)

According to the plate tectonic theory, the earth's lithosphere is divided into an irregular pattern of solid, moving plates that are created at one edge and destroyed at the other edge (see Figures 12-4 and 12-7). The lithospheric plates and their associated continents are thought to be moving at rates of approximately a few centimeters a year. The lithospheric plates move on the plasticlike layer of the upper mantle called the asthenosphere.

Earthquakes, volcanoes, geosynclines, and young continental mountains occur together, as shown in Figure 12-4. It is believed that these zones of frequent crustal activity mark the boundaries of plates. The features and events of these zones are assumed to be the result of plate movements.

Figure 12-7 shows the three major types of plate boundaries. One of these boundary types is where two plates are spreading apart at a mid-ocean ridge. This is called a **divergent plate boundary.** The spreading is due to plate growth from volcanic activity. Another type of plate boundary is where plates collide. This is called a **convergent plate boundary.** The colliding edges of the plates become distorted, and young continental mountains may form between them. An existing geosyncline along a continental margin near the boundary of colliding plates would then be uplifted and changed into folded mountains. Often in plate collisions the edge of one plate is pushed down under the other. The subsiding plate plunges or subducts down into the hot mantle, where it is destroyed. The subsidence or subduction and resultant melting of the plate forms liquid rock, which rises and produces the many volcanic and intrusive features associated with plate collisions. The eruptions of Mount St. Helens are the result of a convergent plate boundary off the western coasts of Washington and Oregon. The third type of plate boundary occurs where the plates slide by each other in a sideways motion. This is called a lateral fault plate boundary. The San Andreas fault in California is an example of a lateral fault plate boundary.

PLATE TECTONICS AND MANTLE CONVECTION.   In order for crustal plates to move, it is assumed that the mantle under the lithosphere and asthenosphere must behave like a fluid. Some geologists believe that there are convection currents within the mantle that cause plate movement. A proposed source of energy for these currents is the decay of radioactive materials within the earth. One form of evidence for these mantle convection currents is that there are variations in heat flow from the earth. The heat flow at the mid-ocean ridges, where it is believed the convection currents are rising, is higher than average, and heat flow decreases as distance from the mid-ocean ridges increases.

EARTHQUAKES

An **earthquake** is a natural, rapid, shaking of the solid earth caused by displacement of rock, such as along faults. The energy of an earthquake is transferred away from its point of origin, which is called the **focus** (plural: *foci*). The energy is transmitted as **seismic** or earthquake **waves,** which are studied by scientists using an instrument called a **seismograph.**

Figure 12-7. Types of plate boundaries. (A) Diverging plate boundary with a mid-ocean ridge, shallow-depth earthquakes, igneous intrusions, extrusions of lava flows, and volcanoes. Plate 1 is moving west and Plate 2 is moving east. **(B)** Converging plate boundary with an oceanic trench, volcanic island arcs, igneous intrusions, young mountains, and subduction of oceanic plate. Earthquake foci exist at various depths, indicating subduction. Plate 1 is moving east and Plate 2 is moving west. **(C)** Lateral fault plate boundary where there is sideways movement of the two plates. This boundary is associated with many shallow-focus earthquakes, no igneous activity, and, if on land, a valley caused by erosion of crushed rocks of the lateral fault.

A

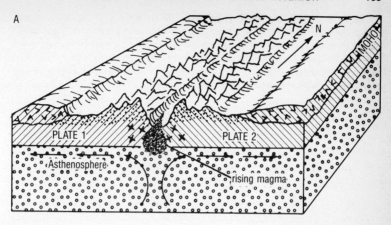

B

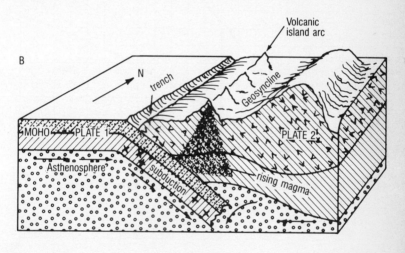

C

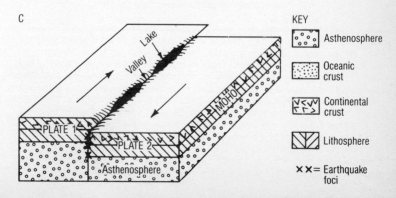

KEY

$\circ$ Asthenosphere

Oceanic crust

Continental crust

Lithosphere

✗ ✗ = Earthquake foci

TYPES OF EARTHQUAKE (SEISMIC) WAVES. Earthquakes create **compressional,** or **primary,** waves **(P-waves),** and **shear,** or **secondary,** waves **(S-waves).** Compressional waves cause the particles of the material through which they travel to vibrate in the direction the waves are moving. Shear waves cause the particles to vibrate at right angles to the direction in which the waves are moving.

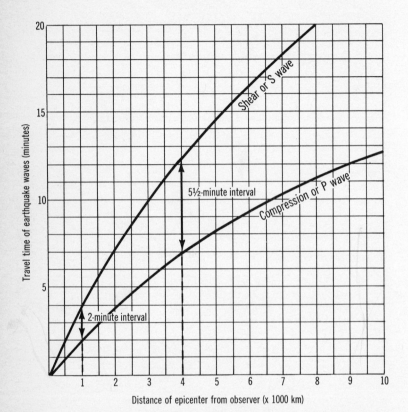

Figure 12-8. Travel times of P and S waves. The two curves in this graph show the time required for P waves and S waves to travel a given distance from the epicenter of an earthquake. Since the S waves travel slower than the P waves, the S waves take longer to reach an observer, and they arrive later than the P waves. For example, if the observer is 1,000 km from the epicenter, the P waves arrive 2 minutes after the earthquake occurs and the S waves arrive 4 minutes after the occurrence. There is thus a 2-minute interval between observation of the P waves and observation of the S waves. At 4,000 km from the epicenter, it takes 7 minutes for the P waves to arrive and 12½ minutes for the S waves; the time interval between them is thus 5½ minutes. The graph can be used to find the distance from the epicenter if the time interval between the arrival of the two waves is known. A similar diagram can be found in the *Earth Science Reference Tables,* page 246.

PROPERTIES OF EARTHQUAKE WAVES

1. In any one medium, *compressional waves travel faster than shear waves*. Thus when an earthquake occurs, compressional waves will reach a seismograph before shear waves (see Figure 12-8).

2. The velocity of seismic waves in the earth depends upon the physical properties of the material they are passing through. Generally, the more dense the material, the greater the velocity of the waves.

3. Within the same material, an increase in pressure increases the velocity of seismic waves.

4. Compressional waves will pass through solids and liquids, while shear waves will pass through solids only.

LOCATION OF AN EPICENTER. The **epicenter** of an earthquake is the place on the earth's surface directly above or closest to the point of origin, or focus, of the earthquake. Epicenters are located by using the velocity differences between compressional (P-waves) and shear (S-waves). P-waves move faster than S-waves; therefore, the farther an observer is from an epicenter, the larger the *time interval* between the arrival of the P-waves and S-waves (see Figure 12-8 or the *Earth Science Reference Tables,* page 246). The distance to the epicenter is determined by comparing the interval with the graph data.

To find the position of the epicenter, at least three seismograph locations must be used, and epicenter distances must be calculated for each. For each of the three locations, the epicenter distance is then used as a radius and circles are drawn on a globe or map, as shown for locations A, B, and C in Figure 12-9. The place where all three circles intersect is the epicenter of the earthquake.

FINDING THE ORIGIN TIME OF EARTHQUAKES. The time at which an earthquake originates can be determined from the epicenter distance and seismic-wave travel time. The farther an observer is from the epicenter, the longer it takes the seismic waves to travel to the observation point. For example, suppose the observer is 4,000 kilometers from the epicenter. Figure 12-8 shows that it took the P-wave seven minutes to arrive; thus the earthquake occurred seven minutes earlier than the time at which the P-waves were observed on the seismograph. As another example, if the S-wave first arrived at a station at 10 hr:12 min:30 sec G.M.T. and the seismograph station is 5,500 kilometers away from the epicenter, when did the earthquake occur, in G.M.T.? (G.M.T. is Greenwich Mean Time.)

A MODEL OF THE EARTH'S INTERIOR

ZONES OF THE EARTH. Analysis of seismic waves indicates that the earth is composed of four major zones—a relatively thin solid **crust,** a solid **mantle,** a liquid **outer core,** and a solid **inner core.** The Moho is the interface between the crust and the mantle. The mantle is considered to be solid when describing short-term events, such as earthquakes. However, in terms of plate tectonics or isostasy, it is considered fluid,

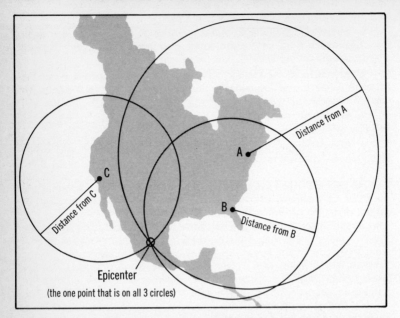

Epicenter
(the one point that is on all 3 circles)

Figure 12-9. Locating the epicenter of an earthquake. Seismograph observations at three widely spaced locations are needed. From the time interval
between the P and S waves, the distance to the epicenter can be determined
for each station. A circle with this radius is then drawn around the station
on a map or globe. The epicenter must lie somewhere on this circle. The
same is done for all three stations. The one point that lies on all three circles
must be the epicenter.

or plastic. Figure 12-10 shows the approximate dimensions and locations
of these zones and how they relate to the velocity and type of earthquake
waves. *The outer core is believed to be liquid because the S-waves do not
penetrate it and because of the sharp decrease in P-wave velocity.*

It is believed that as depth into the earth increases, temperature,
pressure, and density generally increase. Be sure to study the diagram
Inferred Properties of the Earth's Interior in the *Earth Science Reference
Tables* on page 248.

EARTH'S CRUST.   The earth's crust is divided into two major divisions:
the **continental crust** and the **oceanic crust.** The continental crust is usually
much thicker than the oceanic crust (see Figure 12-5 on page 165). The
crust is thickest where it is highest—in mountain regions.

The two crusts are also distinguished by differences in composition
and density. The continental crust is made mostly of granitic rocks, rocks
with a composition similar to granite. The oceanic crust is composed
mostly of basaltic rocks, rocks similar in composition to basalt. The

granitic continental crust is less dense than the basaltic oceanic crust, as shown on the *Scheme for Igneous Rock Identification* of the *Earth Science Reference Tables* (page 250).

COMPOSITION OF THE EARTH'S INTERIOR. The iron and nickel composition of metallic meteorites suggests that the composition of the earth's interior is mostly iron and nickel. A combination of iron and nickel at the temperature and pressure believed to be in the earth's core can account for some of the observed properties of seismic waves in the core.

The high-density iron-nickel composition of the core and the low-density oxygen-silicon composition of the crust indicates that the mantle must have a composition different from the crust and the core. There is no general agreement as to the composition of the mantle.

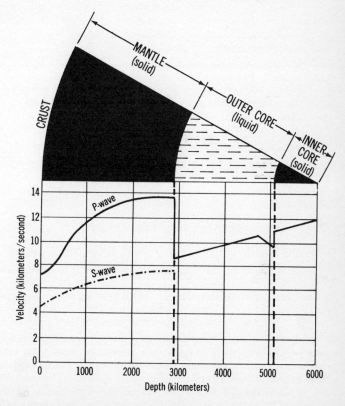

Figure 12-10. Zones of the earth's structure as deduced from characteristics of P and S waves. (Also see *Inferred Properties of the Earth's Interior* in the *Earth Science Reference Tables,* page 248.)

VOCABULARY

original horizontality	convergent plate boundary
strata	earthquake
folded strata	focus (of earthquake)
tilted strata	seismic waves
fault	seismograph
subsidence	compressional wave
bench mark	(primary or P-wave)
geosyncline	shear wave (secondary
isostasy	or S-wave)
continental drift	epicenter
mid-ocean ridge	crust
ocean-floor spreading	mantle
reversal of earth's	outer core
magnetic polarity	inner core
plate tectonic theory	continental crust
divergent plate boundary	oceanic crust

QUESTIONS ON TOPIC XII—THE EARTH'S CRUST AND INTERIOR

Questions in Recent Regents Exams (end of book)

June 1984:   34, 35, 36, 37, 38, 80, 91, 92, 93, 94, 95, 96
June 1985:   37, 38, 39, 40, 86, 88, 96, 97, 98, 99, 102, 104
June 1986:   39–43, 91–95
June 1987:   36–40, 91–95

Questions from Earlier Regents Exams

1. Placing a seismograph on the moon enables us to determine if the moon has ● water   (2) an atmosphere   (3) radioactive rock ● crustal movements

2. The term isostasy refers to a   (1) line of equal air pressure (2) series of anticlines   (3) deflection of winds on the earth caused by rotation   ● condition of balance between segments of the earth's crust

3. Evidence has shown that layers of sedimentary rock thousands of feet thick were formed in shallow seas no deeper than 1,000 feet. Which is the best explanation of how these rocks were formed?   ● the sea bottom gradually sank as sediments were deposited   (2) worldwide sea level increased as the sediments were being deposited   ● the sediment-collecting basins were being uplifted as the sediments were being deposited   (4) great landslides occurred on surrounding mountains and continued to build up sediments in the already filled basins

4. Which is the most logical conclusion to be drawn from marine fossils found on a mountaintop?   (1) marine animals once lived on land   ● sediments once under water were uplifted   ● the fossils were transported there   (4) the mountain is composed of igneous rock

The diagram illustrates how the epicenter of an earthquake is located by observatories in Pasadena, California; Chicago, Illinois; and Washington, D.C. Base your answers to questions 5 through 7 on the diagram and on your knowledge of earth science.

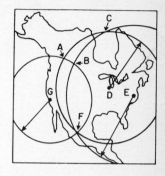

5. The epicenter of the earthquake is located nearest letter   (1) A   (2) B   (3) C   ● F

6. The separation in time between the arrival of primary and secondary waves is   (1) greatest at Pasadena (G)   (2) greatest at Chicago (D)   ● greatest at Washington, D.C. (E)   ● the same at all stations

7. If the method illustrated by the diagram is used to locate the epicenter of an earthquake, it appears unlikely for an individual observatory, operating independently, to determine the   ● direction to the epicenter   (2) distance to the epicenter   (3) distance to an epicenter located under the ocean   (4) interval between the initial and subsequent seismic waves

8. Major mountain systems are believed to have developed on the sites of   ● geosynclines   (2) major ocean basins   (3) eroded mountains   (4) thin sediments

9. Most of the world's volcanoes are located in   ● chains throughout the world   (2) the central regions of the continents   (3) the deepest ocean basins   ● regions in their late stages of erosion

10. In which region is a geosyncline in the process of formation?   (1) Adirondack Mountains   (2) Great Lakes   (3) Colorado Plateau   ● Mississippi River delta

11. Which statement about earthquakes and volcanoes is most nearly correct?   (1) they occur mainly at the poles   ● they occur in the same regions   (3) they occur only in regions where glaciers originate   (4) they occur only in the Southern Hemisphere

12. The place on the earth's surface directly above the point at which an earthquake originates is the   (1) epicenter   ● focus   (3) Moho   (4) zenith

Base your answers to questions 13 through 17 on the graph below and on your knowledge of seismology. The graph shows the velocity of seismic waves at various depths below the earth's surface.

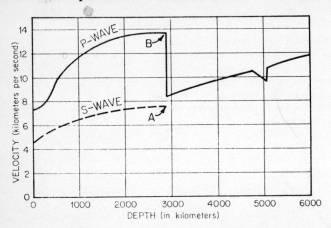

13. At equal depths in the earth, S-waves travel   (1) always faster than P-waves   ● always slower than P-waves   (3) always at the same rate as P-waves   (4) sometimes faster and sometimes slower than P-waves

14. According to the graph, the outer core of the earth would begin at a depth of approximately   ● 200 km   ● 2,900 km   (3) 4,800 km   (4) 5,100 km

15. What is the change in velocity of the P-wave at 2,900 km? (1) 2.0 km/sec   (2) 2.5 km/sec   ● 5.5 km/sec   (4) 8.4 km/sec

16. Which statement concerning the arrival of earthquake waves at a seismic station is true?   ● P-waves arrive first   (2) S-waves arrive first   ● surface waves arrive first   (4) all three waves arrive simultaneously

17. The time lapse between the arrival of the P-waves and S-waves on *one* seismograph recording can be used to determine the (1) magnitude of the earthquake   (2) exact location of the focus (3) exact location of the epicenter   ● distance to the epicenter

18. The diagrams below represent seismographic traces of three different disturbances A, B, and C recorded by the same seismograph.

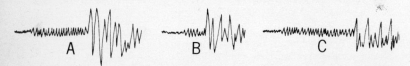

The traces indicate that the distance from the station to the epicenters of the three disturbances is   (1) least for disturbance A   ● least for disturbance B   (3) least for disturbance C   (4) the same for all three disturbances

19. Which part of the earth is probably most responsible for its high average density?   ● core   (2) crust   (3) mantle   (4) mountains

20. In developing a model of the earth's deep interior, most of the evidence was derived from   (1) deep wells   ● mining operations   (3) observing other planets   ● seismic data

21. How does the composition of the oceanic crust compare with the composition of the continental crust?   (1) The oceanic crust is mainly limestone, while the continental crust is mainly sandstone. (2) The oceanic crust is mainly limestone, while the continental crust is mainly granite.   (3) The oceanic crust is mainly basalt, while the continental crust is mainly sandstone.   ● The oceanic crust is mainly basalt, while the continental crust is mainly granite.

22. Which is the best evidence of crustal movement?   (1) molten rock in the earth's outer core   ● tilted sedimentary rock layers ● residual sediments on top of bedrock   (4) marine fossils found below sea level

23. The diagram below represents a vertical cross section of sedimentary rock layers which have not been overturned. Which principle best supports the conclusion that these layers have undergone extensive movement since deposition?

● Sediments are deposited with the youngest layers on top.   ● Sediments are deposited in horizontal layers. (3) Rock layers are older than igneous intrusions.   (4) Sediments containing the remains of marine fossils are deposited above sea level.

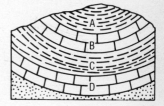

24. Where do most earthquakes originate?   (1) within the earth's outer core   ● along specific belts within the crust   (3) randomly across the entire earth's surface   (4) evenly spaced along the Moho interface

25. In an area of crustal activity, the rate of uplift is 20 centimeters per hundred years and the average rate of erosion is 8 centimeters per hundred years. The elevation of this area is generally   (1) decreasing ● increasing   (3) remaining the same

26. Igneous materials found along oceanic ridges contain magnetic iron particles that show reversal of magnetic orientation. This is evidence that   (1) volcanic activity has occurred constantly throughout history ● the earth's magnetic poles have exchanged their positions   (3) igneous materials are always formed beneath oceans   (4) the earth's crust does not move

27. As one travels from an ocean shore to the interior of a continent, the thickness of the earth's crust generally   (1) decreases   ● increases (3) remains the same

28. The immediate result of a sudden slippage of rocks within the earth's crust will be   (1) isostasy   ● an earthquake   (3) erosion (4) the formation of convection currents

29. A seismograph station records a travel time difference of 7 minutes between *P*-waves and *S*-waves of an earthquake. Approximately how far is the seismic station from the epicenter of the earthquake? (1) 1.9×10^3 km (2) 2.9×10^3 km ● 5.5×10^3 km   (4) 4.0×10^3 km

30. A line of former beaches along a coast, all 50 meters above sea level, is evidence of   (1) present erosion   (2) the present melting of polar icecaps   ● land uplift   (4) a decrease in the deposition of marine fossils

Base your answers to questions 31 through 35 on your knowledge of earth science, the *Earth Science Reference Tables*, and the diagram below. The diagram represents a cross section of the earth showing the paths of earthquake waves from a single earthquake source. Seismograph stations are located on the earth's surface at points *A* through *F*, and they are all located in the same time zone.

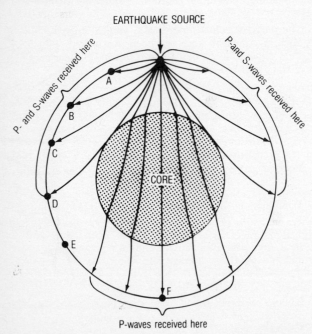

EARTHQUAKE SOURCE

P- and S-waves received here

P-and S-waves received here

CORE

P-waves received here

31. At which station is the difference in time between the arrival of *P*- and *S*-waves the greatest?   (1) *A*   (2) *B*   (3) *C*   ● *D*

32. Station *E* did *not* receive any *P*-waves or *S*-waves from this earthquake because the *P*-waves and *S*-waves   (1) cancel each other out   ● are bent, causing shadow zones   (3) are changed to sound energy   (4) are converted to heat energy

33. What explanation do scientists give for the reason that station *F* did *not* receive *S*-waves?   (1) The earth's inner core is so dense that *S*-waves cannot pass through.   ● The earth's outer core is liquid, which does not allow *S*-waves to pass.   (3) *S*-waves do not have enough energy to pass completely through the earth.   (4) *S*-waves become absorbed by the earth's crust.

34. Seismograph station *D* is 7,700 kilometers from the epicenter. If the *P*-wave arrived at this station at 2:15 p.m., at approximately what time did the earthquake occur?   (1) 1:56 p.m.   (2) 2:00 p.m.   ● 2:04 p.m.   (4) 2:08 p.m.

35. Seismograph station *B* recorded the arrival of *P*-waves at 2:10 p.m. and the arrival of *S*-waves at 2:15 p.m. Approximately how far is station *B* from the earthquake epicenter?   (1) 1400 km   (2) 2400 km   ● 3400 km   (4) 4400 km

36. Shallow-water fossils are found in rock layers that are deep beneath the ocean floor. This suggests that   (1) shallow-water organisms always migrate to the deeper waters to die   (2) parts of the ocean floor have been uplifted   ● parts of the ocean floor have subsided   (4) the surface water cooled off, killing the organisms

37. Which evidence does *not* support the theory that Africa and South America were once part of the same large continent?   (1) correlation of rocks on opposite sides of the Atlantic Ocean   (2) correlation of fossils on opposite sides of the Atlantic Ocean   (3) correlation of coastlines on opposite sides of the Atlantic Ocean   ● correlation of living animals on opposite sides of the Atlantic Ocean

38. Which statement best describes the continental and oceanic crusts?   ● The continental crust is thicker and less dense than the oceanic crust.   (2) The continental crust is thicker and more dense than the oceanic crust.   (3) The continental crust is thinner and less dense than the oceanic crust.   (4) The continental crust is thinner and more dense than the oceanic crust.

39. The composition of some meteorites supports the inference that the earth's core is composed of   (1) aluminum and calcium   ● iron and nickel   (3) silicon and oxygen   (4) magnesium and potassium

40. The temperature of rock located 1,000 kilometers below the earth's surface is about   (1) 1,800°K   ● 2,100°K   (3) 2,500°K   (4) 2,800°K

41. Which evidence best supports the inference that the earth's outer core possesses liquid characteristics?   (1) The velocities of both primary and shear waves increase through the outer core.   (2) The primary wave velocity decreases, while the shear wave velocity increases in the outer core.   ● Primary waves pass through the outer core but shear waves do not.   (4) Both primary waves and shear waves pass through the outer core.

Base your answers to questions 42 through 46 on your knowledge of earth science, the *Earth Science Reference Tables,* and the diagram below. The diagram is a model which represents one possible interpretation of the movements of the earth's rock surfaces according to the theory of plate tectonics (continental drift and sea floor spreading). According to this interpretation, the earth's lithosphere consists of several large "plates" which are moving in relationship to one another. The arrows in the diagram show some of this relative motion of the "plates." The diagram also shows the age of formation of the igneous rocks that make up the oceanic crust of the northern section of the Pacific Plate.

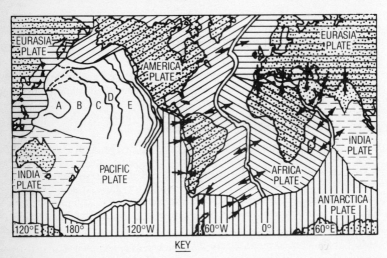

KEY

━┿◄━ Movement of plates toward each other

◄┿━► Movement of plates away from each other

AGE OF ROCKS OF PACIFIC PLATE

A Jurassic   B Early Cretaceous   C Middle Cretaceous   D Late Cretaceous   E Eocene

42. Which statement is best supported by the relative movement shown by the arrows in the diagram? (1) North America and South America are moving toward each other. (2) The India Plate is moving away from the Eurasia Plate. ● The Africa Plate and Eurasia Plate are moving away from the America Plate. (4) The Antarctica Plate is moving away from the America Plate.

43. The boundaries between all of these "plates" are best described as the sites of ● frequent crustal activity (2) deep ocean depths (3) continental boundaries (4) magnetic field reversals

44. Which geologic structure is represented by the double line separating the America Plate from the Africa and Eurasia Plates? (1) thick continental crust (2) thick layers of sediment ● mid-ocean ridge (4) granitic igneous rock

45. Which provides the best explanation of the mechanism that causes these "plates" to move across the earth's surface? ● convection currents in the mantle   (2) faulting of the lithosphere   (3) the spin of the earth on its axis   (4) prevailing wind belts of the troposphere

46. The age of formation of the igneous rocks *A, B, C, D,* and *E* which make up the oceanic crust of the northern half of the Pacific Plate suggests that this section of the Pacific Plate is generally moving in which direction?   (1) from north to south   (2) from south to north   (3) from west to east   ● from east to west

Additional Questions

To answer questions 1 through 12 refer to the diagram below, which represents part of the earth's crust and the underlying mantle as understood by many geologists following the plate tectonic theory.

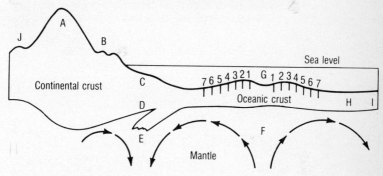

1. According to this explanation of crustal change, heat flow from the mantle is greatest at the earth's surface at location   (1) C   ● G   (3) H   (4) J

2. A present geosyncline is located at   (1) B   ● C   (3) E   (4) G

3. Earthquakes are most common at   (1) J   (2) A   ● D   (4) H

4. The numbered layers around location G indicate   (1) differences in earthquake activity   ● parallel zones of similar magnetic polarity   (3) parallel layers of billion-year-old metamorphic rock   (4) alternate layers of basaltic and granite rock

5. As you go from layer 1 to layer 7 around location G, the age of the igneous rock   ● increases   (2) decreases   (3) remains the same

6. As you go from C to D to E, which does not increase?   ● porosity   (2) density   (3) pressure   (4) temperature

7. The thickest sediments and sedimentary rocks are probably located at   ● C   (2) G   (3) H   (4) I

8. The arrows around E indicate   (1) zones of volcanic activity   (2) areas of frequent earthquake activity   ● convection heat flow   (4) direction of magnetic orientation of minerals in rocks

9. At which location are surface rocks most likely basaltic rocks?
(1) A   (2) B   (3) C   ● G

10. Suppose an earthquake at B was recorded by an observer at J. How would the speed of the compressional waves compare to the speed of the shear waves?   (1) the shear waves would be faster   ● the compressional waves would be faster   (3) the waves would have the same velocity   (4) the comparative velocities could not be determined because the observer would not know the properties of the rock material

11. A subduction zone is most likely found at which location?
(1) J   ● D   (3) G   (4) A

12. Volcanic activity would be most likely at location   (1) J   (2) A   ● G   (4) H

13. According to the plate tectonic theory   (1) mid-ocean ridges have lower-than-normal heat flows   (2) plates are destroyed at mid-ocean ridges   ● continents drift because they rest on plates that are moving   (4) plate thickness equals the thickness of the crust and the mantle combined

Interpreting Geologic History

Geologic history is recorded in the rocks. Observations of the composition, structure, position, and fossil content of the rock record leads to interpretations of the geologic history of the earth. Carefully study the *Geologic Time Scale* (pages 242–243) and the *Generalized Bedrock Geology of New York State* on pages 244–245 of the *Earth Science Reference Tables* before reading further in this topic.

RELATIVE DATING OF ROCKS AND EVENTS

Relative dating is the process of obtaining the chronological sequence of rocks or geologic events in an area. The **relative age** of a rock or event is its age as compared to other rocks or events. It should not be confused with the actual age, called the **absolute age,** which refers to the date when the event actually occurred or the rock was formed. Some of the methods of relative dating are described below.

PRINCIPLE OF SUPERPOSITION. In layers of sedimentary rock and some extrusive igneous rocks, the bottom layer is inferred to be the oldest, with each overlying layer being progressively younger, so that the top layer is the youngest. This inference is called the **principle of superposition,** and it may be used as the basis for relative dating. Superposition is due to the original horizontality of deposited sediments. Exceptions to the principle occur in certain types of rock deformation resulting from crustal change. When there are overturns in folds, or when movement along faults has thrust older rock layers over younger layers, the principle of superposition does not hold true (see Figure 13-1 on page 184).

INTRUSIONS AND EXTRUSIONS. When molten rock (magma) invades pre-existing rocks and crystallizes, it forms a body called an **intrusion.** The intrusion is younger than any rock it cuts through (see Figure 13-2 on page 184). When molten rock (lava) flows on the earth's surface and solidifies, it forms a feature called an **extrusion.** The extrusion or lava flow is younger than any rocks beneath it but will be older than any rocks that may later form on top of it.

ROCK STRUCTURAL FEATURES. A rock is older than any fault, *joint,* or fold that appears in the rock. Like a fault, a **joint** is a crack in rocks. However, a joint differs from a fault because there has been no movement of rocks along the crack. If movement (displacement) of the rocks should occur, the joint would become a fault (see Figure 13-3 on page 185).

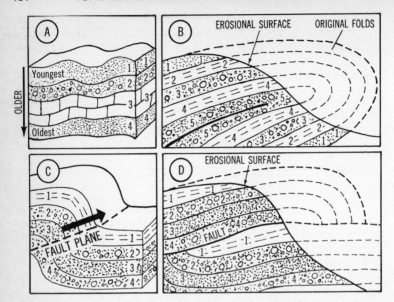

Figure 13-1. The principle of superposition and possible exceptions. (A) Normally, a rock layer is younger than any layers below it. **(B)** Overturned folds can result in an exception to the principle. Layer 1 at lower right is actually a continuation of Layer 1 at upper left. **(C)** and **(D)** Movement of layers along an overthrust fault can result in an exception to the principle. Layers numbered alike are the same age.

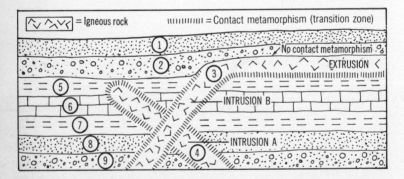

Figure 13-2. Relative ages of intrusions and extrusions. Intrusion A is younger than the layers it intrudes. Intrusion B is younger than A because B cuts A. The layers above the extrusion must be younger than the extrusion because of the absence of contact metamorphism along their common boundary. The rocks are numbered in order of increasing age.

INTERNAL ROCK CHARACTERISTICS. In sedimentary rocks, the sediments are older than the rock itself because they are required to form the rock. In nonsedimentary rocks, individual crystals or fragments are also older than the rock itself.

A **vein** is a mineral deposit, formed from a solution that has filled some crack or permeable zone in rocks. A vein is thus younger than the rock it is in. Mineral cements in sedimentary rocks are also younger than the original sediments in the rock.

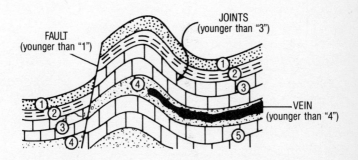

Figure 13-3. Relative ages of structural features of rocks. Folds, faults, joints, and veins are younger than the rocks in which they occur.

CORRELATION

Correlation is the process of showing that rocks or geologic events that occurred in different places are the same age. Correlation is useful in finding mineral deposits, because certain minerals are often found in rocks of a specific age. Correlation is also important in unraveling the sequence of geologic events in an area. Some of the methods of correlation are described below.

CORRELATION BY "WALKING THE OUTCROP." An **outcrop** is local rock, or **bedrock,** that is exposed at the earth's surface. In areas of outcrops, correlation can be accomplished by directly following the continuity of the individual layers or rock formations at the earth's surface; this procedure is called **walking the outcrop** (see Figure 13-4 on page 186). A **formation** is a layer or group of layers of rock and is the basic unit of geologic mapping. The rocks of one formation have similar features, such as rock type, mineral composition, and environment of formation.

CORRELATION BY SIMILARITY IN ROCKS. Where rock formations are separated from one another, they may be tentatively correlated on the basis of similar overall appearance, color, and mineral composition, as indicated in Figure 13-4.

LIMITATIONS OF CORRELATION BY SIMILARITY.   Correlation of rock formations by similarity of the rocks they contain is usually valid over small areas only, and even then may be incorrect. Two rock formations, and even separate parts of the same formation, may be similar and yet be of different ages. For example, Figure 13-5 shows a sedimentary rock formation in which the environment of deposition gradually shifted over a long period of time. Therefore, the rock that formed from the original sediments is much older than the rock that formed in the later stages of deposition, although both parts of the formation are similar in appearance.

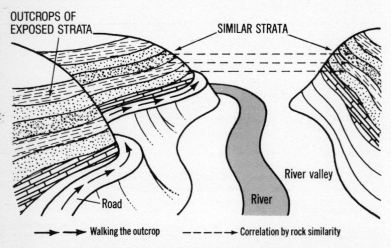

Figure 13-4. Correlation by direct observation. A geologist can follow the strata in an exposed hillside by "walking the outcrop," for example, by walking along the road on the left side of this river valley. The geologist may also be able to correlate strata on opposite sides of the valley by observing similarities in color, texture, and sequence of the rock strata.

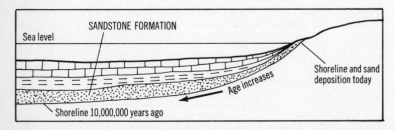

Figure 13-5. Variations in the age of a formation. A sedimentary formation composed of the same type of sediment (for example, sand) may be of different ages in different locations because of movement of the environment of deposition. In this diagram, the sandstone at the left is 10,000,000 years older than the sandstone at the right, even though the formation is continuous and similar in composition.

CORRELATION BY USE OF INDEX FOSSILS. The use of certain *fossils* or groups of fossils is one of the best methods of correlation. A **fossil** is any evidence of former life. With minor exceptions, fossils are found exclusively in sedimentary rocks. Fossils are rarely found in igneous and metamorphic rocks because fossils are usually destroyed by melting and pressure associated with the formation of these nonsedimentary rocks. The fossils used in correlation are called **index fossils.** To be useful as an index fossil, the particular life form must have lived over a large geographic area; that is, it must have a large horizontal distribution throughout rocks formed at the same time. Also, the life form must have lived only a short period of time, thus having a small vertical distribution in the strata in which the fossils occur (see Figure 13-6).

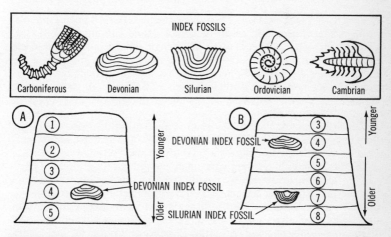

Figure 13-6. Correlation of rocks by means of index fossils. In **A,** a fossil of an organism known to have lived only during the Devonian Period is found in rock layer 4. This layer was therefore deposited during Devonian times. The layers above it are younger and those below it are older. In **B,** a similar fossil is found in one of the layers. This is therefore also a Devonian layer. A second index fossil of the Silurian Period is found in layer 7. This tells us that layers 5 and 6 are not younger than the Devonian and not older than the Silurian. Relative ages of the layers in both formations are indicated by the numbers in order of youngest to oldest.

CORRELATION BY VOLCANIC ASH DEPOSITS. **Volcanic ash** consists of small pieces of extrusive igneous rock that are shot into the air during volcanic eruptions. In large eruptions, volcanic ash is scattered over wide areas of the earth. The ash may then settle among other sediments being deposited in many different regions. If these ash deposits can be detected and identified in rock formations, they are very useful in correlation, because they represent a very small period of time and because they are widely distributed. They can therefore serve as correlating age markers in rock formations that may be hundreds or thousands of kilometers apart.

GEOLOGIC HISTORY FROM THE ROCK RECORD

FOSSILS AND RELATIVE AGE.   Just as the fossils found in rocks can be used to correlate rock strata, they can also be used to place the events in an area in order according to their relative ages. This is possible because the life forms on earth have constantly changed and some forms existed or were dominant only during specific intervals of geologic time. For example, the rock record shows that the dinosaurs as a group existed in a large interval of geologic time (called the Mesozoic Era), but certain types of dinosaurs existed only during smaller intervals. When these life forms appear as fossils in a given rock formation, they serve to establish the relative age of the formation and to give it a specific place in geologic history.

GEOLOGIC TIME SCALE.   Mainly on the basis of such fossil evidence, geologists have been able to divide geologic time into units, called *eras, periods,* and *epochs.* This division of geologic time is called the **geologic time scale** and is often represented as a chart, such as the one in the *Earth Science Reference Tables.* Note that an era, period, or epoch is not an exact unit of measurement such as an hour. A glance at the geologic time scale will show, for example, that no two eras represent the same amount of time.

The Precambrian (pre-Paleozoic) is the earliest division of geologic time and represents about 85% of the total (see the geologic time scale). Fossils are difficult to detect and identify in the Precambrian, because the earliest living things were very small and did not have the hard parts needed to form fossils easily. Fossils are also rare in the Precambrian because many of these ancient rocks have been metamorphosed, melted, or weathered and eroded. Fossils in the rock record indicate that human or humanlike mammals have existed on earth for a relatively extremely short time—only about 0.04% (the Pleistocene Epoch) of the earth's existence.

UNCONFORMITIES.   In attempting to read the rock record, geologists often find evidence of buried erosional surfaces called **unconformities** (see Figure 13-7). An unconformity in the rock record of an area indicates that at some time in the geologic history of the area, crustal movement had produced uplift. This uplift had exposed the rocks to weathering and erosion, and part of the rock record was removed. A later subsidence lowered the area, it was covered by water, and new sediments were deposited on the eroded surface, thus producing the unconformity. In most unconformities, there is a lack of parallelism between the older layers below the erosional surface and the younger ones above it as the result of folding or tilting during the uplift or subsidence. However, this is not always the case.

The presence of an unconformity means that some of the layers of the rock record of an area are missing. Although there is a gap in geologic time, an unconformity is useful in relative dating. The rocks above an unconformity are younger than the unconformity, and the rocks below it are considerably older.

Events producing an unconformity with lack of parallelism.

(A) Deposition forms sedimentary rock layers.

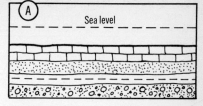

(B) Crustal deformation and uplift occur.

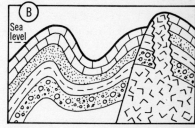

(C) Weathering and erosion remove part of the rock record.

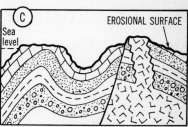

(D) Submergence and new deposition result in an unconformity along the now buried erosional surface.

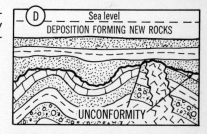

An unconformity in parallel strata.

(E) Uplift, erosion, and submergence have also occurred here, but without deformation. Evidence of a gap in the rock record may be given by widely different ages of the fossils in the layers above and below the unconformity.

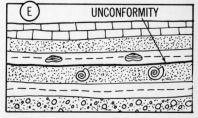

Figure 13-7. Development of an unconformity.

UNIFORMITARIANISM.   One of the basic principles geologists use to interpret geologic history is **uniformitarianism,** or uniformity of process, which implies that "the present is the key to the past"; that is, it is assumed that the geologic processes happening today also happened in the past, and that much of the rock record can be interpreted by observing present geologic processes. Uniformitarianism does not mean that different processes could not have happened in the past or that the geologic processes always occurred at the same rates as they do today.

As an example of uniformitarianism, suppose a geologist finds a sedimentary rock formation that is unsorted, has a wide range of sediment sizes, and has sediments with partly rounded shapes with scratches of various sizes. On the basis of knowledge of glacial processes today, the geologist will infer that this formation was the result of past glaciation.

ABSOLUTE DATING OF ROCKS USING RADIOACTIVE DECAY

The use of fossil evidence, superposition, and similar methods gives geologists only relative dates. *Radioactive dating* is their major way of knowing the actual, or absolute, dates for the events of geologic history.

ISOTOPES.   An *element* is a substance consisting of atoms that are chemically alike. Most elements exist in several varieties called **isotopes.** The difference between one isotope of an element and another is in the mass of its atoms. For example, the mass of an atom of the most common isotope of carbon is 12 units. This isotope is called carbon-12, to distinguish it from other isotopes of carbon, such as carbon-14, in which the atoms have a mass of 14 units.

RADIOACTIVE DECAY.   Almost all the mass of an atom is concentrated in a central region called the *nucleus* (plural, *nuclei*). The nuclei of the atoms of many isotopes are *unstable*. This means that they tend to emit particles and electromagnetic energy, and change to atoms of other elements. This process is called **radioactive decay.** The nucleus that remains after a radioactive decay may also be unstable, and it will decay in its turn. Eventually, a stable isotope (one that does not undergo radioactive decay) is formed.

URANIUM-238.   One of the most important radioactive isotopes for the dating of rocks is **uranium-238,** the isotope of uranium whose atoms have a mass of 238 units. The nuclei of its atoms pass through a series of radioactive decays, eventually producing atoms of *lead-206,* a stable isotope of the element lead.

HALF-LIFE.   The decay of any individual nucleus is a random event. That is, it may occur at any time. However, among the billions of atoms in any sample of an isotope, a certain definite fraction will decay in a given time. In the next time interval of the same length, the same fraction of the remaining atoms will decay. The time required for half the atoms in a given mass of an isotope to decay is called the **half-life** of the isotope. For any isotope, at the end of one half-life period, half the original atoms will have decayed to other elements, and half will remain unchanged. At the end of the next half-life period, half of these remaining atoms will have decayed, leaving one-fourth of the original atoms unchanged. After a third half-life period, half of these will have decayed, leaving one-eighth of the original atoms unchanged. This halving of the number of unchanged atoms during each successive half-life period continues indefinitely.

The half-life is different for each radioactive isotope, but it is always the same for a given isotope. The half-life of an isotope is not affected by any known environmental factors, such as temperature, pressure, or involvement in chemical reaction. Each half-life is assumed to have been the same throughout the earth's history.

Half-lives vary over a wide range, from fractions of a second to billions of years. (See *Radioactive Decay Data* in the *Earth Science Reference Tables,* page 238.)

RADIOACTIVE DATING.   The known half-life period of radioactive isotopes can be used to estimate the age of a rock by determining the ratio between the amount of a radioactive isotope and the amount of its decay products in a rock sample. The method is called **radioactive dating.** For example, suppose a rock formed with crystals of a uranium-238 compound in it. As time passed, the uranium would slowly change to lead-206 (its stable decay product) at its fixed half-life rate. At the end of one half-life period (4.5 billion years for uranium-238), half the uranium-238 atoms would have changed to atoms of lead-206. In terms of number of atoms, there would be equal amounts of uranium-238 and lead-206, where originally the rock was 100% uranium-238 and no lead-206. If a rock is found today with this 1:1 ratio of uranium-238 atoms to lead-206 atoms, it can be concluded that the rock formed 4.5 billion years ago. If there is relatively more uranium and less lead, the rock is less than 4.5 billion years old.

The age corresponding to any particular ratio of uranium to lead can be calculated mathematically. The curves in Figure 13-8 on page 192 show how the percentage of uranium-238 decreases and the percentage of lead-206 increases with time in a given rock.

CARBON-14 DATING.   Radioactive elements with *long* half-lives (such as uranium-238) must be used to date most rocks, because these rocks have ages measured in hundreds of millions, or even billions, of years. In such long periods, any element with a short half-life would have decayed to such an extent that any remaining amounts would be too small to measure. Some radioactive elements with *short* half-lives, such as *carbon-14* (half-life 5,600 years), are useful for dating remains of *organic materials and rocks of relatively recent origin.* For example, **carbon-14 dating** (also called **radiocarbon dating**) can be used for organic remains up to about 50,000 years in age, which is only the last part of the Pleistocene Epoch ice age.

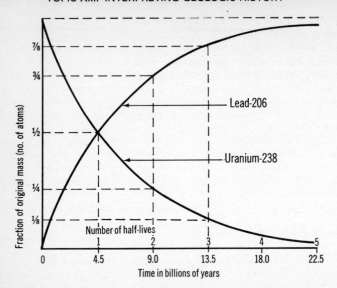

Figure 13-8. Curves showing radioactive decay of uranium-238 and formation of the stable decay product lead-206. After one half-life (4.5 billion years), half the original atoms of uranium have become atoms of lead.

ANCIENT LIFE AND EVOLUTION

VARIATIONS IN FOSSILS AND ENVIRONMENTS.   The fossil record, of mostly sedimentary rocks, shows that a great variety of plants and animals have lived in the past in a great variety of environments. Most of these life forms are now extinct. Comparison of fossils with similar life forms alive today allows geologists to interpret past environments, as shown in Figure 13-9.

The chances of fossilization are very small, so there are probably more types of life forms that have left no evidence of their existence than types of life forms found as fossils.

FOSSILS AND EVOLUTION.   A **species** includes all the life forms that are similar enough to be able to interbreed and produce fertile young. Just by looking around at people, house cats, and dogs, which are three species of life, it can be observed that many *variations* in a species can exist. When graphed, the variations in a species often form bell-shaped curves, as shown in Figure 13-10.

The theory of **organic evolution** assumes that some of the variations within a species give the individuals with those variations a higher chance of surviving and reproducing. If these variations are inheritable, they will be passed on to the offspring, and the favorable variations will be preserved, while unfavorable variations will gradually die out. If this process continues for long periods of time, the accumulated variations may eventually result in a new species—one that can no longer interbreed with the earlier varieties of the species.

The fossil record provides evidence for the theory of evolution. Fossils from adjacent intervals of geologic time show a *gradual transition,* or change, from one species to the next. Recently some scientists have inferred from evidence in the rock record that there are times of rapid organic evolution (punctuated evolution), possibly due to conditions resulting from collisions between celestial bodies and the earth.

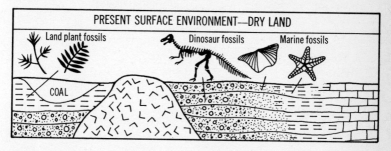

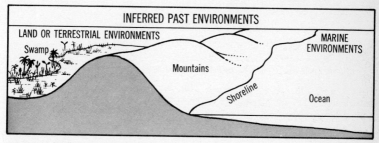

Figure 13-9. Reconstruction of past environments from fossil evidence and rock formations. From the dinosaur and marine fossils and the gradual change in sedimentary rock type as we go further to the right, we infer the former shoreline and ocean. From the types of plant fossils and the occurrence of coal, we infer the former swamp on the left.

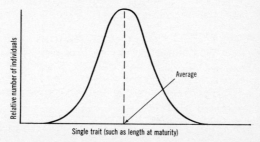

Figure 13-10. Variation in a species trait. In any population of a species, each trait usually has an average value. In most individuals, the trait will be close to the average. In a few, it will be much below average; in a similar number, it will be much above average. If the departure from average in either direction has an advantage for survival and can be inherited, the average will shift in this favorable direction in later generations.

VOCABULARY

relative age
absolute age
principle of superposition
intrusion
extrusion
joint
vein
correlation
outcrop
bedrock
walking the outcrop
rock formation
fossil
index fossil

volcanic ash
geologic time scale
unconformity
uniformitarianism
isotope
radioactive decay
uranium-238
half-life
radioactive dating
carbon-14 (radiocarbon) dating
species
organic evolution

QUESTIONS ON TOPIC XIII
INTERPRETING GEOLOGIC HISTORY

Questions in Recent Regents Exams (end of book)

June 1984: 39, 40, 41, 45, 86, 87, 89, 90, 98, 99, 100, 101
June 1985: 41, 42, 43, 44, 45, 47, 48, 49, 91, 92, 93, 94, 95, 100, 103
June 1986: 44–49, 55, 96, 97, 99, 100
June 1987: 41–46, 96–100, 102

Questions from Earlier Regents Exams

1. The diagram below represents an exposed rock outcrop. Which geologic event occurred *last*?

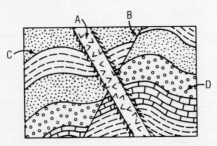

(1) the intrusion of *A*   (2) the fault along line *B*   (3) the fold at *C*
(4) the deposition of gravel at *D*

2. The age of the earth is most accurately estimated from   (1) the salinity of the oceans   (2) the thickness of sedimentary rock   (3) studies of fossils   (4) radioactive dating of rock masses

3. A log is found incorporated in a sequence of layered sediments at the bottom of a lake. Which method would most accurately locate the time period when the tree was living?   (1) counting tree rings (2) counting sedimentary layers   ● radiocarbon dating   (4) uranium-lead dating

Base your answers to questions 4 through 6 on the diagram below and on your knowledge of earth science.

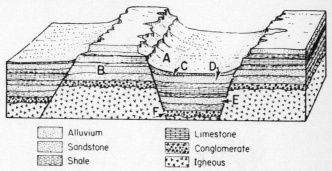

	Alluvium		Limestone
	Sandstone		Conglomerate
	Shale		Igneous

4. The disturbed rock structure shown is probably the result of (1) warping   (2) folding   (3) volcanism   ● faulting

5. Which is the oldest sedimentary rock in this diagram? ● conglomerate   (2) sandstone   (3) shale   (4) limestone

6. Rock layer B is the same age as layer   (1) C   ⊗D   ● E (4) F

7. If a specimen of a given radioactive substance is reduced in size, its half-life   (1) decreases   (2) increases   ● remains the same

8. The physical and chemical conditions which long ago produced changes on the earth's surface are still producing changes. This statement is one way of stating the principle of   (1) catastrophism   (2) diastrophism   ● uniformitarianism   (4) isostasy

9. Rock formation A is located within the Mississippian Period and rests upon formation B. Formation B rests upon formation C, which is located within the Silurian Period. If formation B is neither Mississippian nor Silurian, within which time period is it most probably located? (1) Cambrian   ● Devonian   (3) Pennsylvanian   (4) Permian

10. Below are diagrams of three profile sections showing fossil deposits W, X, Y, and Z, found at widely separated locations. Which would be the best index fossil?   (1) W   ● X   (3) Y   (4) Z

Rock Layer 1	W	W	W Z
Rock Layer 2	W Z	Y	Z
Rock Layer 3	W X	X	X Z
	LOCALITY A	LOCALITY B	LOCALITY C

Base your answers to questions 11 through 15 on the graph below, which shows the radioactive decay curve for uranium to lead, and on your knowledge of earth science.

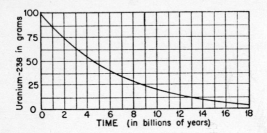

11. The half-life of uranium-238 as shown on this graph is closest to   (1) 2.5 billion years   (2) 3.5 billion years   ● 4.5 billion years (4) 5.5 billion years

12. Because of the half-life nature of the decay process, uranium-238 will theoretically   (1) decay completely before 4.5 billion years (2) decay completely in 18 billion years   (3) decay completely in 20 billion years   ● continue to decay indefinitely

13. A uranium mineral is obtained from an intrusive granite formation. It is then analyzed and found to contain about 1 gram of lead-206 to every 3 grams of uranium-238. Approximately how many billions of years old is the granite?   ● one   (2) two   (3) three   ● four

14. Which curve represents the expected decay rate of uranium-238 if its temperature were raised almost to the melting point?

15. If the decay curve for the element carbon-14 were plotted, the general shape of the curve would be

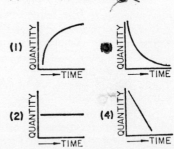

16. "The present is the key to the past." This statement is best interpreted as meaning that   (1) rocks now exposed were formed in the past   ● the processes by which rocks are formed today have been going on throughout the earth's history   (3) activity occurring now will cease in the near future   (4) animals living now are unlike any that lived in the geologic past

17. The best basis for concluding that a certain layer of shale rock in New York State was deposited at the same time as one in California is that both   (1) are the same distance below the surface   ● contain similar fossil remains   (3) are sedimentary rocks   (4) have the same chemical composition

Base your answers to questions 18 through 22 on the diagram below and on your knowledge of earth science.

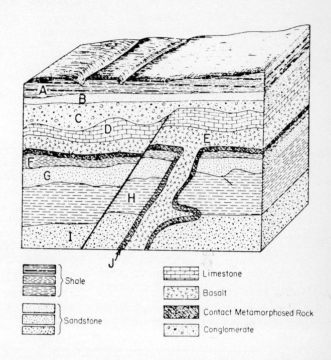

18. Which is the most recently formed rock?   ● A   (2) B   (3) C   (4) D

19. An unconformity is located between   (1) A and B   (2) B and C   ● C and D   (4) F and G

20. The conclusion that the limestone layer (D) is younger than the basalt layer (E) is supported by evidence of   (1) faulting   ● contact metamorphism   (3) igneous intrusion   (4) fossils

21. The last event before faulting occurred was formation of   (1) C   ● D   (3) E   (4) J

22. Which must have preceded the formation of layer D?   (1) faulting   (2) submergence   ● intrusion   (4) uplift

23. In a certain section of sedimentary rock, fossil dating shows that younger rock layers are on top of older rock layers. This relationship indicates that   ● the rock layers were formed according to the principle of superposition   (2) the rock layers have been overturned   (3) fossil dating is often inaccurate   (4) the sediments that formed the rock layers were composed of many different minerals

24. The table below provides information on four samples of igneous rock.

Sample	% of Lead	% of Uranium	% of Other Materials
1	0.307	4.161	95.532
2	1.175	1.175	97.650
3	0.023	0.001	99.976
4	6.044	5.207	88.749

Which sample is oldest?   (1) 1   (2) 2   ● 3   (4) 4

25. Fossils are rarely found in Precambrian rocks. Which is the most probable reason for this?   (1) the fossils are abundant but not readily observable   ● very few living things of that time had hard body parts   (3) no sedimentary rocks were formed during that time   (4) no life existed at that time

26. The fossil remains of organisms which were once common and widespread but which survived only a short period of geologic time might be especially useful for   (1) correlating sedimentary deposits in places distant from each other   ● establishing the absolute age of a deposit   (3) tracing the evolution of organisms related to that species   (4) determining some of the factors that led to extinction

Base your answers to questions 27 through 30 on the following block diagram, which represents a portion of the earth's crust.

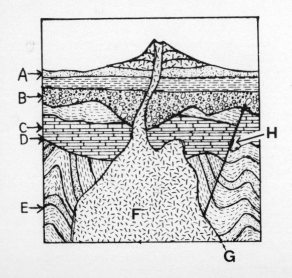

27. Which is the youngest rock?   (1) A   (2) B   (3) C   (4) F

28. An unconformity is located at   (1) A   (2) E   (3) H   (4) D

29. Which rock is least likely to contain fossils?   (1) A   (2) B   (3) C   (4) F

30. Which indicates a fault plane?   (1) E   (2) G   (3) H   (4) D

31. A geologist uses carbon-14 to measure the age of material found in a sedimentary deposit. If the half-life of carbon-14 is 5,700 years and the sample shows that only 25 percent of the original carbon-14 is left, the age of the sample is about   (1) 5,700 years   (2) 11,400 years   (3) 17,100 years   (4) 22,800 years

32. The half-life of a particular radioactive substance   (1) decreases as pressure on it increases   (2) decreases as its mass decreases   (3) increases as the temperature increases   (4) is independent of mass, temperature, and pressure

33. According to the *Generalized Geologic Map of New York State,* what is the geologic age of the bedrock found at the surface at 43° 30′ N. latitude by 75° 00′ W. longitude?   (1) Devonian   (2) Cambrian   (3) Early Ordovician   (4) Middle Proterozoic

34. Why can layers of volcanic ash found between other rock layers often serve as good geologic time markers?   (1) Volcanic ash usually occurs in narrow bands around volcanoes.   (2) Volcanic ash usually contains index fossils.   (3) Volcanic ash usually contains the radioactive isotope carbon-14.   (4) Volcanic ash usually is rapidly deposited over a large area.

35. Which rock layer is *not* found in the rock record of New York State?   (1) Devonian   (2) Silurian   (3) Ordovician   (4) Permian

36. During which time was the majority of the exposed bedrock in New York State deposited?   (1) Precambrian   (2) Mesozoic   (3) Cenozoic   (4) Paleozoic

37. Rocks containing fossils of earliest terrestrial plants could most likely be found in New York State bedrock near   (1) Syracuse   (2) Oswego   (3) Ithaca   (4) Old Forge

38. What process most directly caused the formation of the feature shown by line *AB* in the geologic cross section below?

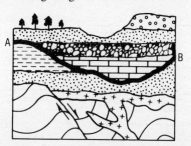

(1) erosion   (2) faulting   (3) igneous intrusion   (4) folding

39. Which conclusion can be made based on existing fossil evidence?   (1) Present life forms have always existed.   (2) The earth's environment has always been the same.   (3) Many life forms have become extinct.   (4) All life forms will remain the same in the future.

40. The Geologic Time Scale has been subdivided into a number of time units called periods on the basis of   (1) fossil evidence   (2) rock thicknesses   (3) rock types   (4) radioactive dating

41. The diagram below represents a section of the earth's crust. The symbols in the diagram indicate the location on a horizontal surface of certain fossils that formed during the Carboniferous Period. For what purpose would the fossil information on the map be most useful?

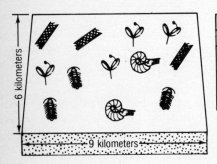

(1) to find the location of the shoreline during the Carboniferous Period
(2) to measure the age of the bedrock by carbon-14 radioactive dating
(3) to provide evidence of the evolution of humans   (4) to indicate the extent of folding that occurred during the Devonian Period

42. Which area in New York State is located on rock formations that contain large amounts of salt deposits?   (1) Syracuse   (2) Long Island   (3) New York City   (4) Old Forge

43. Shark and coral fossils are found in the rock record of certain land areas. What does the presence of these fossils indicate about those areas?   (1) They have undergone glacial deposition.   (2) They were once covered by thick vegetation.   (3) They have undergone intense metamorphism.   (4) They were once covered by shallow seas.

44. According to the Geologic Time Scale in the *Earth Science Reference Tables*, what is the estimated age of the earth as a planet in millions of years?   (1) 570   (2) 4,000   (3) 4,500   (4) 5,000

45. Approximately how long ago were the Taconic Mountains uplifted?   (1) 540 million years ago   (2) 440 million years ago   (3) 310 million years ago   (4) 120 million years ago

46. In which rock type are fossils usually found?   (1) igneous (2) volcanic   (3) sedimentary   (4) metamorphic

47. Uranium-238 is used to date the age of the earth rather than carbon-14 because uranium-238   (1) was more abundant when the earth formed   (2) has a longer half-life   (3) decays at a constant rate   (4) is easier to collect and test

48. Which line is the best representation of the relative duration of each of the geologic time intervals?

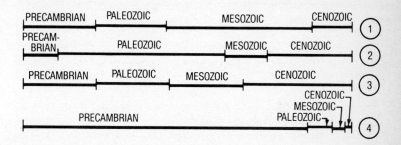

Additional Questions

1. Evidence that New York State had different environments at different times in the past is indicated by   (1) glacial deposits in the Pleistocene   (2) marine fossils in Ordovician rocks   (3) palmlike fossils in Devonian rocks   (4) all of the above

2. If the half-life of radioactive material is 500 years, what part of its original mass will be left after 2,000 years?   (1) ½   (2) ¼   (3) ⅛   (4) ¹⁄₁₆

3. How is the fossil record related to the theory of organic evolution?   (1) it shows that the theory has serious defects   (2) it is the only proof of the theory   (3) it provides supporting evidence for the theory   (4) it neither supports nor conflicts with the theory

4. Which is the youngest aspect of a sedimentary rock composed of sand grains held together by cement?   (1) the rock itself   (2) the cement in the rock   (3) the sand grains in the rock   (4) a crack in the rock

5. Which is the oldest aspect of a sedimentary rock composed of sand grains held together by cement?   (1) a vein in the rock   (2) the sand grains   (3) the rock itself   (4) the bedding of the rock

6. A sedimentary rock formation (sandstone) considered to be a beach deposit is continuously found from New York to Indiana. Which statement is most likely to be true about this formation?   (1) it has the same fossils at all locations   (2) it may be of different ages at different locations   (3) it must be the same age at all locations because it is the same formation   (4) it has the same thickness at all locations

7. It is hard to unravel the history of Precambrian rocks because (1) they are not exposed at the surface   (2) they contain few fossils (3) most Precambrian rocks are found only as sediments in younger rocks   (4) they are found only in the centers of mountains where they have been deformed

8. In the adjoining diagram, sedimentary rock layer A contains fragments of igneous rock. The probable age of the fragments is

(1) 1.3×10^7 years
(2) 1.4×10^7 years
(3) 1.5×10^7 years
(4) 1.6×10^7 years

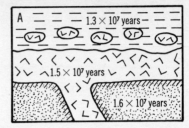

9. Which statement is false?   (1) two members of one species must be exactly alike   (2) the members of a species can vary in physical features   (3) the members of a species can interbreed and produce fertile young   (4) a species may exist on earth for millions of years

10. Differences among the members of a species   (1) may improve the chances that some members will survive   (2) has no effect on survival   (3) causes the different members to fight among themselves   (4) cannot occur according to the theory of organic evolution

11. The simplest way to correlate exposed rock layers in the same general vicinity when they contain no fossils is by   (1) following vertical intrusions   (2) radioactive dating   (3) walking the outcrop   (4) tracing a fault

TOPIC XIV — Landscape Development and Environmental Change

Landscapes (topography) are the features of the earth's surface at the interface between the atmosphere, hydrosphere, and lithosphere (crust). Some of the characteristics of landscapes are the slope of the land, shape of the surface features, stream drainage patterns, stream slope, and soil characteristics. A **stream drainage pattern** is the shape of the aerial view of the stream courses in an area (see Figure 14-6 on pages 210–211).

MEASURING LANDSCAPE CHARACTERISTICS

The shape and slope of the land, stream drainage patterns, and some soil features can be measured using actual observations or models such as contour maps, aerial photographs, satellite images, and the types of maps and diagrams used in this topic. The use of these tools has shown that landscape features such as hills, slopes, and stream drainage patterns have distinctive shapes by which they can be identified.

GRADIENT AND PROFILES. *Slope,* or *gradient,* a measurable characteristic of the land and streams, is described in Topic III. *Profiles,* also described in Topic III, are useful to show the shape and slope of the earth's surface and streams, and the thickness and development of soil horizons.

MOUNTAINS, PLATEAUS, AND PLAINS. On the basis of gradient, elevation, and rock structure, landscapes are divided into three major types—*mountains, plateaus,* and *plains* (see Figure 14-1).

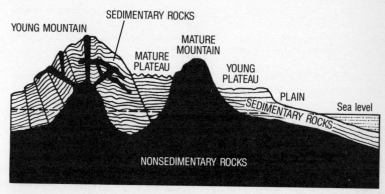

Figure 14-1. Profiles and structures of the major types of landscapes.

A **mountain** is an area of high elevation compared to the surrounding area or sea level, which usually has many changes in slope as well as regions of steep gradient. Internally, mountains are characterized by distorted rock structures such as faults, folds, and tilted rocks, and are often composed of much nonsedimentary rock.

A **plateau** is also an area of high elevation, but it has undistorted horizontal rock structure and often a more level slope or gradient than mountains. A plateau may have steep slopes where streams have cut valleys, such as at the Grand Canyon in the Colorado Plateau.

A **plain** has a generally level surface with little change in slope and has a low elevation. Plains usually have horizontal rock structure unless they are remnants of old mountain areas that have been leveled by erosion and weathering.

SOIL ASSOCIATIONS.   Soils differ in composition, particle size, structure, permeability, porosity, fertility, and degree of horizon development. Soils of similar characteristics are grouped together as a **soil association,** which is similar to a formation in rocks. The boundaries of different associations in an area are often indicated on maps.

LANDSCAPE REGIONS

Landscape characteristics (amount of slope, elevation, stream drainage patterns, and soil characteristics) appear to occur in combinations that form identifiable areas called **landscape regions** or physiographic provinces. For example, the combination of high elevation, steep slopes, thin soils, and trellis, annular, and radial stream patterns is common in mountain landscape regions (see Figure 14-6 on pages 210–211).

CONTINENTAL LANDSCAPE REGIONS.   Any continental land mass has several landscape regions that can be identified. The general landscape regions of the continental United States are shown in Figure 14-2. These types of landscape regions, as well as others, are found in many parts of the earth. You should carefully study the New York State landscape regions on the inside back cover of this book and in the *Earth Science Reference Tables,* page 248.

LANDSCAPE BOUNDARIES.   The boundaries between landscape regions are usually well defined, or distinct, as illustrated on the maps of New York State listed above. Landscape boundaries usually consist of features or characteristics of the landscape that have been brought about by changes in the structure of rocks. Such features and characteristics include the edges of mountains, cliffs, changes in type or amount of slope, or river courses that follow the direction of structural changes.

FACTORS OF LANDSCAPE DEVELOPMENT

The process of landscape development is very complex and involves many factors that may or may not be operating at a particular time and

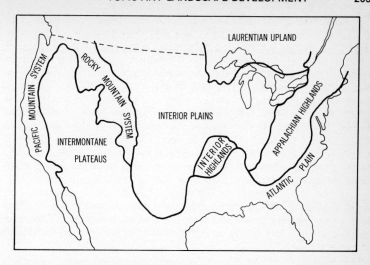

Figure 14-2. Major landscape regions of the continental United States.

place. Therefore, generalizations about landscape development may not apply in any one specific area.

UPLIFTING AND LEVELING FORCES. There are two groups of forces that operate to form and change landscapes—the *uplifting* (or constructional) forces and the *leveling* (or destructional) forces.

Uplifting forces originate beneath or within the earth's crust and displace rock material to raise the land, build mountains, and cause continental growth. The uplifting forces include volcanic action, isostasy, earthquakes, and many plate tectonic events.

Most **leveling forces** operate on the earth's surface. They break down the rocks of land masses and transport material along the earth's surface from higher to lower elevations under the force of gravity, thus tending to level out the land. The leveling forces include weathering, erosion, deposition, and subsidence.

Leveling forces (such as erosion or weathering) are always at work in all areas of the earth's solid surface, but uplifting may or may not be present at the same time. When both groups or forces are present, the landscape will be uplifted or leveled, depending on which forces are dominant (operating at a faster rate).

If uplifting is dominant, level land of low elevation may be changed into mountains with steep hillslopes and high elevations, stream drainage patterns may be altered as the streams begin to erode new landscapes, and wind patterns may change as the mountains act as barriers to the wind. Uplifting forces are usually dominant in plate boundary regions of earthquakes and volcanic action, where mountain building is going on. The landscape reflects the effects of those forces.

In areas where the leveling forces are acting alone or are dominant, elevation is decreasing and the land is becoming flatter or smoother in slope. Weathering and erosion are destroying the rocks faster than uplift (if any) is occurring. Deposition by running water, wind, and glaciers contributes to the leveling and also forms depositional features on the landscape.

TIME AND LANDSCAPE STAGES. The condition of a landscape at any one time is partly the result of the length of time the uplifting and leveling processes have acted on the rocks. Often an area experiences a time when uplifting is dominant, followed by a long time when leveling forces are dominant. When this happens, an area's landscape goes through **stages of development,** with each stage having characteristic conditions.

Figure 14-3 is a model of the stages of landscape development in a mountainous region in a humid climate. In stage A (youth), the uplifting forces are dominant. Uplifting gives the leveling forces such as streams and possibly glaciers a large amount of potential energy, and the rate of

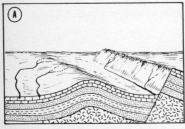

Youth. Uplifting forces are dominant, causing folding and faulting, and forming mountains with high elevations and steep slopes.

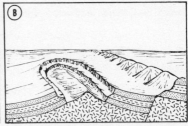

Maturity. Leveling forces are dominant, creating a rugged landscape with lower elevations.

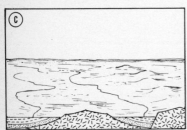

Old age. Leveling forces are still dominant, but less effective because low elevations and gentle slopes provide little potential energy.

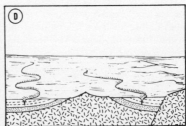

Rejuvenation. Uplifting forces are again dominant. As elevations increase, streams acquire more potential energy and form new valleys and steeper slopes.

Figure 14-3. Stages of landscape development.

leveling is great. As the uplifting forces decrease in effect, the destructional forces carve away the land, creating a rugged landscape of lower elevation characteristic of stage B (maturity). If the leveling forces continue to be dominant for millions of years, the landscape will become progressively smoother in slope and lower in elevation. When the former mountain region is smooth enough to resemble a plain, it is considered to be in stage C (old age). In stage C the leveling forces are usually less active than in earlier stages because of flat slopes and low elevation, so that streams have small potential energy and small gradient.

DYNAMIC EQUILIBRIUM IN LANDSCAPES. Although landscape development is a continuous process leading to gradual change in the landscape, at any one time the landscape condition reflects a state of balance among many environmental factors. This is a condition of **dynamic equilibrium.** If a change occurs in any of the factors, a change in the landscape features will occur until a new equilibrium is established (Stage D in Figure 14-3).

FACTORS OF LANDSCAPE DEVELOPMENT—CLIMATE

The rate of development and the characteristics of the landscape of an area are greatly influenced by the temperature and moisture conditions of the area. Any change in an area's climate will alter the rate of development and characteristics of the landscape. On the other hand, changes in landscape sometimes cause changes in climate. For example, the growth of a new mountain range will block air mass movement and change moisture and temperature patterns, thereby changing the climate of affected areas. In turn, more landscape changes will occur in response to the climatic change. The effect of mountain ranges on climate, called the *orographic effect,* is described in Topic VIII, pages 117-118.

HILLSLOPES IN ARID AND HUMID CLIMATES. The steepness of hillslopes is partly affected by the balance between production of sediments by weathering and the removal of these sediments by erosion. In

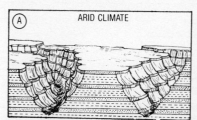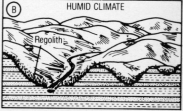

Figure 14-4. Landscape development of a plateau as affected by climate. The rock formations are assumed to be similar in both diagrams. **A** illustrates the steep slopes characteristic of an arid climate. **B** illustrates the smoother, more rounded landscape features of a humid climate, such as the Catskills of New York State.

arid climates there is little vegetation to hold sediments in place on slopes, or as deposits at the base of slopes, so wind and running water can rapidly carry the sediments away. This rapid removal of sediments causes many arid regions to be characterized by the steep slopes and sharp landscape features common in the southwestern United States. Arid regions are also characterized by sand dunes and by bedrock sculptured by wind-blown sand.

In humid climates, sediments on and at the bottom of hillslopes are better held in place by vegetation; therefore, areas with humid climates are characterized by the smoother and more rounded landscape features common in the eastern United States. The greater rate of chemical weathering of bedrock in humid climates contributes to their more rounded landscapes.

GLACIATION AND LANDSCAPES.   In climates where glaciers exist or existed in recent times (such as during the Pleistocene—see the *Geologic Time Scale* in the *Earth Science Reference Tables*, pages 242–243), the landscape will show much evidence of glacial erosion and deposition. Some of the landscape features of glaciation are (1) mountaintops and steep slopes without much soil, (2) transported soil covering large areas, (3) soil with a wide range of particle sizes even at the surface, (4) wide valleys with U-shaped profiles (as compared with a stream's V-shaped profile), (5) many lakes, (6) disrupted stream drainage patterns, (7) many small hills composed of sediment, (8) polished and scratched bedrock, and (9) the features of the glaciers themselves where the glaciers still exist.

STREAMS AND CLIMATE.   Some of the characteristics of streams are controlled by climate. In arid regions, most streams, being temporary, are without water for much of the time; streams in humid regions are permanent, having discharge most or all of the time.

Internal drainage is common in arid regions. Internal drainage occurs when water is channeled into basins that are not connected by streams to the oceans. Examples of such basins include the Great Salt Lake and others in Death Valley, California. Internal drainage is characteristic of arid regions because the streams have not had the time to carve interconnecting valleys for drainage to the oceans.

SOILS AND CLIMATE.   One of the most important factors in determining soil characteristics is climate. Soils in arid regions are often thin or nonexistent, because there is little or no vegetation to make and hold the soil. The soil that does exist is often very sandy, because smaller sediments have been blown away. Arid soils often contain many mineral salts that are not found in the soil of humid regions, where infiltration and runoff dissolve and carry the salts away. In humid regions, the soils tend to be thicker and more acidic; they are also higher in organic content and thus darker in color. If the climate is very hot and humid, the soil will be infertile because chemical weathering and infiltration rapidly remove organic and mineral nutrients, leaving the soil deficient in these components.

FACTORS OF LANDSCAPE DEVELOPMENT—BEDROCK

The composition and structural features of the bedrock are major factors in the rate of development and the characteristics of landscapes.

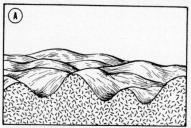

Homogeneous nonsedimentary bedrock. The landscape consists of a random distribution of rounded hills.

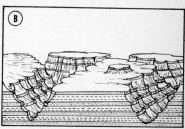

Horizontal sedimentary bedrock (plateau). The landscape has generally uniform elevation, with steep-sided valleys cut by streams.

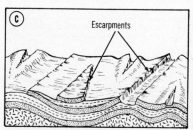

Folded strata of varying resistance. The landscape consists of roughly parallel ridges, with steep-sided escarpments of resistant rock.

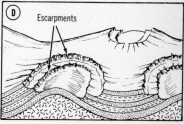

Domed structure. Landscape features resemble **C**, but ridges and escarpments have a generally circular arrangement.

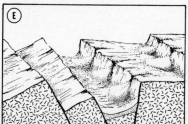

Fault block mountains. The landscape features consist of ridges of varying elevation, with steep slopes along the fault plantes.

Complex bedrock structure. The landscape consists of a great variety of elevations and slopes.

Figure 14-5. Effect of bedrock structure on landscape features.

ROCK RESISTANCE AND HILLSLOPES.   In any one climate, different rock types and formations have varying degrees of **rock resistance,** or resistance to weathering and erosion. If all the rocks in an area exposed to the surface have about the same resistance, the landscape features will be controlled by structural features, such as faults and joints, and the agents of leveling and uplift (E and F in Figure 14-5 on page 209). If there are no special structural features, the landscape features will be random in location and without rapid changes in hillslopes (A in Figure 14-5).

If rocks exposed at the surface have different degrees of resistance, the different rocks will weather and erode at different rates. For example, in sedimentary strata, sandstone layers will generally be more resistant than shale and will weather and erode more slowly. The result will be marked differences in slope between the layers of different resistance, often with a steep slope called an **escarpment** along the eroded edge of the more resistant layer (B, C, and D in Figure 14-5).

Figure 14-6. Effect of bedrock structure on stream drainage patterns. Under each sketch of the landscape there is a corresponding contour map showing the stream drainage.

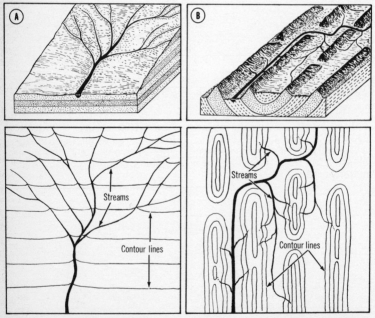

Random or dendritic drainage. This pattern is characteristic of horizontal sedimentary rocks with little difference in rock resistance.

Trellis or block drainage. This is observed in folded rocks with much difference in resistance, and also in faulted or jointed rock.

STRUCTURAL FEATURES AND HILLSLOPES. Often the types of **rock structure,** such as horizontality, folds, faults, and joints, have a major effect on hillslopes. A study of the diagrams in Figure 14-5 will show the influence of horizontal rocks, folded rocks, and faulted rocks. Generally, the greater the variety of structural features found in an area, the more varied the changes in hillslope and types of landscape features (F in Figure 14-5).

STREAMS AND BEDROCK CHARACTERISTICS. The direction, pattern, and gradient of streams are often directly related to the resistance and structure of underlying bedrock. In horizontal rocks with little difference in resistance, the streams will develop a random pattern and have few rapid changes in gradient, as shown in A of Figure 14-6. When the rocks in an area have varying degrees of resistance, or there are tilted, folded, faulted, or jointed rocks, the patterns and directions of the streams will be at least partly if not totally controlled by these rock features, as shown in B, C, and D. In such cases there is often sharp change in gradient, as indicated by falls and rapids.

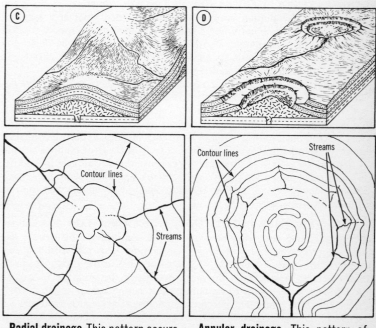

Radial drainage. This pattern occurs in an area of domed structure with little difference in rock resistance.

Annular drainage. This pattern of concentric circles is found in areas of domed structure with much difference in rock resistance.

SOILS AND ROCK COMPOSITION.   The different compositions of the soil associations are due in part to differences in the underlying bedrock or in transported material from which the soil formed. A soil formed from a sedimentary rock such as sandstone will be much different in composition from a soil formed from an igneous rock such as basalt, because of major differences in the mineral and chemical composition of the rocks. A soil association map and a geologic map (like the one in the *Earth Science Reference Tables,* pages 244–245) will often show a close correlation between soil association and rock type.

PEOPLE AND ENVIRONMENTAL CHANGE

People have greatly affected their environment, including the landscape. They have cut down forests and plowed up the land, allowing soil to be carried away or *denuded;* they have carved up or smoothed out the land for mining and construction of roads, buildings, and airports; they have polluted the land with their discards; they have added chemicals to the land, air, and water which aid weathering, and they have even made new land by filling in lakes and parts of the ocean with their garbage. Thus people are a major factor in landscape development.

LANDSCAPE POLLUTION AND POPULATION.   Figure 14-7 is a graph showing that the human population has been increasing at a rapid or exponential rate in recent times. Landscape pollution is generally greatest in areas of high population density. This is so because it is there that people erode and deposit material in concentrations large enough to adversely affect their lives and the life forms and landscape.

Modern people can cause rapid changes in their environment because of **technology**—the application of scientific discoveries to the methods of producing goods and services. Catastrophic events may occur as the environment reacts to the changes caused by technology. The effects of atomic bombs, deforestation of thousands of acres a year, the plowing-up of thousands of acres of grassland a year, the use of millions of tons of pesticides a year, and similar changes cause rapid responses in wildlife, soil and stream characteristics, and rates of landscape evolution. Many of these changes have resulted in the extinction of wildlife and the loss of useful landscapes.

ATMOSPHERIC POLLUTION AND LANDSCAPE CHANGE.   The addition of liquid and solid aerosols to the atmosphere by people can increase reflection and scattering of insolation. This may result in less energy at the surface of the earth for natural landscape-producing processes such as weathering. On the other hand, the addition of carbon dioxide and water vapor to the atmosphere can increase the greenhouse effect and thus cause an increase of energy at the earth's surface for landscape change. Many industrial and community activities add substances to the atmosphere that cause areas to have greater amounts of cloud coverage than would naturally occur. Increased cloud coverage affects precipitation and temperatures and thereby can alter the type and rate of landscape development. The addition of sulfur compounds to the atmosphere, largely by burning fossil fuels and mineral refining,

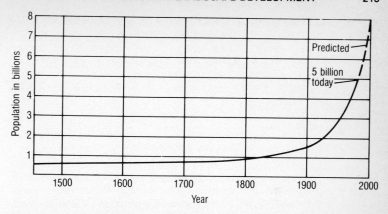

Figure 14-7. Estimated human population of the world in recent centuries (projected to the year 2000).

has significantly increased the acid content of precipitation. This acid precipitation (acid rain) has increased the chemical weathering of rocks, regolith, and vegetation, resulting in changed landscapes.

ENVIRONMENTAL CONSERVATION.   Resources, such as soil for agriculture, land for homesites, pure water for consumption and recreation, and clean air for biologic activity, can be conserved by careful planning and by the control of environmental pollutants.

Some of the goals of environmental planning are elimination of landscape pollution and a net elimination of *denudation*. **Denudation** is the loss or removal of regolith (soil and sediments) and life forms, such as trees, due to leveling forces. Often denudation is due to or accelerated by human activities. Another goal is the reclaiming of landscapes that have been made unusable by misuse.

For successful programs in conservation of the environment, there must be education to make people aware of the problems and to change attitudes that lead to misuse of the environment. Finally, people must *act* to stop further misuse and to repair former destruction.

VOCABULARY

landscape	leveling forces
stream drainage pattern	stages of landscape development
mountain	dynamic equilibrium in landscape
plateau	rock resistance
plain	escarpment
soil association	rock structure
landscape region	technology
uplifting forces	denudation

QUESTIONS ON TOPIC XIV—LANDSCAPE DEVELOPMENT AND ENVIRONMENTAL CHANGE

Questions in Recent Regents Exams (end of book)

June 1984: 43, 44, 46, 54, 55, 97
June 1985: 36, 46, 50, 51, 52, 53, 89
June 1986: 50–54, 88, 101–105
June 1987: 47–52

Questions from Earlier Regents Exams

1. Rounded-bottom valleys with almost vertical sides, small hills and ridges composed of unsorted sediments, and exposed bedrock with small, parallel grooves and scratches are observed. Which events probably produced these features? (1) extensive glaciation (2) widespread earthquakes and associated faulting (3) a period of active volcanoes and lava flows (4) extensive flooding followed by periods of wind erosion

2. Which factor is most important in determining the evolution of a landscape? (1) surface topography (2) plant cover (3) climate (4) development of drainage

3. What is the only difference between the Adirondacks and the Catskills that can be distinguished from the *Earth Science Reference Tables?* (1) The Adirondacks have metamorphic bedrock, but the Catskills have sedimentary bedrock. (2) The Adirondacks have mostly rounded hilltops and the Catskills have jagged hilltops. (3) The Catskills have vegetation, but the Adirondacks do not. (4) The Catskills are much higher in elevation than the Adirondacks.

4. Which graph best represents human population growth?

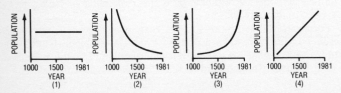

5. Landscape regions are generally determined by (1) underlying rock structure and elevation (2) amount of stream discharge and direction of flow (3) method of surface sediment deposition (4) amount of yearly precipitation

6. Which feature would most likely indicate the boundary between two landscape regions? (1) a highway cutting through a mountain region (2) resistant bedrock composed of more than one type of mineral (3) two adjoining massive bedrock types that have different structures (4) a long meandering stream flowing across a large, level region

7. Which change would be occurring in a landscape region where uplifting forces are dominant over leveling forces? (1) topographic features that are becoming smoother with time   (2) a state of dynamic equilibrium existing with time   (3) streams that are decreasing in velocity with time   (4) hill slopes that are increasing in steepness with time

8. Which of the following stream patterns is most characteristic of horizontal rock structure?

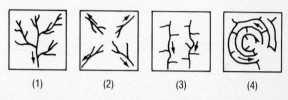

(1)   (2)   (3)   (4)

9. Soil formed from local bedrock of the Adirondack Highlands is observed to be different from soil formed from local bedrock in the Appalachian Uplands. Which statement best explains this observation? (1) The elevation of the bedrock in the Adirondacks is different from the elevation of the bedrock of the other region.   (2) The type of agriculture found in the Adirondacks is different from the agriculture in the other region.   (3) The type of bedrock of the Adirondacks is different from the bedrock of the other region.   (4) The stream drainage patterns of the Adirondacks are different from the stream drainage patterns of the other region.

10. The Catskills are a part of which New York State landscape region?   (1) the Hudson-Mohawk Lowlands   (2) the Appalachian Uplands   (3) the Adirondack Highlands   (4) the Taconic Mountains

11. When most landscape regions are uplifted, the amount of weathering and erosion that occurs will generally   (1) decrease   (2) increase   (3) remain the same

12. In the cross section of the hill shown below, which rock units are probably most resistant to weathering?

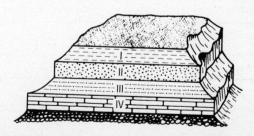

(1) I and II   (2) II and III   (3) I and III   (4) II and IV

13. Which diagram best represents a cross section of a valley which was glaciated and then eroded by a stream?

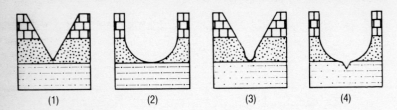

(1)   (2)   (3)   (4)

14. According to the *Earth Science Reference Tables*, which New York State landscape region has the lowest elevation, the most nearly level land surface, and is composed primarily of Cretaceous through Pleistocene unconsolidated sediments?   (1) the Hudson-Mohawk Lowlands   (2) the Atlantic Coastal Lowlands   (3) the Champlain Lowlands   (4) the Erie-Ontario Lowlands

15. The boundaries between landscape regions are usually determined by the location of   (1) state boundaries   (2) major cities   (3) population density   (4) well-defined surface features

16. The most recent major influence on New York State landscape development was   (1) volcanic activity   (2) crustal subsidence   (3) continental glaciation   (4) the folding of the Catskills

17. In an area of crustal activity, the rate of uplift is 20 centimeters per hundred years and the average rate of erosion is 8 centimeters per hundred years. The elevation of this area is generally   (1) decreasing   (2) increasing   (3) remaining the same

18. According to the *Earth Science Reference Tables*, which New York State landscape region contains mostly Devonian bedrock? (1) Adirondack Highlands   (2) Atlantic Coastal Lowlands   (3) Appalachian Uplands   (4) Tug Hill Plateau

19. On the diagram below, the present surface features known as Peters, Blue, Third, and Second Mountains were mainly the result of (1) intrusion of igneous material   (2) faulting   (3) different erosion rates   (4) metamorphism

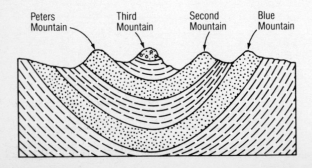

Peters Mountain   Third Mountain   Second Mountain   Blue Mountain

Base your answers to questions 20 and 21 on your knowledge of earth science and on the diagram below of a section of the earth's crust.

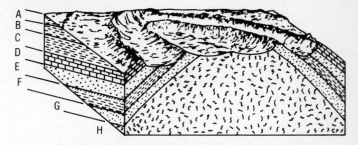

20. Which kind of stream pattern would most likely be found on the type of landscape shown in the diagram?

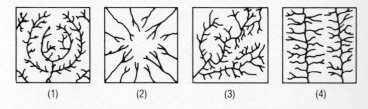

(1)   (2)   (3)   (4)

21. According to the surface landscape development indicated in the diagram, which rock type or types are most resistant to weathering and erosion in this environment?   (1) rock *E*   (2) rock *H*   (3) rocks *C* and *F*   (4) rocks *D* and *G*

Additional Questions

1. Which of the following would *not* explain why soils are different in separate locations?   (1) different climates   (2) different compositions of the rocks the soils formed from   (3) different amounts of time for soil formation   (4) different ages of the rocks the soil formed from

2. If a new mountain range were to form where the Mississippi River is today, the landscape east of this new mountain range would become more angular and less rounded because the climate would become   (1) drier and warmer   (2) drier and cooler   (3) moister and warmer   (4) moister and cooler

3. The development of a landscape with large amounts of transported soil, polished and scratched bedrock, and valleys much wider than the streams in them is most related to   (1) uplifting   (2) glacial erosion   (3) stream erosion   (4) subsidence

4. In a warm, humid climate, if the leveling forces have been dominant many millions of years without any uplifting, what characteristics would the landscape have?   (1) rugged slopes with thin soil

(2) rugged slopes with thick soil   (3) smooth slopes with thin soil
(4) smooth slopes with thick soil

5. If an area became more arid, the steepness of the slopes and
the sharpness of landscape features would   (1) increase   (2) decrease
(3) remain the same

6. Models of hillslopes and landform shapes can be made with the
use of   (1) isobars   (2) contour lines   (3) isotherms   (4) parallels

7. The different types of soil found at the earth's surface are
classified as   (1) soil profiles   (2) soil horizons   (3) soil associations
(4) soil formations

Refer to the diagram below to answer questions 8 through 15.

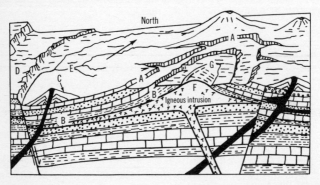

8. The climate of this area is most likely   (1) arid   (2) humid
(3) hot   (4) cold

9. The cliffs around locations A are most directly the result of
(1) igneous intrusion   (2) resistant rock layers   (3) the different ages
of the rocks   (4) movement along faults

10. What can be said about rock layer B compared to rock layer
F?   (1) B is younger   (2) B is more resistant   (3) B is less resistant
(4) B is lower because of its environment of deposition

11. The landscape characteristics of this area are most like the
landscapes found in what part of the continental United States?
(1) northeast   (2) southeast   (3) midwest   (4) southwest

12. How would you classify the geologic forces producing the landscapes at locations C and G?   (1) at both places uplifting forces are
dominant   (2) at both places leveling forces are dominant   (3) at C
uplifting is dominant, and at G leveling is dominant   (4) at C leveling
is dominant, and at G uplifting is dominant

13. What immediate effects would increased rainfall have on the
rate of leveling of this landscape?   (1) increase   (2) decrease   (3) remain
the same

14. The primary reason for the cliff at D is   (1) volcanic action   (2) resistant rock layers   (3) movement along a fault   (4) joints in the rock layers

15. The steepness of the slopes in this area is *not* due to (1) vegetation holding sediments in place   (2) local bedrock composition   (3) uplifting forces   (4) the type of stream drainage pattern in the area

16. If a landscape is in dynamic equilibrium and uplift occurs, (1) there can never again be dynamic equilibrium in the area   (2) the dynamic equilibrium will remain the same   (3) a new dynamic equilibrium will be established   (4) a new landscape will form without dynamic equilibrium

17. If people's addition of aerosols to the atmosphere decreases insolation, the amount of landscape change due to weathering would (1) increase   (2) decrease   (3) remain the same

18. What is the most practical way to control pollution?   (1) slowing down the rate of technological growth   (2) decreasing the population   (3) careful planning of environmental usage   (4) more government control of industry

19. The most practical way individuals can help fight pollution is by   (1) becoming aware of the problems and thus changing their attitudes and actions   (2) recycling paper   (3) using fewer products produced by technology   (4) changing their life-styles to conform to that of nineteenth-century rural America

Refer to the graphs below to answer questions 20 through 27. The first variable listed in the question corresponds to the X axis and the second variable corresponds to the Y axis. For each of the questions choose the number of the graph that best matches the statement.

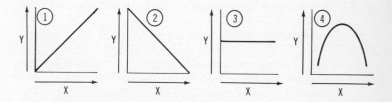

20. Population density and amount of landscape pollution.

21. People's addition of carbon dioxide to the atmosphere and absorption of terrestrial electromagnetic energy from the earth.

22. Erosion of sediments and steepness of slopes.

23. Degree of similarity of bedrock composition and the amount of variation in slopes in an area's landscape.

24. Variation in rock types in an area and number of soil associations.

25. Time and elevation of an area during a cycle of landscape development.

26. Equal rates of uplift and leveling and change in the average elevation of an area.

27. Positive $P-E_p$ and steepness of hillslopes in an area.

Refer to the diagrams below of five different landscapes to answer questions 28 through 36.

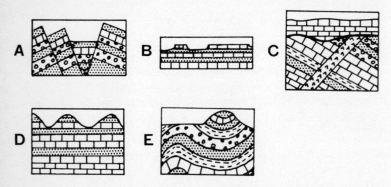

28. Which two landscapes are most likely the product of a humid climate?   (1) A & B   (2) A & C   (3) B & E   (4) D & E

29. Which of the landscapes appears to have been produced in an arid climate?   (1) B   (2) C   (3) D   (4) E

30. Where is rock resistance more important than rock structure in producing the present landscape?   (1) B   (2) C   (3) D   (4) E

31. In which landscape region was the dynamic equilibrium among the landscape-producing forces most recently disturbed by uplifting? (1) A   (2) B   (3) D   (4) E

32. Which landscape has the most characteristics of a mountainous region?   (1) A   (2) B   (3) C   (4) D

33. In which landscape would rock structure have the greatest effect on stream patterns?   (1) A   (2) B   (3) C   (4) D

34. In which diagram does the present landscape show the most evidence of a long period of leveling?   (1) A   (2) B   (3) D   (4) E

35. Which diagram has evidence for a former period of landscape development?   (1) B   (2) C   (3) D   (4) E

36. In which landscape is faulting a dominant reason for the present landscape?   (1) A   (2) B   (3) D   (4) E

Glossary

absolute age: The actual age of an object (rock) or geologic event in years. Often determined by radioactive dating methods. See **relative age.**

absolute humidity: The actual amount (weight) of water vapor in a given volume of air. Directly related to vapor pressure.

absolute zero: Theoretically, the lowest possible temperature. No heat energy can be extracted from matter at this temperature.

absorption: The interception or taking in of electromagnetic energy by a material. When electromagnetic energy is absorbed by a material it is usually changed into other forms of energy, often heat, which causes a temperature rise.

actual evapotranspiration (E_a): In reference to the water budget, the total amount of water lost through evaporation and transpiration from an area in a given period of time. Usually expressed as a depth (mm of water).

adiabatic temperature change: A change in temperature that occurs without heat being added or removed. The cooling of air as it rises and expands and the warming of air as it descends are adiabatic temperature changes.

aerobic bacteria: Bacteria that require the presence of free oxygen to carry on their life functions.

aerosol: Small solid or liquid particles suspended in a gas. Suspended solid or liquid water particles are the aerosols in fog and clouds.

air mass: A large body of air in the lower atmosphere (troposphere) with approximately uniform air temperature, pressure, and moisture at any given level.

air pressure: See **atmospheric pressure.**

altitude: (1) The vertical distance (elevation) between a point and sea level. (2) The angle of a celestial object above the horizon. Usually expressed in degrees; often measured with a sextant.

anaerobic bacteria: Bacteria that do not require the presence of free oxygen to carry on their life functions. They are associated with polluted water.

angle of insolation: The angle at which the sun's rays hit the earth's surface. The higher the sun is in the sky, the higher the angle of insolation.

anticyclone: A high-pressure mass of air within the troposphere in which air moves out from the center. They rotate clockwise in the Northern Hemisphere and counterclockwise in the Southern Hemisphere. Anticyclone Also called *HIGHS.*

aphelion: The point in a planet's orbit when it is farthest from the sun. For the earth, aphelion occurs about July 4th, when it is about 152,000,000 kilometers from the sun.

apparent diameter: The diameter a celestial object (such as the sun or a planet) appears to have, depending on its distance from an observer; not the actual diameter. It is usually expressed in angular units. The closer a celestial object is to the earth, the larger its apparent diameter.

apparent solar day: A day of varying length determined by the time it takes for the sun to arrive at its highest point in the sky on two consecutive days at the same location. It is always slightly longer than the time it takes for one complete rotation of the earth. Can be measured by a sundial. See also **mean solar day.**

apparent solar time: Time based on the apparent solar day. Also called *local* or *sundial time.*

arc: A curved line that is part of a circle. An arc is the shape of the path of most celestial objects, such as the sun, in their daily paths through the earth's sky.

arid climate: A dry climate where the precipitation (P) is less than the potential evapotranspiration (E_p) for a large part of the year. Thus there is a deficit (D) of moisture and a drought much of the time.

astronomical unit: The mean distance of the earth from the sun—about 150,000,000 kilometers. Commonly used as a unit of distance in astronomy.

atmosphere: The shell of gases surrounding the earth. It is divided into layers according to differences in chemical and physical properties.

atmospheric pressure: The weight of the overlying atmosphere pushing down on a given unit of area. It is affected by changes in temperature, moisture, and altitude. Also called *air pressure* or *barometric pressure.*

atmospheric variables: The changeable conditions in the atmosphere that cause weather. The variables include temperature, air pressure, wind, and moisture.

axis: An imaginary line through the earth from the north to the south geographic poles, about which the earth rotates.

banding: The layered arrangement of mineral crystals in some metamorphic rocks due to the alignment and separation of like minerals.

barometric pressure: See **atmospheric pressure.**

bedrock: The solid and largely unweathered portion of the crust and lithosphere in an area that is underneath the soil and other loose material. Also called the *local rock.*

benchmark: A permanent marker, usually metal, at a specific location, that indicates an exact elevation or altitude at the time of installation.

calorie: A unit of heat energy defined as the quantity of heat needed to raise the temperature of 1 gram of water 1°C.

capillarity: The process by which water is drawn into pores due to molecular attraction.

capillary migration: The upward movement of water, against gravity, in part of the soil, regolith, or bedrock due to capillarity. Also called *capillary action.*

capillary water: The water held in pores in the soil and rocks in the zone of aeration as a result of the process of capillarity.

carbon-14: A radioactive isotope of carbon with a short half-life (5600 years). Used only to date recent (up to 50,000-year-old) remains of organic material.

celestial object: Any object outside the earth's atmosphere, including moons, comets, planets, stars, and galaxies.

cementation: The process by which solid sediments are "glued" together by precipitated minerals, forming a sedimentary rock.

change: The observation or inference that the characteristics of a portion of the environment have altered.

change in soil storage (ΔSt): In reference to the water budget, the amount of water added to or taken from an area's soil storage. A positive change in soil storage is called *recharge,* and a negative change is called *usage.*

chemical weathering: The process whereby chemicals, such as oxygen and water, alter rocks and other earth materials, resulting in new minerals (chemicals). Rusting is a common example.

classification: The grouping together of objects and/or events with similar observed properties to make them more meaningful for study.

clay: See **colloids.**

climate: The total view or concept of an area's weather over a long period of time. It includes not only averages but also extremes.

cloud: A mass of suspended liquid water droplets and/or ice crystals in the atmosphere.

cold front: A weather front in which the colder air mass is pushing the warmer air mass. Cold fronts are characterized by a steep slope, rapid changes in weather, and often thunderstorms.

colloids: Very small solid particles (less than 0.0004 cm in diameter) that remain suspended in water for long periods of time. They make muddy water muddy. Also called **clay.**

compression: The process by which deposited sediment is pressed down by overlying sediments, water, and/or earth movements, resulting in the formation of sedimentary or metamorphic rocks.

compression waves: In earthquakes, the waves that cause particles through which the waves travel to vibrate in the direction the waves are moving. Compression waves are the fastest-moving of earthquake waves. Also called *primary*, or *P, waves.*

condensation: The change in phase from a gas to a liquid, such as when water vapor changes to liquid water droplets as clouds form.

condensation surface: A solid surface required for the condensation of water. Aerosols, such as dust, salt crystals, and ice, act as condensation surfaces in the formation of clouds. In dew and frost formation, the condensation surfaces are the earth's surface features.

conduction: The transfer of heat energy from atom to atom, in any state of matter, through contact when atoms collide. Conduction of energy occurs most readily in solids, especially metals.

conservation of energy: The concept that energy is neither created nor destroyed, but remains the same in total amount in a closed system.

constituent unit: Those parts that make up a material, such as the minerals or sediments in a rock or the crystal structure of a mineral.

contact metamorphic zone: A special type of *transition zone* between rock types caused by the baking or altering of older bedrock by contact with molten rock (lava or magma). Changes older rock into nonsedimentary metamorphic rock.

continental climate: The climate of inland areas not moderated by a large body of water; characterized by hot summers and cold winters, and thus having a wide annual temperature range.

continental crust: The part of the earth's crust (upper lithosphere) that makes up the continental blocks. Compared to oceanic crust, it is thicker, lower in density, and granitic rather than basaltic in composition.

continental drift: The concept that the continents have been and are presently shifting their position on the earth's surface; really due to plate tectonics.

continental polar air mass (cP): Very common cold and dry air masses that invade the contiguous United States from Canada.

continental tropical air mass (cT): Relatively rare hot and dry air masses that form in the southwestern United States or Mexico, that may affect weather of the contiguous United States in the summer.

contour line: An isoline on contour, or topographic, maps that represents points of equal elevation on the earth's surface.

contour map: A model of the elevation field of the earth's surface using contour lines and other symbols. Also called a *topographic map.*

convection: The transfer of heat energy by circulatory movements in a fluid (liquid or gas) that results from differences in density within the fluid.

convection current: A circulatory motion in a fluid due to convection. Also called *convection cell.*

convergence: (1) the coming together of air currents at the earth's surface and at the top of the troposphere. (2) The direct collision of lithospheric plates in the **plate tectonic theory.**

coordinate system: A grid or system of lines for determining the location of a point on a surface.

core: The innermost region of the earth, thought to be composed of iron and nickel. The outer part of the core is thought to be liquid and the inner part solid.

Coriolis effect: The deflection of all moving particles of matter at the earth's surface, which provides evidence for the earth's rotation; the deflection is to the right in the Northern Hemisphere and to the left in the Southern Hemisphere.

correlation: In geology, the process of showing that rocks or geologic events in different places are the same in relative or absolute age.

crust: The outermost portion of the earth's solid lithosphere. It is separated from the uppermost mantle by the Moho interface.

crystal: (1) The individual mineral constituent units of rocks. (2) A solid with a definite internal structure because its constituent atoms are arranged in a characteristic, regular, repeating pattern.

crystalline: A term used to describe a rock that is composed of intergrown mineral crystals.

crystallization: A type of solidification in which molten rock (magma or lava) cools to form nonsedimentary igneous rocks composed of minerals that have a definite arrangement of their atoms. Also see **solidification.**

cyclic change: Orderly changes in the environment in which the events constantly repeat themselves with reference to time and space.

cyclone: A low-pressure portion of the troposphere that has air moving toward its center. Cyclones in the Northern Hemisphere rotate counterclockwise and in the Southern Hemisphere they rotate clockwise. Types of cyclones include hurricanes, tornadoes, and mid-latitude cyclones. Also called a *LOW.*

daily motion: The apparent east-to-west movement of celestial objects in the sky at 15 degrees per hour actually caused by the earth's west-to-east rotation. Daily motion causes the sun, stars, etc. to appear to move in circular or arc-shaped paths in the sky.

deficit (D): The condition in the local water budget when actual evapotranspiration (E_a) does not equal potential evapotranspiration (E_p) because there is not enough water from precipitation (P) and soil storage (St). A long period of deficit is a drought.

density: The ratio of the mass of an object to its volume. $\text{density} = \dfrac{\text{mass}}{\text{volume}}$

denudation: The stripping off and removal (erosion) of the plants, soil, and regolith at the earth's surface. Denudation is often caused or increased by the careless activities of human beings.

deposition: The process by which sediments are released, dropped, or settled from erosional systems; it includes the precipitation of dissolved minerals from water in the formation of evaporite sedimentary rocks. Also called *sedimentation.*

desert: A region with an arid climate where the average yearly precipitation (P) is much smaller than potential evapotranspiration (E_p).

dew point: The temperature at which the air is saturated with moisture and the relative humidity is 100%. At temperatures below the dew point, condensation of water vapor occurs.

direct rays: Rays of sunlight that strike the earth at an angle of 90°. Also called *vertical rays* or *perpendicular insolation.*

distorted structure: The curving and folding of the banded layers in nonsedimentary metamorphic rocks due to heat and compression.

divergence: (1) The spreading out of air from rising or falling currents of air in the troposphere. (2) The type of plate movement in which lithospheric plates move away or spread from each other, according to the **plate tectonic theory.**

duration of insolation: The length of time insolation is received at a location in a day, or how long the sun is in the sky in a day.

dynamic equilibrium: A condition of changing balance between opposing processes, such as evaporation and condensation or erosion and deposition.

earthquake: A natural, rapid shaking of the crust or lithosphere of the earth caused by the displacement of rocks; most often associated with fault movement, but also associated with other causes, such as volcanic eruptions.

eccentricity: The degree of ovalness of an ellipse, or how far an ellipse is from being a circle. Eccentricity is computed using the formula

$$\text{eccentricity} = \frac{\text{distance between foci}}{\text{length of the major axis}}$$

electromagnetic energy: Energy that is emitted (radiated) in the form of transverse waves, into any part of the universe. Electromagnetic energy radiates from all objects not at a temperature of absolute zero. Examples include visible light, radio waves, and infrared energy.

electromagnetic spectrum: A model, such as a chart, that shows the full range of the types of electromagnetic energy, usually in order of wavelength.

ellipse: A closed curve around two fixed points, called foci, in which the sum of the distances between any point on the curve and the foci is a constant. All planetary orbits, including the earth's, are elliptical in shape.

energy: The ability to do work.

environmental equilibrium: The balance that exists among the natural parts of the environment even though all parts of the environment are constantly changing.

epicenter: The place on the earth's surface lying directly above the point at which an earthquake originates (the focus).

equator: The parallel on earth midway between the geographic north and south poles with a latitude of 0 degrees.

equinox: A time when the sun is directly overhead at noon at the equator, and there are 12 hours of daylight and 12 hours of darkness over the whole earth. The spring (vernal) equinox is about March 21st, and the fall (autumnal) equinox is about September 23rd.

erosion: The carrying away of soil and pieces of rock by wind, water, ice, etc. Erosion is the process by which sediments are obtained and transported. Erosion also refers to the wearing away and lowering of the earth's surface.

error: The amount of deviation or incorrectness in a measurement. See also **percent error.**

escarpment: A steep slope or cliff in layered (stratified) rocks. Formed from certain rock layers that are resistant to weathering and erosion.

evaporation: The change in phase from liquid to a gas, such as liquid water into water vapor (steam). Also called *vaporization.*

evaporite: A type of sedimentary rock formed directly by precipitation of dissolved minerals from water. Evaporites, which include rock salt and gypsum, are composed of intergrown mineral crystals.

evapotranspiration: The combination of the processes of evaporation and transpiration.

event: The name used to describe the occurrence of a change in the environment.

extrusion: A body of nonsedimentary igneous rock formed by the cooling and solidification of liquid rock (lava) at the earth's surface.

extrusive igneous rock: Igneous rocks, such as basalt and rhyolite, that form through the cooling and solidification of liquid rock (lava) at the earth's surface.

fault: A crack in a mass of rock with displacement, or movement, of rock along the crack.

field: Any region of space that has some measurable value of a given quantity at every point, such as the earth's magnetic field.

focus (plural **foci**): (1) In an ellipse, either of two fixed points located so that the sum of their distances to any point on the ellipse is a constant. The sun is at one of the two foci of the orbit of each of the planets. (2) The place where an earthquake actually originates.

folded strata: The bends in layered rock due to movement in the lithosphere; a type of deformed strata.

formation: See **rock formation.**

fossil: Any evidence of former life, either direct or indirect.

Foucault pendulum: A freely swinging pendulum whose path appears to change in a predictable way, thus providing evidence for the earth's rotation.

frames of reference: Properties or characteristics by which something can be described, studied, or compared. Time and space are frames of reference for studying change.

frictional drag: Friction at the interface of the atmosphere and the earth's surface caused by wind, air-mass movement, the Coriolis effect, etc. Heat produced by frictional drag minimally heats the atmosphere.

front: The interface between two air masses of different characteristics.

geocentric model: An early concept of celestial objects and their motions in which all celestial objects revolved around the earth, which was stationary and was the center of the universe.

geographic poles: The North and South poles of the earth, with a latitude of 90 degrees. The geographic poles are located at opposite ends of the earth's axis of rotation.

geologic time scale: A chronological model of the geologic history of the earth using divisions called eras, periods, and epochs. See the *Earth Science Reference Tables* on page 242 for details.

geosyncline: A large, shallow ocean basin near continental margins that slowly subsides under large quantities of sediment. It is thought that geosynclines are eventually uplifted, forming mountains and continental areas.

graded bedding: A layering of sediment or sedimentary rock that shows a gradual change in particle size, with the largest particles on the bottom and the smallest ones on top.

gradient: The rate of change from place to place within a field. Also called *slope.*

$$\text{gradient} = \frac{\text{amount of change in the field}}{\text{distance through which change occurs}}$$

gravitation: The attractive force that exists between any two objects in the universe. It is proportional to the product of the masses of the objects and inversely proportional to the square of the distance between their centers.

$$\text{force} \propto \frac{\text{mass}_1 \times \text{mass}_2}{(\text{distance between their centers})^2}$$

gravity: The force that pulls objects toward the center of the earth.

greenhouse effect: A process that warms the atmosphere and reduces heat loss by terrestrial radiation from the earth's surface. It results from the fact that the atmosphere transmits the short-wave radiation received from the sun, but absorbs and is heated by the long-wave radiation from the earth's surface.

ground water: The portion of the subsurface water found beneath the water table; the water in the zone of saturation. Also see **subsurface water.**

half-life: The time required for one half of the atoms in a given mass of a radioactive isotope to decay, or change, to a different isotope.

heat energy: Energy that is transferred from one body to another as a result of a difference in temperature between the two bodies; also called *thermal energy*.

heliocentric model: The modern concept of celestial objects and their motions, in which the rotating earth and other planets revolve around the sun.

HIGH: See **anticyclone**.

horizontal sorting: The sorting of particles of sediments into layers in which particle size and density decrease in one horizontal direction—the direction toward which the erosional system was moving.

humid climate: A moist or wet climate where precipitation (P) equals or is greater than potential evapotranspiration (E_p) on a yearly average.

hydrosphere: The liquid water that rests on much of the earth's surface. The oceans constitute most of the hydrosphere.

igneous rock: A nonsedimentary rock formed by the cooling and solidification of molten material (lava or magma) above or below the earth's surface.

index fossil: A fossil used in correlation and relative dating of rocks. A species used as an index fossil generally lived for only a short time and was distributed over a large geographic area.

inference: An interpretation (conclusion, theory, or explanation) of observation(s).

infiltration: The seeping and entering of liquid water from the earth's surface into the ground (bedrock and soil), where the water becomes subsurface water.

inner core: The innermost zone of the earth's core, which is thought to be composed of iron and nickel in a solid state.

insolation (INcoming SOLar radiATION): The part of the sun's radiation that is received by the earth.

instrument: A device made by people, that aids or extends the human senses beyond their normal limits in order to obtain more accurate observations.

intensity of insolation: The relative strength energy of the sun's radiations intersecting a specific area of the earth in a specific amount of time, such as calories per square meter per minute. The higher the angle of insolation the greater the intensity of insolation and the sun's heating effect.

interface: The boundary zone between regions with different properties. Energy is usually exchanged across an interface.

intrusion: A mass of nonsedimentary igneous rock formed by the cooling and solidification of liquid rock (magma) below the earth's surface.

intrusive igneous rock: An igneous rock, such as granite or gabbro, that forms by the cooling and solidification of liquid rock beneath the earth's surface.

isobar: An isoline used on weather and climatic maps to connect points of equal air pressure.

isoline: A line used on a model of a field, such as a map, which connects points of equal value of a field quantity. Examples of isolines are isotherms, isobars, and contour lines.

isostasy: A principle that states that the earth's crust is in a state of equilibrium and that any change in the mass of one part of the crust will be offset by a change in mass of another part to maintain the equilibrium. Isostasy is often used to explain why the continental crust floats higher than the denser oceanic crust and why mountains and other continental areas rise as they are eroded.

iso-surface: A surface in a model of a three-dimensional field in which all points on the surface have the same field value.

isotherm: An isoline used on weather and climatic maps to connect points of equal air temperature.

isotope: One of the varieties of an element. The various isotopes of an element all have the same atomic number and chemical properties. However, they differ in their atomic masses and physical properties. For example, carbon-12 and carbon-14 are isotopes of carbon.

joint: A crack in rocks along which there has been no relative movement or displacement, such as there is in a fault.

kinetic energy: The energy of movement of a mass or object. The greater the velocity or speed of an object, the greater the kinetic energy.

landscape: The characteristics of the earth's surface at the interface between the atmosphere and the hydrosphere and lithosphere. Also called *topography*.

landscape region: A portion of the earth's surface with landscape characteristics that distinguish it from other areas. Some of the distinguishing characteristics are rock structure, elevation, degree of slope, and stream patterns. Also called a *physiographic region*.

latent heat: Energy absorbed or released by a substance during a change of phase. This transfer of energy occurs without a change in temperature.

latitude: Angular distance north or south of the equator; usually expressed in degrees. Minimum latitude is at the equator (0°), and maximum is at the geographic poles (90°N or 90°S).

latitudinal climatic patterns: East-west belts, or zones, of climate types on the earth caused by latitudinal changes in climatic factors, such as temperature, moisture, winds, and ocean currents.

leveling forces: Forces that operate constantly at or near the earth's surface and that break down rocks, transport material from higher to lower elevations, and tend to level off and lower the land. Leveling forces include weathering, erosion, denudation, deposition, and subsidence. Also called *destructional forces*.

lithosphere: The outer, solid, rocky part of the earth as distinguished from the hydrosphere and atmosphere. The crust is the part of the lithosphere above the mantle.

local noon: Noon, determined by when the sun is at its highest position on a given day at a specific location; it is also called *sundial noon* or *apparent solar noon*.

local water budget: See **water budget.**

longitude: Angular distance east or west of the prime meridian; usually expressed in degrees. Minimum longitude (0°) is at the prime meridian, which runs through Greenwich, England, and maximum longitude is 180°E or W. The International Date Line, which runs through the Pacific Ocean, follows the 180° meridian along most of its length.

LOW: See **anticyclone.**

mantle: Solid intermediate zone between the earth's crust and the outer part of the core.

marine climate: A coastal climate moderated by the effects of a large body of water (ocean, lake, etc.). Such areas have warmer winters and colder summers than areas of similar latitude not near a large body of water, thus they have a small annual temperature range.

maritime polar air mass (mP): Cool and humid air masses that invade the contiguous United States from the oceans to the northeast and the northwest.

maritime tropical air mass (mT): A very common warm and humid air mass that invades the contiguous United States from the oceans to the south, east, and west.

mass: The quantity of matter in an object. Unlike weight, mass is not affected by location.

mean solar day: The 24-hour day established for convenience in time-keeping; it was derived by averaging the apparent solar days in a year.

measurement: An observational process of obtaining more precise or accurate dimensions of properties of objects and events by making comparison with some standard of reference, often using instruments. An example would be using a ruler.

meridian: North-south trending lines on maps or globes of the earth that have constant longitude.

metamorphic rock: A nonsedimentary rock formed without melting from other rocks (igneous, sedimentary, or other metamorphic rocks) within the lithosphere in response to heat, pressure, or chemical action. Metamorphic rocks are often associated with mountain-building processes.

mid-ocean ridge: Huge chain of largely underwater mountain ranges in the oceans; associated with lithospheric plate divergence, ocean-floor spreading, earthquakes, and volcanoes.

mineral: A naturally occurring, crystalline, inorganic solid with physical and chemical properties that vary within certain specified limits.

model: Any way of representing (illustrating) the properties of an object, event, or system. Models include graphs, drawings, charts, mental pictures, numerical data, or scaled physical objects.

Moho: Short for *Mohorovicic discontinuity*. The interface, or boundary zone, between the crust and the mantle.

moisture: Water vapor in the atmosphere or subsurface water.

moisture capacity: See **absolute humidity.**

monomineralic: A rock composed of just one mineral, such as gypsum or halite.

mountain: A landscape characterized by relatively high elevations, many changes in slope, and steep slopes. Internally, mountains are characterized by distorted rock structures, such as faults, folds, and tilted rocks. Often composed of much nonsedimentary rock. Old mountains may be low in elevation and have little slope.

nonsedimentary rock: Rocks that do not form directly from sediments. Igneous and metamorphic rocks are nonsedimentary rocks.

North Star: See **Polaris.**

oblate spheroid: A sphere that is slightly flattened at the top and bottom (the polar regions) and slightly bulging at the middle (the equatorial region); the shape of the earth.

observation: An interaction of one of the human senses, with or without the aid of instruments, to an aspect of the environment; a reaction that is not an inference.

occluded front: Formed when an advancing cold weather front pushes into a warm front, causing the warm air mass to be lifted off the earth's surface, forming mid-latitude cyclones (LOWs).

ocean-floor spreading: The principle that the oceanic crust spreads outward (plate divergence) at mid-ocean ridges. Also called *sea-floor spreading*.

oceanic crust: The portion of the earth's crust that is usually below the oceans and not associated with the continental blocks. Oceanic crust is thinner and higher in density than continental crust and is basaltic rather than granitic in composition.

orbit: The path of an object revolving around another object, such as the path of the earth around the sun.

orbital speed: The speed of an orbiting body along its orbit at a given time. Also called *orbital velocity*.

organic: Refers to an earth material that is composed of and/or was formed by life forms. *Inorganic* means "not organic."

organic evolution: The theory that new species of organisms arise by gradual transitional changes from existing species.

original horizontality: A principle that states that sedimentary rocks and some extrusive igneous rocks are originally formed in horizontal layers. There are exceptions to this principle, but most sedimentary rock not found in horizontal layers is thought to have been deformed after formation by crustal change.

orographic effects: The effects that mountains have on climate.

outcrop: Exposed bedrock without a cover of soil or regolith.

outer core: The zone of the earth between the mantle and the inner core. It is thought to be a liquid because shear waves from an earthquake do not go through it. It is believed to be composed of iron and nickel.

parallel: East-west trending lines on maps and globes that have constant latitude.

percent error or **percent deviation:** The numerical amount, expressed as a percent, that a measurement differs from a given, standard, or accepted value.

perihelion: The point in a planet's orbit when it is closest to the sun. Perihelion for the earth occurs about January 3, when it is about 147,000,000 kilometers from the sun.

period: (1) The amount of time it takes a planet to make one orbit, or revolution, around the sun. This amount of time is called the *year* for that planet. (2) In geology, a part of the geologic time scale smaller than an era.

permeability: The degree to which a porous material (such as rock or soil) will allow fluids, such as water, to pass through it.

permeability rate: The speed at which fluids, like water, can pass through a porous material. The speed at which water moves from above to below the earth's surface, becoming subsurface water, is a special type called *infiltration rate.*

perpendicular insolation: See **direct rays.**

phase: (1) One of the three main forms of matter—liquid, solid, or gas. Also called *state.* (2) The varying amount of the lighted portion of the moon, Venus, or Mercury visible from the earth.

phase change: The change of a substance from one phase, or state, to another.

physical weathering: The mechanical or physical alteration of rock and other earth materials at or near the earth's surface into smaller fragments (sediments) without a change in the mineral or chemical composition of the materials. Frost action is the most common type.

plain: A landscape of low elevation and gentle slopes; usually characterized by horizontal rock structure, unless it is a remnant of an old mountain region.

planetary wind belts: East-west zones on the earth where the wind blows from one direction much of the time. An example is the prevailing southwest winds that blow over much of the United States.

plateau: A landscape of relatively high elevation with generally undistorted horizontal sedimentary rocks or extrusive igneous lava flows.

plate tectonic theory: A theory stating that the earth's lithosphere is divided into about 20 sections called plates. The plates can move up and down or sideways on a plastic part of the upper mantle called the asthenosphere. Plates diverging, converging, and sliding by each other result in many of the earth's physical features and events, including continent and mountain formation, volcanoes, and earthquakes; includes the concepts of continental drift and ocean-floor spreading.

Polaris: The star that is almost directly over the geographic North Pole of the earth. Also called the *North Star.*

pollutants: Substances or forms of energy that pollute the environment; they include solids, liquids, gases, life forms, heat, sound, and nuclear radiation.

pollution: The occurrence in the environment of a substance or form of energy in concentrations large enough to have an adverse effect on people, their property, or plant and animal life.

polymineralic: Refers to rocks that contain more than one mineral.

porosity: Amount of open space (pores) in rocks or soils compared to total volume.

potential energy: The energy possessed by an object as a result of its position or location, chemical conditions, or phase of matter.

potential evapotranspiration (E_p): The amount of water that would be lost from an area through evaporation and transpiration over a given time if the water were available. Potential evapotranspiration is determined by the amount of heat energy available and the amount of surface area for evapotranspiration.

precipitation: (1) The falling of liquid or solid water from clouds toward the earth's surface. (2) A type of deposition in which dissolved substances come out of solution to form solids, as in formation of evaporite sedimentary rocks.

present weather: The conditions or state of atmosphere for a short period of time at a location determined by comparison with a standard list produced by the U.S. Weather Service. A partial abbreviated list is found on the sample station model on page 95.

pressure gradient: The amount of difference in air pressure over a specific distance; the greater the pressure gradient, the greater the speed of the wind.

primary waves: See **compression waves.**

probability: The odds of some environmental change, such as rain or an earthquake, taking place.

P-waves: See **compression waves.**

radiation: (1) The emission or giving off of energy in the form of electromagnetic energy. (2) The method by which electromagnetic energy moves from place to place by way of transverse waves.

radiative balance: A condition in which an object gives off as much energy as it receives. Under such conditions its average temperature remains the same.

radioactive dating: The use of radioactive isotopes to determine the absolute age of rocks of geologic events.

radioactive decay: The natural spontaneous breakdown of the nucleus of unstable atoms into more stable atoms of the same or other elements. The process releases energy, continues at a constant rate for any particular radioactive isotope, and is not affected by changes in temperature, pressure, or other environmental conditions. Also called **radioactivity.**

recharge $(+\ \Delta St)$: In reference to the water budget, the addition of water to the soil storage by infiltration. Recharge can occur only if the soil is not saturated and if precipitation (P) is greater than potential evapotranspiration (E_p).

recrystallization: A process in the formation of many metamorphic rocks by which some mineral crystals grow in size at the expense of other crystals or sediments without true melting.

reflection: A change in direction of waves when the waves strike the surface of a material, in which the waves leave the surface at the same angle at which they arrived.

refraction: A change in direction and velocity of waves when they pass from one medium into another with a different density.

regolith: All the unconsolidated material at the earth's surface, including the soil.

relative age: The age of rocks or geologic events as compared to other rocks or events with no reference to a specific year or absolute date.

relative humidity: The ratio of the actual amount of water vapor in the air to the maximum amount of water vapor the air can hold. It is often expressed as a percent. Relative humidity can be calculated by the following formula:

relative humidity (%) =

$$\frac{\textbf{vapor pressure of dew point temperature}}{\textbf{vapor pressure of dry bulb temperature}} \times 100$$

residual sediment: Weathered material that has remained in its place of origin.

residual soil: Soil formed from rocks and/or regolith under the soil; soil that has not been transported from its place of origin.

reversal of earth's magnetic polarity: The fact that the earth's magnetic field and poles switch polarity (north for south and south for north) in intervals of thousands of years but in no known cycle.

revolution: Movement of one body about another in a path called an *orbit*.

rock: Any naturally formed solid that is part of the earth's lithosphere. Most rocks are composed of one or more minerals; a few rocks, such as coal, volcanic glass, and coral, are not composed of minerals at all.

rock cycle: A model of the interrelationships of the different rock types, the materials they form from, and the processes that produce them.

rock formation: The basic unit of geologic mapping, consisting of a body of rocks with similar features.

rock-forming mineral: Any one of a small number of minerals (20–30) that are commonly found in rocks; most of them are silicates.

rock resistance: The ability of a body of rock to withstand erosion and weathering.

rock structure: The features of rock that can be observed in an outcrop. Structural features include folds, faults, joints, and tilting and thickness of strata.

rotation: The spinning of an object on its own axis, like a top.

runoff: All natural flowing of water at the earth's surface, including stream flow.

saturation: The condition of being filled to capacity. When the atmosphere contains all the water vapor it can hold, it is filled to saturation and the relative humidity is 100%.

saturation vapor pressure: The vapor pressure of a parcel of air when it is filled or saturated with water vapor; the vapor pressure when relative humidity is 100%.

scalar field: A field that can be totally described in terms of magnitude (amount) alone. Temperature and relative humidity are scalar fields.

scattering: The refraction and/or reflection of waves in various directions.

seasons: The divisions of the year with characteristic weather conditions.

secondary wave: The type of earthquake wave that causes particles through which it travels to vibrate at right angles to the direction of the wave motion. Secondary waves will travel only through solids, not through liquids or gases. Also called *shear waves* or *S-waves*.

sediment: Particles or materials formed by the weathering or erosion of rocks or organic materials; particles or materials transported by erosional systems.

sedimentary rock: The rocks that form directly from sediments by processes of cementation, precipitation of minerals, drying out, and compression.

seismic waves: The energy waves generated by an earthquake, including primary and secondary waves. Also called *earthquake waves*.

seismograph: An instrument used to record seismic waves.

senses: The five abilities or faculties—sight, touch, hearing, taste, and smell—by which one observes.

shear waves: See **secondary waves**.

silicon-oxygen tetrahedron: The most common constituent unit of minerals. This four-sided pyramid unit contains four atoms of oxygen and one atom of silicon.

sink: In an energy system, a region that has a lower energy concentration than its surroundings. Energy flows toward a sink.

soil: The part of the regolith that will support rooted plants. Soil is produced by weathering and the action of bacteria, plants, and animals.

soil association: A basic mapping unit or unit of soil classification composed of soils with similar characteristics, such as composition, structure, porosity, permeability, and fertility.

soil horizon: A vertical layer of soil with certain characteristics such as the high organic content of the top soil horizon. The combination of all the horizons in an area is called the area's *soil profile*.

soil storage (St): In terms of the water budget, the amount of liquid water stored in the soil.

solar noon: See **local noon.**

solar system: Our star, the sun, and the portion of the universe occupied by the objects that revolve around the sun, including planets, comets, and asteroids.

solidification: The processes by which a liquid changes phase to a solid, such as when molten rock (lava and magma) changes into igneous rocks. In the case of the igneous rock volcanic glass, there are no minerals, thus no orderly arrangement of atoms, because the lava solidified so rapidly. Most igneous rocks are produced by a type of solidification called crystallization. Also see **crystallization.**

solstices: The two times of the year when the vertical rays of the sun fall the farthest from the equator. At the summer solstice (about June 21st) the vertical rays fall on 23½° north latitude and the duration and angle of insolation are greatest for most of the Northern Hemisphere and least in the Southern Hemisphere. At the winter solstice (about December 21st) the vertical rays fall on 23½° south latitude and the duration and angle of insolation are greatest for most of the Southern Hemisphere and least in the Northern Hemisphere.

sorted particles: See **sorting of sediments.**

sorting of sediments: The degree of similarity of size in the particles in a mass of sediments or sedimentary rocks. The greater the degree of similarity of particles the more **sorted** the sediments; the greater the difference in the size of particles the more **unsorted** the material.

source: In an energy system, a region that has a higher energy concentration than its surroundings. Energy flows from the source.

source region: The area of the earth's surface over which an air mass forms and acquires its characteristics.

species: The basic unit in the classification of life forms. All members of the same species are similar in body features, environment, and life habits. Our species is *sapien.*

specific heat: The amount of heat, in calories, needed to raise the temperature of 1 gram of a substance 1 degree C; or the degree of difficulty a material offers to heating up or cooling off. Liquid water has the highest specific heat (1 cal/g/degree C) of all common substances.

stages of landscape development: The stages (including Youth, Maturity, Old Age, and Rejuvenation) in the evolution of a landscape feature or region. The stage is characterized by certain features, including the types of dominant forces, the amount of slope, elevation, and the amount of change in slope.

stationary front: A weather condition in which the boundary between two air masses remains in the same position without moving.

strata: The layers, or beds, of sedimentary rock; *stratum* is the singular form.

stream bed: The bottom, or floor, of a stream.

stream discharge: The volume of water passing a certain spot in a stream in a given amount of time.

stream drainage pattern: An aerial view of the stream courses in an area. The patterns are determined by the shape of the landscape, rock structure, and rock resistance.

structure: See **rock structure.**

sublimation: The phase change from a gas directly to a solid or from gas to a solid with no intermediate liquid phase. Frost forms by sublimation.

subsidence: The sinking or depression of a part of the earth's surface.

subsurface water: All water found in the soil, regolith, and bedrock beneath the earth's surface. Also see **ground water.**

sundial: An ancient time-keeping device that uses the position of the sun to determine apparent solar, local, or sundial time.

superposition: A principle applied in the relative dating of layered sedimentary and some extrusive igneous rocks. It states that the youngest rock layer is found on top and that rock age increases with depth. There are many instances where this theory does not apply, such as in deformed rocks, and where there are igneous intrusions.

surplus (S): In terms of the water budget, liquid water that is not removed from the surface by infiltration or evapotranspiration and thus becomes runoff. There is always a surplus when the soil is saturated (maximum St) and when precipitation (P) is greater than potential evapotranspiration (E_p).

S-waves: See **secondary waves.**

technology: The application of scientific discoveries to the methods of producing goods and services; the means by which a society provides objects required for human subsistence and comfort.

temperature: A measure of the average kinetic energy of the particles of a body of matter. Heat energy always flows from a higher temperature to a lower temperature.

terrestrial: (1) Relating to the earth as compared to any other part of the universe. (2) Relating to land or continental environments as compared to air or water environments.

terrestrial motions: The motions of the whole earth, including rotation and revolution about the sun.

terrestrial radiation: The electromagnetic energy given off by the earth's surface; it is mostly long wavelength infrared energy.

texture: Size, shape, and arrangement of mineral crystals or sediments in a rock.

thermal energy: See **heat energy.**

tilted strata: A type of deformed rock in which the strata, or layers, have been forced out of a horizontal position, usually by crustal movement.

topographic maps: See **contour maps.**

topography: See **landscape.**

track: The path of movement of an air mass and/or front. Tracks are often predictable, which helps in weather forecasting.

transformation of energy: The changing of energy from one form to another.

transition zone: An area where a mass of rock changes from one class (sedimentary, metamorphic, or igneous) to another. In many cases in a transition zone it is impossible to determine which class a particular segment belongs to. Also see **contact metamorphic zone.**

transpiration: A process by which plants release water vapor into the atmosphere as part of their life functions.

transported sediment: Weathered or eroded rock and organic materials that have been moved by an erosional system from their place of origin.

transported soil: Soil that has been moved from its place of original formation. Examples would be glacial soils common in the northern United States and the alluvial soils found around rivers and deltas.

transporting system: A system that accomplishes erosion. It includes an agent of erosion, a driving force, and the material that is transported.

transverse wave: A wave that vibrates at right angles to its direction of motion. Examples are electromagnetic radiations and secondary earthquake waves.

ultraviolet radiation: A form of electromagnetic energy of shorter wavelength than visible light. Most of the ultraviolet energy insolation is absorbed by gases of the atmosphere, such as ozone, before reaching the earth's surface.

unconformity: A break, or gap, in the rock record caused by the burial of an erosion surface by newer rocks or sediments. The rocks below an unconformity are older than those above it, unless there has been overturning of strata.

uniformitarianism: A principle stating that the geologic processes taking place today also took place in the past, and that we can interpret past events by studying present geologic processes. Uniformitarianism does not mean that geologic processes always occur at the same rate. Also, it does allow for the possibility that there were processes that occurred in the past (such as the earth's formation) that are not happening today.

unsorted particles: See **sorting of sediments.**

uplifting forces: Forces that originate beneath or within the earth's crust that raise the land, build mountains, and cause continental growth. The uplifting forces include volcanic action, isostasy, earthquakes, continental drift, ocean-floor spreading, and plate tectonics. Also called *constructional forces.*

uranium-238: A radioactive isotope of uranium that decays to lead-206 with a half-life of 4.5 million years. Because of its long half-life, U-238 is useful for dating very old rocks.

usage $(-\Delta St)$**:** In terms of the water budget, the loss of water from soil storage by evapotranspiration. Usage occurs when potential evapotranspiration (E_p) is greater than precipitation (P) and soil storage (St) is greater than zero.

vaporization: See **evaporation.**

vapor pressure: The pressure exerted by water vapor in a given volume of air. It is a measure of the amount of water vapor in the atmosphere and is directly related to the absolute humidity of the atmosphere.

vector field: A field that must be described in terms of both magnitude and direction. Gravitational, magnetic, and wind fields are examples of vector fields.

vein: A sheetlike mineral deposit formed from a solution that has filled a crack or permeable zone in previously formed rocks; thus a vein is younger than the rocks into which it intrudes.

vertical rays: See **direct rays.**

visibility: The farthest distance that one can see a prominent object at the horizon with the naked eye. Fog, air pollution, and precipitation are common causes of low visibility.

volcanic ash: Small pieces of extrusive igneous rock shot into the air during a volcanic eruption. Volcanic ash is very important in geologic dating because all the ash from one eruption will be about the same age, no matter what type of rock it is found associated with; thus it is a time marker useful in correlation.

volume: The amount of space an object occupies.

walking the outcrop: A method of correlation done by actually following the continuity of the individual layers of formations in outcrops of bedrock. Generally, this is useful only for short distances, except in arid regions where a large expanse of bedrock may be uncovered.

warm front: A weather front in which a warmer air mass is pushing a colder air mass. Warm fronts are characterized by a gentle slope and long periods of precipitation.

water budget: A numerical model of an area's water supply. Often shown on a monthly basis using the average figures from date gathered over many years.

water cycle: A model, often in diagram form, used to illustrate the movement and phase changes of water at and near the earth's surface.

water table: The interface between the zone of saturation and the zone of aeration; the top of the zone below which the regolith and/or bedrock is saturated with liquid water.

water vapor: Water in the form of a gas.

wavelength: The distance between a point on a wave and the corresponding point on the next wave, such as the distance between two successive peaks in an electromagnetic wave.

weather: The condition of the atmospheric variables, such as temperature, pressure, wind, and moisture, at a location for a relatively short period of time.

weathering: The chemical and physical alterations of rock and other earth materials at or near the earth's surface. Weathering occurs through the action of water, chemical agents, and living things.

wind: The horizontal movement of air over the earth's surface.

year: The time it takes for a planet to make one revolution around the sun. The earth's year is 365¼ days. Also see **period.**

zone of aeration: The soil, regolith, or bedrock from the earth's surface down to the water table, where the pores are only partly filled with subsurface (capillary) water; air fills the rest of the pores.

zone of saturation: The portion of the earth near the earth's surface that is below the water table, where the pores in the soil, regolith, or bedrock are filled with subsurface water (ground water).

EARTH SCIENCE REFERENCE
TABLES AND CHARTS

PROPORTIONS

Kepler's harmonic law of planetary motion : (Period of Revolution)$^2 \propto$ (mean Radius of Orbit)^3 : $T^2 \propto \overline{R}^3$

Universal law of gravitation : Force $\propto \dfrac{mass_1 \times mass_2}{(\text{distance between their centers})^2}$: $(F \propto \dfrac{m_1 m_2}{d^2})$

Potential energy : Potential Energy $\propto$ mass x acceleration due to gravity x height : $PE \propto mgh$

Kinetic energy : Kinetic Energy $\propto$ mass x (velocity)^2 : $(KE \propto mv^2)$

EQUATIONS

Per cent deviation from accepted value : Deviation (%) = $\dfrac{\text{difference from accepted value}}{\text{accepted value}} \times 100$

Circumference of a circle : Circumference = 2π radius : $(C = 2\pi r)$ Note: $\pi = 3.14$

Volume of a sphere : Volume = $\frac{4}{3}\pi$ (radius)^3 : $(V = \frac{4}{3}\pi r^3)$

Volume of a rectangular solid : Volume = length x width x height : $(V = lwh)$

Density of a substance : Density = $\dfrac{mass}{volume}$: $(D = \dfrac{m}{v})$

Eccentricity of an ellipse : Eccentricity = $\dfrac{\text{distance between foci}}{\text{length of major axis}}$: $(e = \dfrac{d}{L})$

Gradient : Gradient = $\dfrac{\text{change in field value}}{\text{change in distance}}$

Relative humidity : RH(%) = $\dfrac{\text{vapor pressure of dewpoint temp}}{\text{vapor pressure of dry-bulb temp}} \times 100$

Latent Heat {solid ↔ liquid : Heat (cal) = mass x heat of fusion
liquid ↔ gas : Heat (cal) = mass x heat of vaporization

Heat energy (lost or gained) : Heat (cal) = mass x temp change x specific heat

PHYSICAL CONSTANTS

RADIOACTIVE DECAY DATA

Radioactive Element	Disintegration	Half-life
Carbon 14	$C^{14} \rightarrow N^{14}$	5.6×10^3 years
Potassium 40	$K^{40} \rightarrow Ar^{40}$	1.4×10^9 years
Uranium 238	$U^{238} \rightarrow Pb^{206}$	4.5×10^9 years
Rubidium 87	$Rb^{87} \rightarrow Sr^{87}$	6.0×10^{10} years

PROPERTIES OF WATER

Heat of fusion of water = 80 cal/g
Heat of vaporization of water = 540 cal/g
Density of water (3.98°C) = 1.00 g/ml

SPECIFIC HEATS OF COMMON MATERIALS (in cal/g C°)

Water	= 1.0
Ice	= .5
Water Vapor	= .5
Dry Air	= .24
Basalt	= .20
Granite	= .19
Iron	= .11
Copper	= .09
Lead	= .03

ASTRONOMY MEASUREMENTS

Measurement	Earth	Sun	Moon
Mass (m)	5.98×10^{24} kg	1.99×10^{30} kg	7.35×10^{22} kg
Radius (r)	6.37×10^3 km	6.96×10^5 km	1.74×10^3 km
Average density	5.52 g/cm^3	1.42 g/cm^3	3.34 g/cm^3

MEASUREMENT SCALES

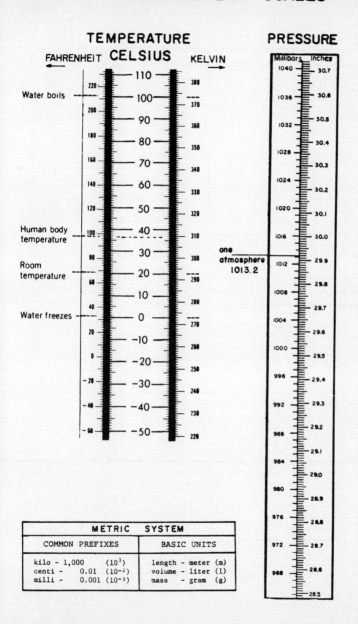

TEMPERATURE

FAHRENHEIT CELSIUS KELVIN

Water boils

Human body
temperature

Room
temperature

Water freezes

PRESSURE

Millibars Inches

one
atmosphere
1013.2

METRIC SYSTEM	
COMMON PREFIXES	BASIC UNITS
kilo - 1,000 (10^3) centi - 0.01 (10^{-2}) milli - 0.001 (10^{-3})	length - meter (m) volume - liter (l) mass - gram (g)

PHYSICAL PROPERTIES

DEWPOINT TEMPERATURE CHART

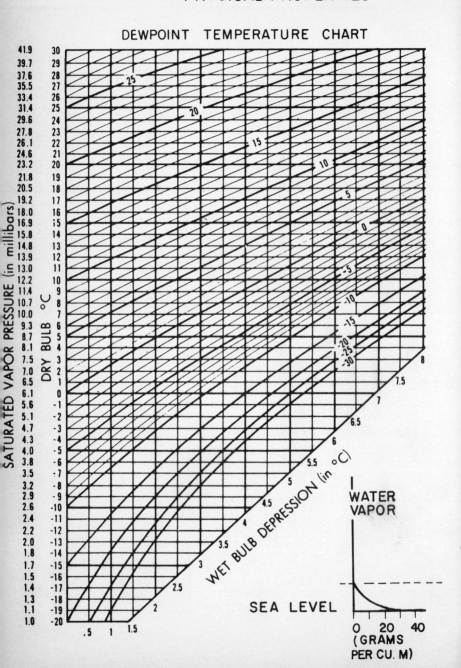

OF THE ATMOSPHERE

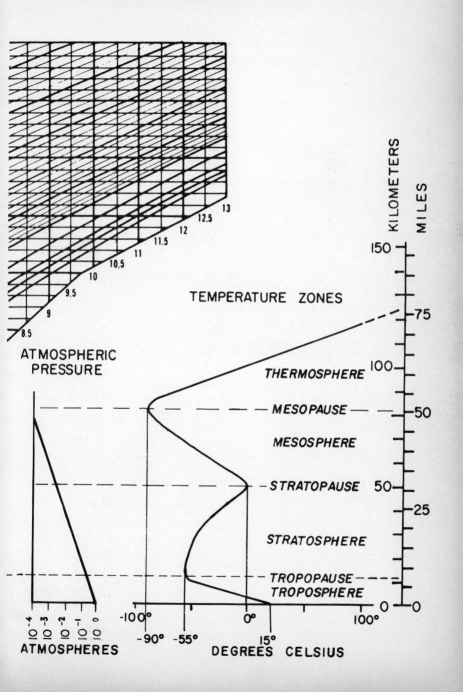

KILOMETERS

MILES

TEMPERATURE ZONES

ATMOSPHERIC
PRESSURE

150

75

THERMOSPHERE   100

MESOPAUSE   50

MESOSPHERE

STRATOPAUSE   50

25

STRATOSPHERE

TROPOPAUSE
TROPOSPHERE

0   0

10^{-4} 10^{-3} 10^{-2} 10^{-1} 10^{0}

ATMOSPHERES

-100°   0°   100°

-90° -55°   15°

DEGREES CELSIUS

Geologic time scale, showing

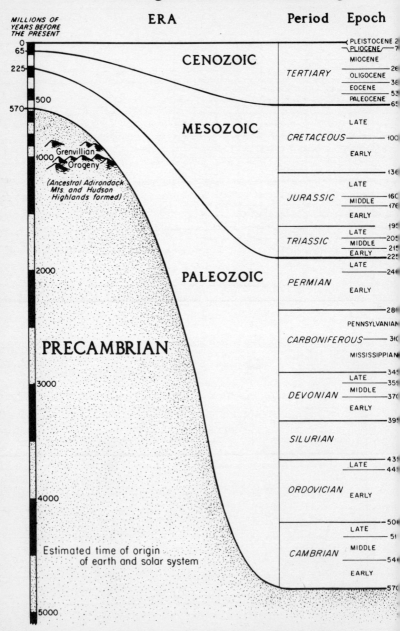

ERA	Period	Epoch

MILLIONS OF
YEARS BEFORE
THE PRESENT

CENOZOIC

TERTIARY — PLEISTOCENE, PLIOCENE, MIOCENE, OLIGOCENE, EOCENE, PALEOCENE

MESOZOIC

CRETACEOUS — LATE, EARLY

JURASSIC — LATE, MIDDLE, EARLY

TRIASSIC — LATE, MIDDLE, EARLY

PALEOZOIC

PERMIAN — LATE, EARLY

CARBONIFEROUS — PENNSYLVANIAN, MISSISSIPPIAN

DEVONIAN — LATE, MIDDLE, EARLY

SILURIAN

ORDOVICIAN — LATE, EARLY

CAMBRIAN — LATE, MIDDLE, EARLY

Grenvillian Orogeny
(Ancestral Adirondack Mts. and Hudson Highlands formed)

PRECAMBRIAN

Estimated time of origin of earth and solar system

major events in geological history

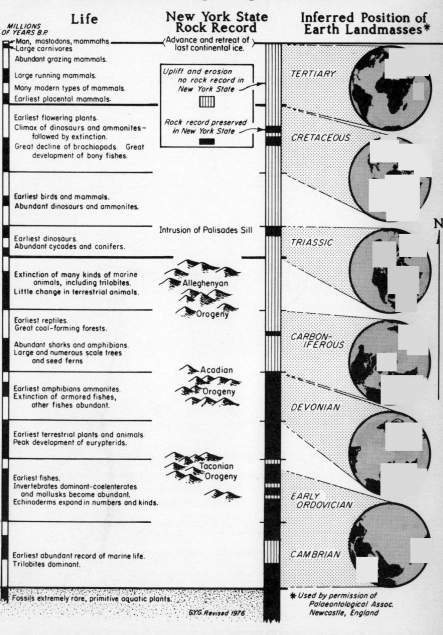

MILLIONS OF YEARS B.P.	Life	New York State Rock Record	Inferred Position of Earth Landmasses*

Life

Man, mastodons, mammoths.
Large carnivores
Abundant grazing mammals.

Large running mammals.

Many modern types of mammals.

Earliest placental mammals.

Earliest flowering plants.
Climax of dinosaurs and ammonites—
followed by extinction.
Great decline of brachiopods. Great development of bony fishes.

Earliest birds and mammals.
Abundant dinosaurs and ammonites.

Earliest dinosaurs.
Abundant cycades and conifers.

Extinction of many kinds of marine animals, including trilobites.
Little change in terrestrial animals.

Earliest reptiles.
Great coal-forming forests.

Abundant sharks and amphibians.
Large and numerous scale trees and seed ferns

Earliest amphibians ammonites.
Extinction of armored fishes, other fishes abundant.

Earliest terrestrial plants and animals.
Peak development of eurypterids.

Earliest fishes.
Invertebrates dominant-coelenterates and mollusks become abundant.
Echinoderms expand in numbers and kinds.

Earliest abundant record of marine life.
Trilobites dominant.

Fossils extremely rare, primitive aquatic plants.

New York State Rock Record

Advance and retreat of last continental ice.

Uplift and erosion no rock record in New York State

Rock record preserved in New York State

Intrusion of Palisades Sill

Alleghenyan Orogeny

Acadian Orogeny

Taconian Orogeny

E.Y.G. Revised 1976

Inferred Position of Earth Landmasses*

TERTIARY

CRETACEOUS

N

TRIASSIC

CARBON-IFEROUS

DEVONIAN

EARLY ORDOVICIAN

CAMBRIAN

* Used by permission of Palaeontological Assoc. Newcastle, England

GENERALIZED BEDROCK GEOLOGY
OF
NEW YORK STATE

COMPILED BY
GEOLOGICAL SURVEY
OF THE
NEW YORK STATE MUSEUM AND SCIENCE SERVICE
1972

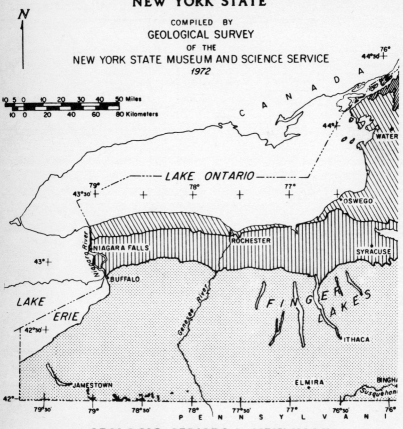

GEOLOGIC PERIODS in NEW YORK

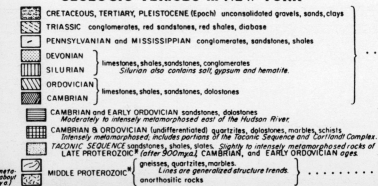

CRETACEOUS, TERTIARY, PLEISTOCENE (Epoch) unconsolidated gravels, sands, clays

TRIASSIC conglomerates, red sandstones, red shales, diabase

PENNSYLVANIAN and MISSISSIPPIAN conglomerates, sandstones, shales

DEVONIAN
SILURIAN } limestones, shales, sandstones, conglomerates
Silurian also contains salt, gypsum and hematite.

ORDOVICIAN
CAMBRIAN } limestones, shales, sandstones, dolostones

CAMBRIAN and EARLY ORDOVICIAN sandstones, dolostones
Moderately to intensely metamorphosed east of the Hudson River.

CAMBRIAN & ORDOVICIAN (undifferentiated) quartzites, dolostones, marbles, schists
Intensely metamorphosed; includes portions of the Taconic Sequence and Cortlandt Complex.

TACONIC SEQUENCE sandstones, shales, slates. *Slightly to intensely metamorphosed rocks of*
LATE PROTEROZOIC* *(after 900 m.y.a.),* CAMBRIAN, and EARLY ORDOVICIAN ages.

MIDDLE PROTEROZOIC* { gneisses, quartzites, marbles.
Lines are generalized structure trends.
anorthositic rocks }

(regional metamorphism about 1,000 mya)

* Subdivisions of Precambrian

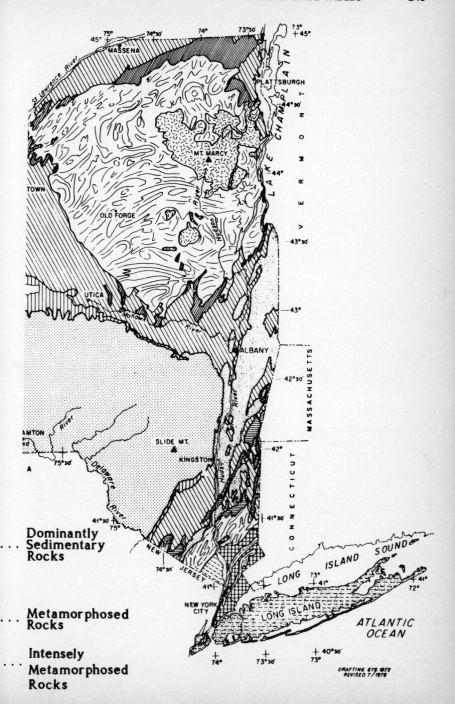

Dominantly
Sedimentary
Rocks

Metamorphosed
Rocks

Intensely
Metamorphosed
Rocks

DRAFTING GYS 1972
REVISED 7/1978

EARTHQUAKE S-WAVE & P-WAVE TIME TRAVEL GRAPH

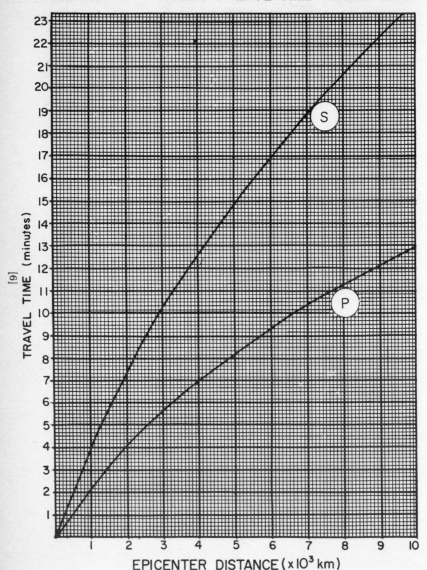

AVERAGE CHEMICAL COMPOSITION OF CRUST, HYDROSPHERE AND TROPOSPHERE

Element	Symbol and Common Oxidation State(s)	Percentage by Volume		
		Crust	Hydrosphere	Troposphere
Aluminum	Al^{+3}	0.47	-	-
Calcium	Ca^{+2}	1.03	-	-
Hydrogen	H^{+1}	-	66	-
Iron	$Fe^{+2},^{+3}$	0.43	-	-
Magnesium	Mg^{+2}	0.29	-	-
Nitrogen	$N^{+2},^{-3}$	-	-	78
Oxygen	O^{-2}	93.77	33	21
Potassium	K^{+1}	1.83	-	-
Silicon	Si^{+4}	0.86	-	-
Sodium	Na^{+1}	1.32	-	-
Others		-	1	1

AIR MASSES

cA   Continental Arctic

cP   Continental polar

cT   Continental tropical

mT   Maritime tropical

mP   Maritime polar

ROCK CYCLE

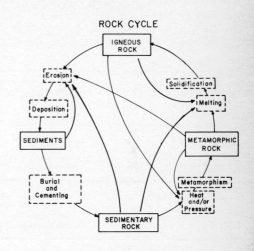

WEATHER MAP INFORMATION
STATION MODEL

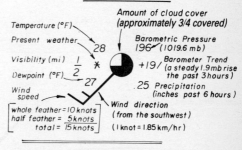

FRONT SYMBOLS

COLD

WARM

STATIONARY

OCCLUDED

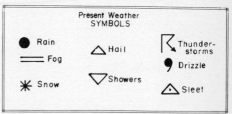

Present Weather SYMBOLS

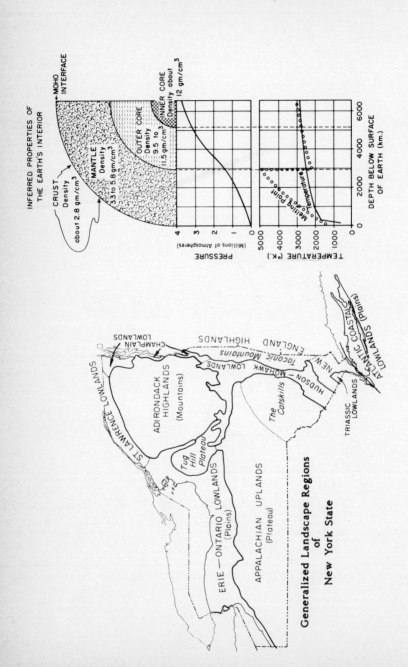

INFERRED PROPERTIES OF THE EARTH'S INTERIOR

MOHO INTERFACE

CRUST Density about 2.8 gm/cm³

MANTLE Density 3.3 to 5.8 gm/cm³

OUTER CORE Density 9.5 to 11.5 gm/cm³

INNER CORE Density about 12 gm/cm³

PRESSURE (Millions of Atmospheres)

TEMPERATURE (°K.)

Melting Point

Temperature

DEPTH BELOW SURFACE OF EARTH (km.)

Generalized Landscape Regions of New York State

ST. LAWRENCE LOWLANDS

CHAMPLAIN LOWLANDS

ADIRONDACK HIGHLANDS (Mountains)

Tug Hill Plateau

ERIE-ONTARIO LOWLANDS (Plains)

APPALACHIAN UPLANDS (Plateau)

The Catskills

MOHAWK LOWLANDS

HUDSON-MOHAWK LOWLANDS

Taconic Mountains

NEW ENGLAND HIGHLANDS

TRIASSIC LOWLANDS

ATLANTIC COASTAL LOWLANDS (Plains)

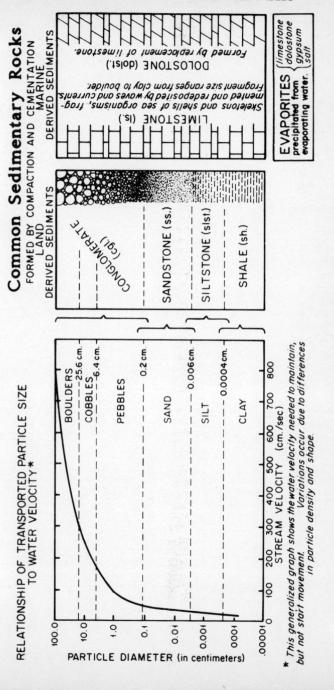

Common Sedimentary Rocks

FORMED BY COMPACTION AND CEMENTATION

LAND DERIVED SEDIMENTS

CONGLOMERATE (cgl.)

SANDSTONE (ss.)

SILTSTONE (slst.)

SHALE (sh.)

MARINE DERIVED SEDIMENTS

LIMESTONE (ls.)

Skeletons and shells of sea organisms, fragmented and redeposited by waves and currents. Fragment size ranges from clay to boulder.

DOLOSTONE (dolst.)

Formed by replacement of limestone.

EVAPORITES precipitated from evaporating water.
{ limestone
  dolostone
  gypsum
  salt

RELATIONSHIP OF TRANSPORTED PARTICLE SIZE TO WATER VELOCITY*

BOULDERS
— 25.6 cm.
COBBLES
— 6.4 cm.
PEBBLES
— 0.2 cm.
SAND
— 0.006 cm.
SILT
— 0.0004 cm.
CLAY

PARTICLE DIAMETER (in centimeters)
100.0   10.0   1.0   0.1   0.01   0.001   .0001   .00001

STREAM VELOCITY (cm./sec)
0   100   200   300   400   500   600   700   800

* This generalized graph shows the water velocity needed to maintain, but not start movement. Variations occur due to differences in particle density and shape.

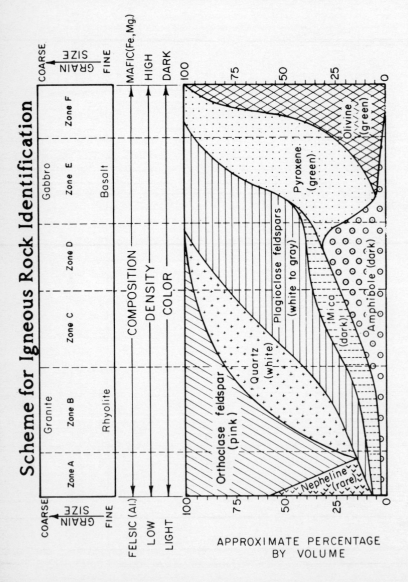

Scheme for Igneous Rock Identification

MINERAL COMPOSITION   CHARACTERISTICS

APPROXIMATE PERCENTAGE
BY VOLUME

Index

Absolute age (absolute dating), of rocks and geologic events, 183; methods of determining, 190–191

Absolute humidity, and air pressure, 83; and atmospheric moisture, 87–88

Absolute zero, 53

Absorption, of electromagnetic radiation, 53–54, 66–67; and temperature of atmosphere, 82

Abyssal areas, and deposition, 139

Actual evapotranspiration, and water budget, 111

Adiabatic temperature change, 83

Aeration, zone of, 107

Aerobic bacteria, and water pollution, 108–109

Aerosols, and insolation, 66

Age, of rocks and geologic events, 183–191

Air; see Atmosphere

Air masses, and weather, 91–93

Air pressure; see Atmospheric pressure

Altitude, of celestial object, 13; and air pressure, 83

Anaerobic bacteria, and water pollution, 109

Angle of insolation, defined, 66; and intensity, 67

Annular drainage patterns, 211 (Fig. 14-6D)

Anticyclones, and air masses, 92

Aphelion, defined, 38; and orbital speed, 39

Apparent diameter, defined, 30

Apparent motion, of celestial objects, 29, 30

Apparent solar day, defined, 40

Apparent solar time, 40

Arc, 29

Arid climates, defined, 113; and landscapes, 207–208

Ash, volcanic, 187

Astronomical Unit, defined, 40

Atmosphere, defined, 16; zones of, 16; and insolation, 65–66; and weather, 82–94; pollution of by people, 9, 212–213

Atmospheric pressure, and weather, 83–84

Atmospheric variables, 82

Atoms, and isotopes, 190

Axis, of earth, 74–75

Bacteria, and water pollution, 108–109

Balance, radiative, 72–73

Banding, in metamorphic rocks, 150

Barometric pressure, 83

Basaltic rocks, and oceanic crust, 167, 172–173

Bedding, graded, 139

Bedrock, and outcrops, 185; and landscape features, 209–212

Beds, and deposition, 139

Bench marks, and elevation, 162

Biologic processes, and rock formation, 147

Block drainage patterns, 210 (Fig. 14-6B)

Calorie, defined, 57

Capillarity, and infiltration, 108

Capillary migration, 108

Capillary water, 108

Carbon-14, and radioactive dating, 190, 191

Celestial objects, defined, 29

Cells, convection, 54

Cementation, and sedimentary rocks, 146

Change, environmental, 8–9

Chemical weathering, 127

Circulation, of atmosphere, 85

Classification, as a scientific process, 1

Clay, 129, 132, 138

Cleavage, of minerals, 154

Climate, 113–118; and weathering, 128; and landscape development, 207–208

Clouds, and insolation, 66; and atmospheric moisture, 91

Coal, as sedimentary rock, 147

Cold front, 93

Colloids, and sediment, 129, 132, 138

Color, of minerals, 154

Compounds, and composition of minerals, 154

Compression, and sedimentary rocks, 146

Compressional waves, and earthquakes, 170

Condensation, and temperature of atmosphere, 82; and dew point, 89, 91, 94

Condensation surfaces, and clouds, 91

Conduction, and transfer of energy, 54; and temperature of atmosphere, 82

Conservation, of energy, 55; of environmental resources, 213

Constituent units, of minerals, 154

Constructional forces, and landscape development, 205–207

Contact metamorphic zone, in rocks, 153

Continental climate, 115

Continental crust, 163, 165, 172–173

Continental drift, 165–166

Continental polar air mass, 92

Continental tropical air mass, 92

Continents, and climate, 115–116

252

254   INDEX

REGENTS EXAMINATIONS

EARTH SCIENCE
June 20, 1984

Part I

Answer all 55 questions in this part.   [55]

Directions (1-55): For *each* statement or question, select the word or expression that, of those given, best completes the statement or answers the question.

1. An interpretation based upon an observation is called (1) a fact (2) an inference (3) a classification (4) a measurement

2. Which is the *least* probable source of atmospheric pollution in heavily populated cities? (1) human activities (2) industrial plants (3) natural processes (4) automobile traffic

3. A student calculates the densities of five different pieces of aluminum, each having a different volume. Which graph best represents this relationship?

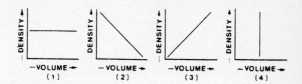

4. To an observer on the Moon, the Earth in full phase would appear to be shaped like (1) an egg (2) a basketball (3) a pear (4) a football

5. An observer recorded the barometric pressure while traveling up the west side of a mountain and down the other side. Which graph best represents the probable air pressure changes that were observed?

6. An observer on a moving ship notices that the altitude of Polaris increases each night. Local solar noon occurs at the same time each day. In what direction is the ship moving? (1) due east (2) due south (3) due west (4) due north

7. According to the *Earth Science Reference Tables,* nitrogen is the most abundant element in the (1) crust (2) hydrosphere (3) troposphere (4) mantle

8. The diagram below represents two photographs of the Moon, *A* and *B*, taken at full moon phase several months apart. The photographs were taken using the same magnification. Each photograph was cut in half and the halves placed next to each other.

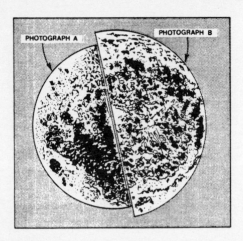

What most likely caused the difference in the apparent size of the Moon in photographs *A* and *B*? (1) The phases of the Moon changed. (2) The Moon expanded. (3) The distance from the Earth to the Moon changed. (4) The Moon rotated.

9. Which planetary model allows a scientist to predict the exact positions of the planets in the night sky over many years? (1) The planets' orbits are circles in a geocentric model. (2) The planets' orbits are ellipses in a geocentric model. (3) The planets' orbits are circles in a heliocentric model. (4) The planets' orbits are ellipses in a heliocentric model.

10. Based on observations made in the Northern Hemisphere, which statement is the best supporting evidence that the Earth rotates on its axis? (1) The stars appear to follow daily circular paths around Polaris. (2) The apparent solar diameter varies throughout the year. (3) The length of the daylight period varies throughout the year. (4) The seasons (spring, summer, fall, and winter) repeat in a cyclic pattern.

11. On March 21, two observers, one at 45° north latitude and the other at 45° south latitude, watch the "rising" Sun. In which direction(s) must they look? (1) Both observers must look westward. (2) Both observers must look eastward. (3) The observer at 45°N. must look westward while the other must look eastward. (4) The observer at 45° S. must look westward while the other must look eastward.

12. Infrared, ultraviolet, and visible light are all part of the solar spectrum. The basic difference between them is their (1) wavelength (2) speed (3) source (4) temperature

13. By which process does starlight travel through space? (1) absorption (2) conduction (3) convection (4) radiation

14. In New York State, the longest period of insolation occurs on or about (1) January 21 (2) March 21 (3) June 21 (4) August 21

15. Between the years 1850 and 1900, records indicate that the Earth's mean surface temperature showed little variation. This would support the inference that (1) the Earth was in radiative balance (2) another ice age was approaching (3) more energy was coming in than was going out from the Earth (4) the Sun was emitting more energy

16. The rate of evaporation of water can be increased by (1) increasing the amount of moisture in the air (2) decreasing the temperature of the water (3) increasing the temperature of the air (4) decreasing the circulation of the air

17. A mT airmass would most likely originate over which type of Earth surface? (1) cold and moist (2) warm and moist (3) cold and dry (4) warm and dry

18. The diagram below shows the direction of movement of air over a mountain.

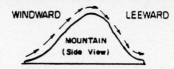

As the air moves down the leeward side of the mountain, the air will (1) warm due to compression (2) warm due to expansion (3) cool due to compression (4) cool due to expansion

19. Which natural event directly results in the periodic cleaning of the atmosphere? (1) volcanic eruptions (2) transpiration (3) radiation (4) precipitation

20. When rain falls on a soil surface, flooding at that location would most likely occur if the (1) soil surface is permeable (2) soil surface is covered with vegetation (3) soil pore spaces are filled to capacity (4) infiltration rate exceeds the precipitation rate

21. At which location will a low-pressure storm center most likely form? (1) along a frontal surface between different airmasses (2) near the middle of a cold airmass (3) on the leeward side of mountains (4) over a very dry, large, flat land area

22. Stream discharge would normally be highest during a period of (1) recharge (2) deficit (3) usage (4) surplus

23. The main source of moisture for the local water budget is (1) potential evapotranspiration (2) actual evapotranspiration (3) ground water storage (4) precipitation

24. What effect does a large body of water usually have on the climate of a nearby landmass? (1) The water causes cooler summers and colder winters. (2) The water causes cooler summers and warmer winters. (3) The water causes hotter summers and warmer winters. (4) The water causes hotter summers and colder winters.

25. Which is the best example of physical weathering? (1) the cracking of rock caused by the freezing and thawing of water (2) the transportation of sediment in a stream (3) the reaction of limestone with acid rainwater (4) the formation of a sandbar along the side of a stream

26. In which climate would chemical weathering occur at the greatest rate? (1) cold and dry (2) cold and humid (3) warm and dry (4) warm and humid

27. The velocity of a stream is 100 centimeters per second. According to the *Earth Science Reference Tables,* what is the largest diameter particle that can be transported? (1) 1.0 cm (2) 0.1 cm (3) 0.01 cm (4) 0.0001 cm

28. The diagram at the right represents a core sample of a sedimentary deposit found at a particular location. The deposition most likely occurred as a result of (1) dropping directly from a glacier (2) an avalanche on a mountainside (3) a decrease in the velocity of a stream (4) dropping of weathered rock fragments from a cliff

29. The chart below indicates the densities of four different minerals.

Mineral	Density (g/cm³)
Calcite	2.8
Diamond	3.5
Hematite	5.3
Quartz	2.7

If spheres 5 millimeters in diameter of these four minerals are dropped at the same time into a large tube filled with water, which would settle to the bottom first? (1) calcite (2) diamond (3) hematite (4) quartz

30. According to the *Earth Science Reference Tables,* sedimentary rocks formed by compaction and cementation of land-derived sediments are classified on the basis of (1) composition (2) type of cement (3) particle size (4) rate of formation

31. According to the *Earth Science Reference Tables,* which is a fine-grained igneous rock made up primarily of pyroxene and plagioclase feldspar? (1) gabbro (2) basalt (3) granite (4) rhyolite

32. Which rock is most likely a nonsedimentary rock? (1) a rock showing mud cracks (2) a rock containing dinosaur bones (3) a rock consisting of layers of rounded sand grains (4) a rock composed of distorted light-colored and dark-colored mineral bands

33. The diagram below represents a single silicon-oxygen tetrahedron unit. Two different minerals have these same units arranged in different patterns. How will the minerals differ?

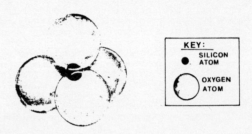

(1) One mineral will have some physical properties different from the other. (2) One mineral will be more radioactive than the other. (3) One mineral will have the silicon atom outside the tetrahedron while the other will have it inside the tetrahedron. (4) One mineral will have larger silicon atoms than the other.

34. According to the Inferred Position of Earth Landmasses information shown in the *Earth Science Reference Tables,* on what other landmass would you most likely find fossil remains of the late Paleozoic reptile called Mesosaurus shown below?

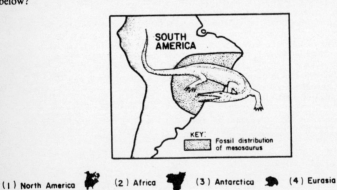

35. A seismograph station records a difference in arrival time between the *S*- and *P*- wave of 4 minutes. About how far away is the earthquake epicenter? (Refer to the *Earth Science Reference Tables.*) (1) 1,000 km (2) 1,900 km (3) 2,600 km (4) 5,200 km

36. An observer discovers shallow-water marine fossils in rock strata at an elevation of 5,000 meters. What is the best explanation for this observation? (1) The level of the ocean was once 5,000 meters higher. (2) Violent earthquakes caused crustal subsidence. (3) Marine organisms have evolved into land organisms. (4) Crustal uplift has occurred in this area.

37. According to the *Earth Science Reference Tables,* as the depth within the Earth's interior increases, the (1) density, temperature, and pressure increase (2) density, temperature, and pressure decrease (3) density and temperature increase, but pressure decreases (4) density increases, but temperature and pressure decrease

38. The inference that the inner core of the Earth is solid is based on analysis of (1) seismic data (2) crustal rock (3) radioactive data (4) meteorite composition

39. According to the *Earth Science Reference Tables,* which radioactive substance has the longest half-life? (1) carbon-14 (2) potassium-40 (3) rubidium-87 (4) uranium-238

40. Which statement about dinosaurs is supported by information provided in the *Earth Science Reference Tables?* (1) Dinosaur fossils first appeared in rocks of the Paleozoic Era. (2) The number of dinosaurs increased before dinosaurs became extinct. (3) Dinosaur fossils and trilobite fossils may be found in the same rocks. (4) Dinosaurs lived only on land.

Base your answers to questions 41 and 42 on the block diagram below of a portion of the Earth where the rock layers have not been overturned.

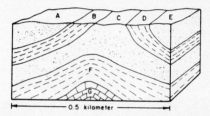

41. The evidence present in the diagram supports the inference that (1) rock *B* is the same age as rock *F* (2) rock *B* is the same age as rock *D* (3) rock *C* is older than rock *G* (4) rock *D* is younger than rock *A*

42. Rock layers *A* and *C* are sandstones that have the same texture. Layer *A* contains quartz grains, but layer *C* does not. This information suggests that layers *A* and *C* probably (1) are part of the same formation (2) have different types of cementing material (3) have undergone different amounts of metamorphism (4) were formed by sediments originating from different sources

43. Which landscape characteristic indicates a landscape has been formed primarily by streams? (1) residual soil covering a large area (2) coastal sand dunes (3) V-shaped valleys (4) parallel hills of unsorted sediments

44. According to the *Earth Science Reference Tables,* which New York State landscape region has the lowest elevation, the most nearly level land surface, and is composed primarily of Cretaceous through Pleistocene unconsolidated sediments? (1) the Hudson-Mohawk Lowlands (2) the Atlantic Coastal Lowlands (3) the Champlain Lowlands (4) the Erie-Ontario Lowlands

45. The diagram below represents cross sections of three rock outcrops approximately 100 kilometers apart. What would be the best method of correlating the rock layers of each outcrop?

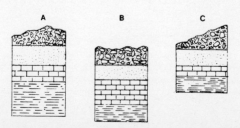

(1) comparing rock types (2) comparing mineral composition (3) comparing index fossils (4) comparing thickness of rock layers

46. The major landscape regions of the United States are identified chiefly on the basis of (1) similar surface characteristics (2) similar climatic conditions (3) nearness to major mountain regions (4) nearness to continental boundaries

47. According to the *Earth Science Reference Tables,* what is the straight-line distance in kilometers from Elmira, New York, to Buffalo, New York? (1) 100 km (2) 120 km (3) 150 km (4) 190 km

Note that questions 48 through 55 have only three choices.

48. The information below is a classification of six common rocks, based on how they were formed. In which group would conglomerate rock be placed in this classification?

Group A	Group B	Group C
basalt	sandstone	marble
granite	shale	gneiss

(1) *Group A* (2) *Group B* (3) *Group C*

49. If equal masses of water in various phases (states) are compared, which phase will contain the greatest amount of stored energy (latent heat)? (1) solid ice (2) liquid water (3) water vapor

50. The diagram at the right represents a ray of sunlight striking the Earth at point *P.* Angle *A* is the angle between the ray and the surface of the Earth at point *P.* As angle *A* increases, the intensity of insolation at point *P* will (1) decrease (2) increase (3) remain the same

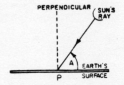

51. Two weather stations are located near each other. The air pressure at each station is changing so that the difference between the pressures is increasing. The wind speed between these two locations will probably (1) decrease (2) increase (3) remain the same

52. How does the average annual surface temperature compare from latitude to latitude? (1) As latitude increases, the average annual surface temperature decreases. (2) As latitude increases, the average annual surface temperature increases. (3) As latitude increases, the average annual surface temperature remains the same.

53. Larger crystal size in one of two igneous rocks of similar composition usually indicates that the rock with the larger crystals cooled for (1) a shorter period of time than the other (2) a longer period of time than the other (3) the same amount of time as the other

54. If the rate of erosion in a particular landscape on the Earth's surface increases and the uplifting forces remain constant, the elevation of that landscape will (1) decrease (2) increase (3) remain the same

55. The human population of the Earth is (1) decreasing (2) increasing (3) remaining the same

Part II

This part consists of ten groups, each containing five questions. Each group tests a major area of the course. Choose seven of these ten groups. Be sure that you answer all five questions in each group chosen.   [35]

Group 1

If you choose this group, be sure to answer questions 56-60.

Base your answers to questions 56 through 60 on your knowledge of earth science, the *Earth Science Reference Tables,* and the diagrams below. The diagrams represent three solid objects made of the same uniform material. The name of each shape is shown, along with its mass (*M*) and volume (*V*).

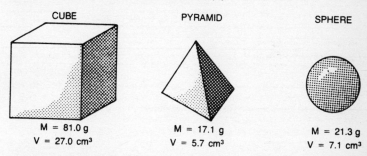

CUBE	PYRAMID	SPHERE
M = 81.0 g	M = 17.1 g	M = 21.3 g
V = 27.0 cm³	V = 5.7 cm³	V = 7.1 cm³

56. What is the *actual* length of any one side of the cube?   (1) 1.0 cm   (2) 2.0 cm   (3) 3.0 cm   (4) 8.0 cm

Note that question 57 has only three choices.

57. Which line on the graph below best represents the density of the three samples?

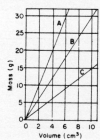

(1) *A*   (2) *B*   (3) *C*

58. If the cube were cut into four smaller cubes, the density of one of the small cubes, compared to that of the original cube, would be   (1) the same   (2) one-fourth as great   (3) one-sixteenth as great   (4) four times as great

59. If the pyramid is ground into a powder, the rate at which the powder would chemically weather, compared to the original pyramid, would be   (1) slower because the surface area will be less   (2) slower because the surface area will be greater   (3) faster because the surface area will be less   (4) faster because the surface area will be greater

60. If the sphere is heated to a temperature below its melting point, which is most likely to occur?   (1) Both the volume and density of the sphere will increase.   (2) Both the volume and density of the sphere will decrease.   (3) The volume of the sphere will increase, but its density will decrease.   (4) The volume of the sphere will decrease, but its density will increase.

Group 2

If you choose this group, be sure to answer questions 61-65.

Base your answers to questions 61 through 65 on your knowledge of earth science, the *Earth Science Reference Tables,* and on the data table below. The table lists some information about the planets in the solar system. The revolution period of the planet Uranus has been deliberately left blank.

DATA TABLE OF SOLAR SYSTEM

	MERCURY	VENUS	EARTH	MARS	JUPITER	SATURN	URANUS	NEPTUNE	PLUTO
Mean Distance from Sun (millions of kilometers)	57.9	108.2	149.6	227.9	778.3	1,427	2,869	4,496	5,900
Period of Revolution	88 days	224.7 days	365.26 days	687 days	11.86 years	29.46 years		164.8 years	247.7 years
Rotation Period	59 days	243 days	23 hours 56 minutes 4 seconds	24 hours 37 minutes 23 seconds	9 hours 50 minutes 30 seconds	10 hours 14 minutes	11 hours	16 hours	6 days 9 hours
Eccentricity of Orbit	.206	.007	.017	.093	.048	.056	.047	.009	.250
Equatorial Diameter (kilometers)	4,880	12,104	12,756	6,787	142,800	120,000	47,100	48,400	2,400(?)

Known Data as of June, 1980

61. Which orbital path model correctly shows the relative positions of the Sun and its four nearest planets? [Distances and planet sizes are not to scale.]

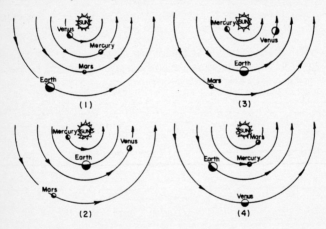

62. Which of the following takes the longest time to make one complete spin on its axis? (1) Uranus (2) Mercury (3) Earth (4) Jupiter

63. What would be the most likely period of revolution for Uranus? (1) 6 years (2) 18 years (3) 84 years (4) 171 years

64. Which planet has the most eccentric orbit? (1) Venus (2) Mars (3) Saturn (4) Pluto

65. Which planet has a diameter most similar to the Earth's? (1) Venus (2) Mars (3) Saturn (4) Pluto

Group 3

If you choose this group, be sure to answer questions 66-70.

Base your answers to questions 66 through 70 on your knowledge of earth science and on the diagrams below. The diagrams represent plastic hemisphere models. Lines have been drawn to show the apparent path of the Sun across the sky on June 21 for observers at four different Earth locations. The zenith (Z) is the point in the sky directly over the observer.

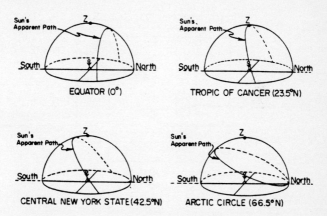

66. At which location will the longest noontime shadow be observed? (1) Equator (2) Tropic of Cancer (3) central New York State (4) Arctic Circle

67. Which location will experience the *shortest* duration of insolation? (1) central New York State (2) Tropic of Cancer (3) Equator (4) Arctic Circle

68. The Arctic Circle has the coolest climate of these four locations because the Arctic Circle (1) is usually farthest from the Sun (2) receives the fewest hours of daylight (3) reflects the least amount of insolation (4) receives mostly low-angle, slanting insolation rays

69. Which location will receive the greatest intensity of insolation at solar noon? (1) Equator (2) Tropic of Cancer (3) central New York State (4) Arctic Circle

70. In three months, the length of a day in central New York State will be (1) shorter, because the Sun will rise and set farther south (2) shorter, because the Sun will rise and set farther north (3) longer, because the Sun will rise and set farther south (4) longer, because the Sun will rise and set farther north

Group 4

If you choose this group, be sure to answer questions 71-75.

Base your answers to questions 71 through 75 on your knowledge of earth science, the *Earth Science Reference Tables,* and the diagram below. The diagram represents a closed energy system consisting of air and equal masses of copper, granite, and water in a perfectly insulated container. The temperatures were taken at the time the materials were placed inside the closed system.

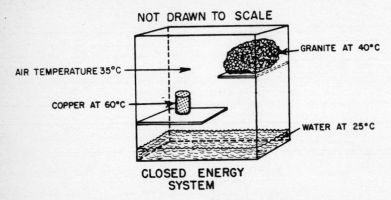

NOT DRAWN TO SCALE

GRANITE AT 40°C

AIR TEMPERATURE 35°C

COPPER AT 60°C

WATER AT 25°C

CLOSED ENERGY SYSTEM

71. In this system, which material is a heat sink for another material? (1) The water is a heat sink for the air. (2) The copper is a heat sink for the granite. (3) The granite is a heat sink for the water. (4) The copper is a heat sink for the air.

72. Which material in the energy system has the highest specific heat? (1) copper (2) granite (3) dry air (4) water

73. The mass of the granite is 2,000 grams. How much heat would have to be added to raise its temperature 20 C°? (1) 76 cal (2) 4,000 cal (3) 5,400 cal (4) 7,600 cal

Note that questions 74 and 75 have only three choices.

74. In the first day after the materials were placed in the system, the temperature of the water would probably (1) decrease (2) increase (3) remain the same

75. As time passes, the total energy in the system will (1) decrease (2) increase (3) remain the same

Group 5

If you choose this group, be sure to answer questions 76-80.

Base your answers to questions 76 through 80 on your knowledge of earth science, the *Earth Science Reference Tables,* and the map and information below.

One eruption of Mt. St. Helens in Washington State resulted in the movement of volcanic ash across the northwestern portion of the United States. The map shows the movement of the ash along paths at three different altitudes above sea level: path *A* at 1.5 km, path *B* at 3.0 km, and path *C* at 5.5 km. The lines across each path indicate the time interval between the eruption and the position of the leading edge of the ash. Points *X* and *Y* are places on the Earth's surface.

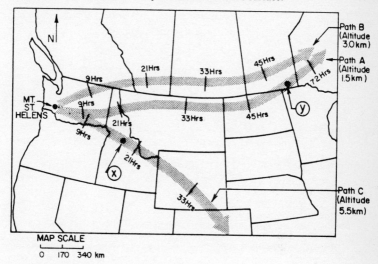

76. The data for paths *A*, *B*, and *C* were collected in which region of the atmosphere? (1) troposphere (2) stratosphere (3) mesosphere (4) thermosphere

Note that question 77 has only three choices.

77. How would the amount of insolation reaching point *X* 24 hours after the eruption compare with the amount of insolation this point usually receives? (1) The amount of insolation would be less. (2) The amount of insolation would be greater. (3) The amount of insolation would be the same.

78. Approximately how many hours did it take for the ash front of path *A* to arrive at point *Y*? (1) 39 (2) 45 (3) 59 (4) 72

79. Why did the general direction of the ash front along path *C* *not* follow the general direction of the ash fronts along path *A* and path *B*? (1) The eruption threw material toward the southeast. (2) Northwest winds existed at the 5.5-kilometer level. (3) Mountain ranges southeast of the volcano are 1.5 kilometers high. (4) Only the ash along path *C* was affected by the Earth's rotation.

80. Approximately how long would it take for an earthquake *P*-wave caused by the eruption to travel from Mt. St. Helens to point *Y*? (Use the map scale.) (1) 7 minutes (2) 2 minutes (3) 11 minutes (4) 4 minutes

Group 6

If you choose this group, be sure to answer questions 81-85.

Base your answers to questions 81 through 85 on your knowledge of earth science, the *Earth Science Reference Tables,* and the diagram below which represents a surface weather map of a portion of the United States. The map shows a low-pressure system with frontal lines and five weather stations *A* through *E*. Note that part of the weather data is missing from each station. [All temperatures are in °F.]

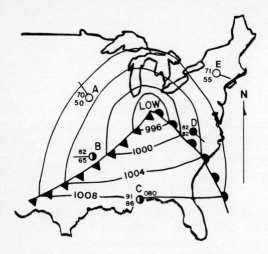

81. Which weather station has a relative humidity of 100%? (1) *A* (2) *B* (3) *C* (4) *D*

82. The weather at station *C* would most likely be (1) partly cloudy, windy, and very cold (2) partly cloudy and warm (3) overcast, humid, and cool (4) very dry and extremely hot

83. The atmospheric pressure at the center of the low would most likely be (1) 988 millibars (2) 990 millibars (3) 994 millibars (4) 997 millibars

84. The wind direction at station *A* is (1) northwest (2) northeast (3) southwest (4) southeast

85. Assuming that the low-pressure system follows a normal storm track, which weather station is probably located in the path of the approaching center of the low? (1) *A* (2) *B* (3) *C* (4) *E*

Group 7

If you choose this group, be sure to answer questions 86-90.

Base your answers to questions 86 through 90 on your knowledge of earth science, the *Earth Science Reference Tables,* and the diagram below which shows matching geologic columns from three different locations, *A, B,* and *C.* The locations are about 5 kilometers apart and the layers have not been overturned.

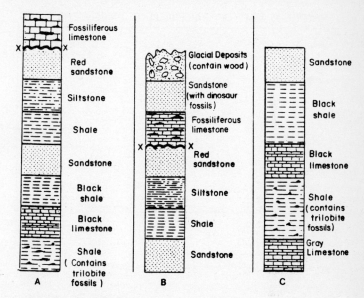

86. Which is the oldest layer shown? (1) gray limestone (2) sandstone (3) glacial till containing wood (4) shale containing trilobite fossils

87. The shale which contains the trilobite fossils was most likely deposited during which geologic period? (1) Cretaceous (2) Tertiary (3) Triassic (4) Ordovician

88. The formation of the fossiliferous limestone in column *B* was probably due to (1) heat and pressure which has metamorphosed the limestone and fossils (2) deposition of a variety of glacial sediments (3) compaction and cementation of skeletons and shells of sea organisms (4) cooling and solidification of molten material containing fossils

89. The feature at *X* is a buried erosional surface. Based on this, what inference can best be supported? (1) Faulting has occurred along the boundary between the red sandstone and the fossiliferous limestone. (2) No rock layers were ever formed between the red sandstone and the fossiliferous limestone. (3) An igneous intrusion has destroyed part of the fossiliferous limestone layer. (4) The red sandstone and the fossiliferous limestone do not provide a continuous geologic record.

90. Radioactive carbon-14 would be most useful in determining the age of the (1) trilobite fossils in the shale (2) wood in the glacial till (3) calcite in the black limestone (4) iron oxide in the red sandstone

Group 8

If you choose this group, be sure to answer questions 91-95.

Base your answers to questions 91 through 95 on your knowledge of earth science, the *Earth Science Reference Tables,* and on the world map below. The dots on the map indicate the locations of epicenters of major earthquakes over a five-year period. Points *A* through *G* are locations on the map.

WORLD MAP OF EARTHQUAKE EPICENTERS

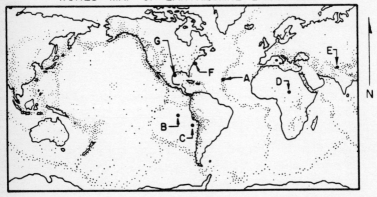

91. Where do most major earthquakes occur? (1) in the continental interiors (2) at the mantle-core boundary (3) randomly over the Earth's surface (4) in specific earthquake belts within the crust

92. How would a map showing the location of active volcanoes compare to the map showing the location of earthquake epicenters? (1) Only a small percentage of volcano locations would be in the same regions as the epicenters. (2) A large percentage of volcano locations would be in the same regions as the epicenters. (3) There would be no match between the locations of the volcanoes and the epicenters. (4) The location of the volcanoes and the epicenters would only match in the ocean regions.

93. The crust of the Earth is most likely the thickest at which location? (1) *A* (2) *B* (3) *C* (4) *E*

94. Rising mantle convection currents would most likely be located at which location on the map? (1) *A* (2) *B* (3) *C* (4) *G*

95. Continental growth (formed from the deposition of land-derived sediments) would most likely occur at which location? (1) *A* (2) *B* (3) *G* (4) *D*

Group 9

If you choose this group, be sure to answer questions 96-100.

Base your answers to questions 96 through 100 on your knowledge of earth science, the *Earth Science Reference Tables,* and on the block diagram below which shows a section of the Earth's crust. The rock layers have not been overturned, I, II, III, IV, and V are locations on the Earth's surface.

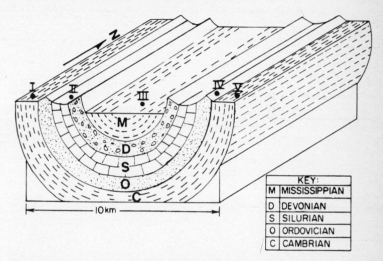

KEY:	
M	MISSISSIPPIAN
D	DEVONIAN
S	SILURIAN
O	ORDOVICIAN
C	CAMBRIAN

96. The deformed rock strata in the block diagram above are primarily the result of (1) faulting (2) folding (3) volcanism (4) ground water

97. Which rock layer appears to be the most resistant to weathering? (1) Mississippian shale (2) Silurian limestone (3) Ordovician sandstone (4) Cambrian shale

98. Which diagram best represents the rocks crossed when traveling across the surface from location III to location V?

III | V
M D S O C
(1)

III | V
C O S D M
(3)

III | V
D
(2)

III | V
C S D M O
(4)

99. Near which location in New York State would rocks similar in age to those at location III in the diagram be found?
(1) 42° N. lat., 79° W. long.
(2) 41° N. lat., 72° W. long.
(3) 44° N. lat., 74° W. long.
(4) 44° N. lat., 75° W. long.

100. Fossils of the earliest fishes could be found in the bedrock at location (1) I (2) II (3) III (4) IV

Group 10

If you choose this group, be sure to answer questions 101-105.

Base your answers to questions 101 through 105 on your knowledge of earth science and the *Earth Science Reference Tables.*

101. During which time was the majority of the exposed bedrock in New York State deposited? (1) Precambrian (2) Mesozoic (3) Cenozoic (4) Paleozoic

102. What is the approximate elevation of the stratopause? (1) 10 km (2) 30 km (3) 50 km (4) 80 km

103. What is the location of Binghamton, New York?
(1) 42° 06′ N. lat., 75° 55′ W. long.
(2) 42° 06′ N. lat., 76° 05′ W. long.
(3) 42° 54′ N. lat., 76° 05′ W. long.
(4) 42° 54′ N. lat., 75° 55′ W. long.

104. Which material would require the greatest amount of heat energy to raise its temperature from 5°C to 10°C? (1) 10 g of granite (2) 10 g of dry air (3) 10 g of lead (4) 10 g of iron

105. What is the approximate dewpoint temperature if the dry-bulb temperature is 25°C and the wet-bulb temperature is 20°C? (1) 7°C (2) 11°C (3) 17°C (4) 20°C

EARTH SCIENCE

JUNE 19, 1985

Part I

Answer all 55 questions in this part.   [55]

Directions: (1-55): For *each* statement or question, select the word or expression that, of those given, best completes the statement or answers the question. Record your answer on the separate answer sheet in accordance with the directions on the front page of this booklet.

1. Which statement about a burning candle is most likely an inference? (1) Carbon dioxide and water vapor are produced by the burning. (2) The wick gets shorter as the candle burns. (3) The candle wax is melting. (4) The flame is yellow.

2. The diagram below represents a rectangular object with a mass of 450 grams. According to the *Earth Science Reference Tables,* what is the density of the object?

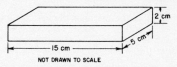

NOT DRAWN TO SCALE

(1) 1 gram per cubic centimeter (2) 2 grams per cubic centimeter (3) 3 grams per cubic centimeter (4) 4 grams per cubic centimeter

3. A beaker of water at 50°C is placed in a room where the air temperature is 20°C. Which graph best represents the change in the water temperature?

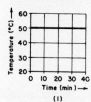 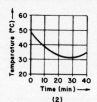 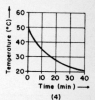

4. A student calculates the specific heat of ice to be 0.40 cal/g C°. According to the *Earth Science Reference Tables,* what is the student's percent deviation from the accepted value? (1) 2.5% (2) 2.0% (3) 20.% (4) 25.%

5. The best evidence of the Earth's nearly spherical shape is obtained through (1) telescopic observations of other planets (2) photographs of the Earth from an orbiting satellite (3) observations of the Sun's altitude made during the day (4) observations of the Moon made during lunar eclipses

6. What is the elevation of the highest contour line shown on the map below?

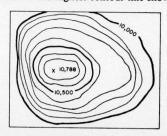

(1) 10,000 feet (2) 10,688 feet (3) 10,700 feet (4) 10,788 feet

7. According to the *Earth Science Reference Tables,* nearly all the water vapor in the atmosphere is found within the (1) mesosphere (2) thermosphere (3) troposphere (4) stratosphere

8. The Sun is approximately 141,000,000 kilometers from the Earth. This distance correctly expressed in scientific notation (powers of ten) would be (1) 1.41×10^6 km (2) 1.41×10^8 km (3) 1.41×10^9 km (4) 1.41^9 km

9. Which diagram below best represents the illumination of the Earth on the first day of summer in the Northern Hemisphere?

10. Upon which frame of reference is time based? (1) the motions of the Earth (2) the longitude of an observer (3) the motions of the Moon (4) the real motions of the Sun

11. Cities located on the same meridian (longitude) must have the same (1) altitude (2) latitude (3) length of daylight (4) solar time

12. The Earth reaches its greatest orbital speed when it is (1) closest to the Moon (2) farthest from the Moon (3) closest to the Sun (4) farthest from the Sun

13. The various forms of electromagnetic energy are distinguished from one another by their (1) temperature (2) wavelengths (3) longitudinal wave properties (4) speed of travel

14. Which energy transformation occurs as a rock falls freely from the top of a vertical cliff? (1) The rock's potential energy and kinetic energy decrease. (2) The rock's potential energy decreases and the rock's kinetic energy increases. (3) The rock's potential energy increases and the rock's kinetic energy decreases. (4) The rock's potential energy and kinetic energy increase.

15. The diagram below shows temperature values at various points in a solid piece of aluminum. Toward which point will heat flow from point P?

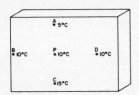

(1) A (2) B (3) C (4) D

16. Which graph below best represents the relationship between the angle of insolation and the intensity of insolation?

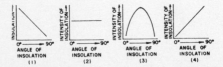

17. The temperature of the atmosphere may increase as the carbon dioxide content of the atmosphere increases. Which statement best explains this increase? (1) More ultraviolet radiation will be absorbed by the atmosphere. (2) More infrared radiation will be absorbed by the atmosphere. (3) Less light will be reflected by the atmosphere. (4) Less heat will be transferred to the atmosphere.

18. Which factor is most directly related to wind velocity? (1) dewpoint (2) relative humidity (3) cloud type (4) pressure gradient

19. What is the approximate dewpoint temperature if the dry-bulb temperature is 26°C and the wetbulb temperature is 21°C? (1) 5°C (2) 12°C (3) 18°C (4) 23°C

20. In the diagram below, at which location would the vapor pressure of the air most likely be greatest?

(1) *A* (2) *B* (3) *C* (4) *D*

21. The diagram below shows the Earth's high and low air pressure belts and direction of prevailing winds for a particular time of the year. The winds do *not* appear to blow in a straight line from the high-pressure belts to the low-pressure belts. Which statement best explains this observation?

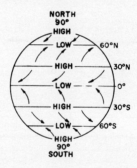

(1) Wind direction is modified by the Earth's rotation. (2) Wind direction is modified by land forms. (3) Wind direction is modified by water areas. (4) Wind direction is modified by the Sun's motion.

22. Condensation of water vapor in the atmosphere is most likely to occur when a condensation surface is available and (1) a strong wind is blowing (2) the temperature of the air is below 0°C (3) the air is saturated with water vapor (4) the air pressure is rising

23. Compared to a maritime tropical airmass, a maritime polar airmass has (1) lower temperature and less water vapor (2) lower temperature and more water vapor (3) higher temperature and less water vapor (4) higher temperature and more water vapor

24. Which graph best represents the relationship between porosity and particle size for soil samples of uniform size, shape, and packing?

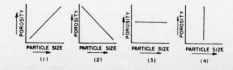

Base your answers to questions 25 and 26 on the graph below which represents the relationship between the time of year and the average monthly discharge of a stream located in New York State.

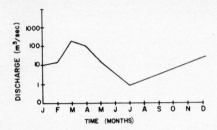

25. According to the graph, when will maximum surface runoff occur? (1) February through April (2) April through June (3) June through August (4) October through December

26. The stream discharge in June most likely occurred during a period of (1) minimum evapotranspiration (2) maximum ground water surplus (3) ground water recharge (4) ground water depletion

27. Which single factor generally has the greatest effect on the climate of an area on the Earth's surface? (1) the distance from the Equator (2) the extent of vegetative cover (3) the degrees of longitude (4) the month of the year

28. Transported rock materials are more common than residual rock materials in the soils of New York State. Which statement best explains this observation? (1) Solid rock must be transported to break. (2) Weathering changes transported rock materials more easily than residual rock materials. (3) Most rock materials are moved by some agent of erosion at some time in their history. (4) Residual rock material forms only from bedrock that is difficult to change into soil.

29. According to the *Earth Science Reference Tables,* a stream flowing at a velocity of 100 centimeters per second can transport (1) silt, but not sand, pebbles, or cobbles (2) silt and sand, but not pebbles or cobbles (3) silt, sand, and pebbles, but not cobbles (4) silt, sand, pebbles, and cobbles

30. A glass sphere and a lead sphere have the same volume. Each sphere is dropped into a container of water. Which statement best explains why the lead sphere settles faster? (1) The lead sphere has a higher density. (2) The glass sphere has a smoother surface. (3) The lead sphere takes up less space. (4) The glass sphere has more surface area.

31. Which situation exists in a section of a river where the amount of deposition is the same as the amount of erosion? (1) The water is flowing swiftly in that section. (2) That section of the river is a delta region. (3) Dynamic equilibrium has been reached in that section. (4) Lowest elevation has been reached in that section.

32. According to the *Earth Science Reference Tables,* which element is most abundant in the Earth's crust? (1) nitrogen (2) silicon (3) oxygen (4) hydrogen

33. The diagrams below represent magnifications of rocks. Which is most likely a diagram of a *nonsedimentary rock?*

34. According to the *Earth Science Reference Tables,* the sedimentary rock, gypsum, forms as a result of (1) faulting and folding of shale (2) metamorphism of limestone (3) weathering of siltstone (4) evaporation of seawater

35. According to the "Scheme for Igneous Rock Identification" in the *Earth Science Reference Tables,* which statement best describes the percentage of plagioclase feldspars in a sample of gabbro? (1) The percentage of plagioclase feldspars in gabbro can vary. (2) Gabbro always contains less plagioclase than pyroxene. (3) Plagioclase feldspars always make up 25% of a gabbro sample. (4) Gabbro contains no plagioclase feldspars.

36. According to the *Earth Science Reference Tables,* in which part of New York State is anorthositic bedrock found? (1) Long Island (2) the Adirondacks (3) the Catskills (4) the Tug Hill Plateau

37. Two geologic surveys of the same area, made 50 years apart, showed that the area had been uplifted 5 centimeters during the interval. If the rate of uplift remains constant, how many years will it take for this area to be uplifted a total of 70 centimeters? (1) 250 years (2) 350 years (3) 500 years (4) 700 years

38. Where are earthquakes most likely to take place? (1) along the core-mantle interface (2) where the composition of the Earth tends to be uniform (3) near the Earth's Equator (4) near a fault zone

39. The composition of the Earth's core is thought to be the same as the composition of (1) certain meteorites (2) most basalts (3) most granites (4) volcanic ash

40. Which best describes a major characteristic of both volcanoes and earthquakes? (1) They are centered at the poles. (2) They are located in the same geographic areas. (3) They are related to the formation of glaciers. (4) They are restricted to the Southern Hemisphere.

41. The most complete fossil record of past invertebrate life in New York State can be found in rocks of which era? (1) Cenozoic (2) Mesozoic (3) Precambrian (4) Paleozoic

42. Which feature in a rock layer is older than the rock layer? (1) igneous intrusions (2) mineral veins (3) rock fragments (4) faults

43. Geologists have subdivided geologic time into units based on (1) rock type (2) fossil evidence (3) erosion rates (4) landscape development

44. According to the *Earth Science Reference Tables,* which of the following cities is located on the youngest bedrock? (1) Watertown (2) Syracuse (3) Albany (4) Binghamton

Base your answers to questions 45 and 46 on the diagram below which shows a geologic cross section and landscape profile of a section of the Earth's crust.

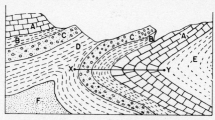

45. Which graph best represents the age of the rocks along line *XY*?

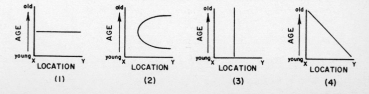

46. Based on the profile of this landscape, which statement is most likely correct? (1) The folding of rock layers creates level landscapes. (2) Rock layer *C* is more resistant to erosion than rock layer *B*. (3) Glaciers have been the major agent of erosion in this area. (4) The erosional surface was formed before the rock layers were folded.

47. According to the *Earth Science Reference Tables,* approximately how many years ago did the Palisades Sill form? (1) 195 million (2) 2 million (3) 570 million (4) 1,650 million

48. What characteristics of fossils are most useful in correlating sedimentary rock layers? (1) limited geographic distribution but found in many rock formations (2) limited geographic distribution and limited to a particular rock formation (3) wide geographic distribution but limited to a particular rock formation (4) wide geographic distribution and found in many rock formations

49. Which radioactive substance would probably be used in dating the recent remains of a plant found in sedimentary deposits (1) carbon-14 (2) potassium-40 (3) rubidium-87 (4) uranium-238

50. The Catskills landscape region is classified as a plateau because the region has (1) deep gorges (2) shallow valleys (3) rock type similar to the Adirondack Highlands (4) landscape characteristics most similar to the Appalachian Uplands

51. Which characteristics of a landscape region would provide the best information about the stage of development of the landscape? (1) the age and fossil content of the bedrock (2) the type of hillslopes and the stream patterns (3) the amount of precipitation and the potential evapotranspiration (4) the type of vegetation and the vegetation's growth rate

52. Which factor has the *least* influence on the development of a landscape over a number of years? (1) average amount of rainfall (2) average rate of uplift (3) composition of bedrock (4) geologic age of bedrock

53. According to the *Earth Science Reference Tables,* which two mineral grains would most likely be found in soil formed from granite? (1) olivine and pyroxene (2) orthoclase and quartz (3) plagioclase and pyroxene (4) olivine and nepheline

Note that questions 54 and 55 have only three choices.

54. As the amount of reflection caused by dust particles in the atmosphere increases, the amount of insolation reaching the Earth's surface (1) decreases (2) increases (3) remains the same

55. A large rock is broken into several smaller pieces. Compared to the rate of weathering of the large rock, the rate of weathering of the smaller pieces is (1) less (2) greater (3) the same

Part II

This part consists of ten groups, each containing five questions. Choose seven of these ten groups. Be sure that you answer all five questions in each group chosen. Record the answers to these questions on the separate answer sheet in accordance with the directions on the front page of this booklet. [35]

Group I

If you choose this group, be sure to answer questions 56-60.

Base your answers to questions 56 through 60 on your knowledge of earth science and the air pollution field map shown on the next page. The isolines represent the concentration of pollutants measured in particles/cm^3.

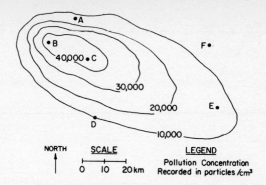

56. The major source of air pollution is most likely at point   (1) A   (2) B   (3) E   (4) D

57. The winds responsible for this air pollution pattern are most likely blowing from the   (1) northeast   (2) northwest   (3) southeast   (4) southwest

58. The most rapid increase in air pollution would be encountered when traveling between points   (1) A and B   (2) A and F   (3) C and D   (4) D and E

59. The air pollution field illustrated by the map is located in a heavily populated area. Which is the *least* probable source of the pollution?   (1) human activities   (2) industrial plants   (3) automobile traffic   (4) natural processes

60. Which graph best represents the relationship between the pollution concentration and distance from point B toward point E?

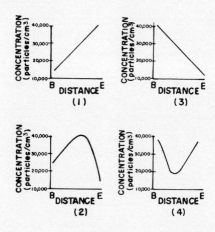

Group 2

If you choose this group, be sure to answer questions 61-65.

Base your answers to questions 61 through 65 on your knowledge of earth science and the diagrams on the next page. The diagrams represent observers at four different locations A, B, C, and D on the Earth's Surface and the altitude of Polaris at each location.

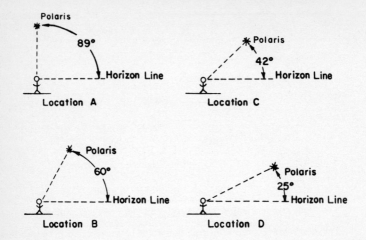

61. All four observers must be (1) located at the same longitude (2) located in the Northern Hemisphere (3) able to see Polaris for the same length of time each day (4) able to observe the rotation of Polaris around the Earth

62. The observer at location *A* is nearest to the (1) Equator (0°) (2) Tropic of Cancer (23$\frac{1}{2}$° N.) (3) Arctic Circle (66$\frac{1}{2}$° N.) (4) North Pole (90° N.)

63. The observations of the altitude of Polaris made by the four observers provide information about the (1) shape of the Earth (2) density of the Earth (3) time at the observers' locations (4) longitude of the observers' locations

Note that question 64 has only three choices.

64. The observer at location *C* travels 200 kilometers directly west. As he moves away from location *C*, the altitude of Polaris will (1) decrease (2) increase (3) remain the same

65. When viewed from the Northern Hemisphere of the Earth, all stars appear to circle Polaris. Which statement best explains this observation? (1) The Earth's orbit is an elliptical path around the Sun. (2) The Sun is one of the stars which revolves around Polaris. (3) The Sun is at the center of the solar system and rotates on its axis. (4) The northern end of the Earth's axis of rotation points in the direction of Polaris.

Group 3

If you choose this group, be sure to answer questions 66-70.

Base your answers to questions 66 through 70 on your knowledge of earth science, the *Earth Science Reference Tables,* and the diagram and graph on the next page. In the diagram, equal masses of water and soil are located at identical distances from the lamp. Both were heated for ten minutes and then the lamp was removed. The water and soil were then allowed to cool for ten minutes. The graph shows the temperature data obtained during the investigation.

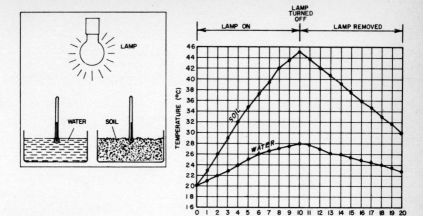

66. What were the temperature readings of the water and soil at the time the lamp was turned off? (1) The water was 20°C and the soil was 20°C. (2) The water was 23°C and the soil was 30°C. (3) The water was 28°C and the soil was 45°C. (4) The water was 45°C and the soil was 28°C.

67. By which process was most of the energy transferred between the lamp and the water during the first 10 minutes of the investigation? (1) conduction (2) convection (3) reflection (4) radiation

68. What was the rate at which the soil temperature changed during the first ten minutes of the investigation? (1) 0.8 C°/min (2) 2.5 C°/min (3) 8 C°/min (4) 25 C°/min

69. Compared to the water, the soil became warmer during the heating period because the soil (1) has a lower specific heat (2) was closer to the lamp (3) reradiated less heat (4) has a lower density

70. Assume that the soil and water in this investigation heat and cool in the same manner as the land and water on the map below. At the time of highest temperature readings, in which direction would the wind most likely be blowing?

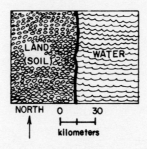

(1) south to north (2) north to south (3) east to west (4) west to east

Group 4

If you choose this group, be sure to answer questions 71-75.

Base your answers to questions 71 through 75 on your knowledge of earth science, the *Earth Science Reference Tables,* and the map below which represents a weather system located over the central United States. Letters *A, B, C, D,* and *E* locate weather stations on the map.

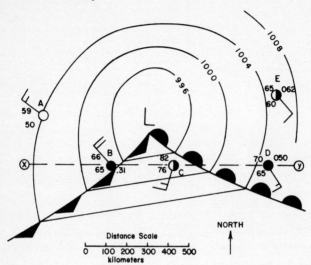

71. What is the air pressure at weather station *A*? (1) 1069 mb (2) 1064 mb (3) 1004 mb (4) 1000 mb

72. Which weather station is experiencing clouds, heavy precipitation, and rapidly decreasing air temperature? (1) *A* (2) *B* (3) *E* (4) *D*

73. In which diagram do the arrows best represent the wind direction in the weather system?

74. Which diagram best represents a cross section of the Earth's atmosphere showing the fronts between airmasses as they would appear along line *x – y*?

75. If the weather system follows a normal storm track at a speed of 50 kilometers per hour, which best describes the atmospheric changes which will most likely occur at weather station *C* in about six hours? (1) air temperature increase, air pressure increase, and clearing sky (2) air temperature decrease, air pressure increase, and precipitation (3) air temperature increase, no change in air pressure, and clearing sky (4) little atmospheric change with a low probability of precipitation

Group 5

If you choose this group, be sure to answer questions 76-80.

Base your answers to questions 76 through 80 on your knowledge of earth science and the data below. The chart is a record of the monthly average temperature and average precipitation for a locality in New York State. The graph is provided for your use in plotting the given data and to assist you in answering the questions.

Temperature °C	Month	Precipitation cm
−3.1	January	6.0
−2.1	February	6.4
2.7	March	7.5
8.8	April	7.7
14.8	May	8.3
20.1	June	11.0
22.4	July	9.8
21.5	August	8.7
17.9	September	6.8
12.0	October	7.1
5.8	November	10.6
−0.3	December	8.6

FOR STUDENT USE

KEY TO CLIMATE

Total Yearly Precipitation

Dry—less than 50 cm
Moderate—50 cm–200 cm
Wet—more than 200 cm

76. During which months does the *least* total amount of precipitation occur in this area? (1) January, February, March (2) April, May, June (3) July, August, September (4) October, November, December

77. Which graph best represents the relationship between the average precipitation and the time of year for this location?

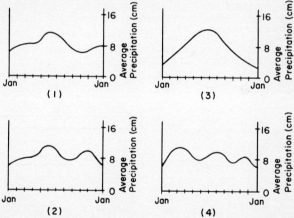

78. The stream discharge in this area is observed to remain relatively low during September, October, and early November, even though the precipitation increased during this time. The best explanation for this observation is that much of the precipitation (1) evaporated because of increased potential evapotranspiration (2) was absorbed by plants due to an increased air temperature (3) recharged the soil moisture storage that was used during the dry months (4) was used to fill large nearby lakes

79. Which statement best describes the climate of this location during the time that the data in the chart were recorded? (1) constant monthly temperatures with moderate yearly precipitation (2) a cold, dry summer and a warm, wet winter (3) a cold, wet summer and a warm, dry winter (4) warm summer and cool winter temperatures, with a moderate yearly precipitation

80. During which month is the potential evapotranspiration for this location highest? (1) January (2) March (3) July (4) December

Group 6

If you choose this group, be sure to answer questions 81-85.

Base your answers to questions 81 through 85 on your knowledge of earth science, the *Earth Science Reference Tables,* and the cross-sectional diagram below. The diagram shows a sediment-laden stream entering the ocean. The ocean is divided into four zones *A, B, C,* and *D.*

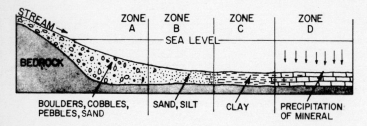

81. In which zone would the stream normally deposit particles of largest size? (1) *A* (2) *B* (3) *C* (4) *D*

82. Which material would most likely be held in suspension in zone *D*? (1) cobbles (2) sand (3) silt (4) colloids

83. Which change in the stream system would most likely cause the deposition of larger particles to be farther offshore? (1) a decrease in the stream's gradient (2) a decrease in the quantity of large particles (3) an increase in the stream's velocity (4) an increase in the density of large particles

84. Limestone would most likely form in zone (1) *A* (2) *B* (3) *C* (4) *D*

85. Which zone would contain particles mostly in the range of 0.05 to 0.10 centimeter in diameter? (1) *A* (2) *B* (3) *C* (4) *D*

(continued on next page.)

Group 7

If you choose this group, be sure to answer questions 86-90,

Base your answers to questions 86 through 90 on your knowledge of earth science, the *Earth Science Reference Tables,* and the map on the next page. The map shows the epicenters and intensities of recent earthquakes within New York State. The State has been subdivided into four regions (*A,B,C,D*). In the key, VIII represents the most intense earthquakes and IV represents the least intense.

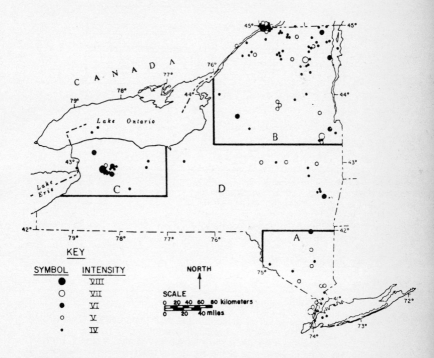

86. Which levels of earthquake intensity have occurred most frequently in New York State? (1) V and VII (2) IV and VIII (3) VI and VII (4) IV and V

87. Which is the best approximation of the length of the northern boundary line of zone *A*? (1) 80 km (2) 100 km (3) 120 km (4) 155 km

88. Which city is most likely to experience an earthquake at some future time? (1) Massena (2) Elmira (3) Jamestown (4) Utica

89. Which landscape region occupies most of earthquake region *B*? (1) Erie-Ontario Lowlands (2) Adirondack Highlands (3) Appalachian Uplands (4) New England Highlands

90. What type of rocks are found surrounding the epicenters of region *C*? (1) intensely metamorphosed (2) slightly metamorphosed (3) igneous (4) sedimentary

Group 8

If you choose this group, be sure to answer questions 91-95.

Base your answers to questions 91 through 95 on your knowledge of earth science, the *Earth Science Reference Tables,* and the diagram on the next page. The diagram represents a geologic cross section in which overturning has not occurred.

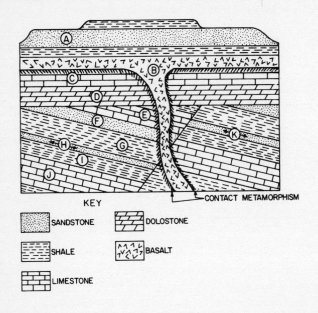

KEY

SANDSTONE   DOLOSTONE

SHALE   BASALT

LIMESTONE

CONTACT METAMORPHISM

91. Which rock is the same age as rock *K*? (1) *A* (2) *E* (3) *F* (4) *H*

92. Which rock is *least* likely to contain fossils? (1) *A* (2) *B* (3) *E* (4) *G*

93. What is the relative age of the fault? (1) older than rock *D* (2) older than rock *G* (3) younger than rock *B* (4) younger than rock *C*

94. Dinosaur bones and ammonite shells have been found in several of the rocks shown. What is the probable age of these rocks? (1) Devonian (2) Jurassic (3) Oligocene (4) Permian

95. A buried erosion surface (unconformity) most likely exists between rocks (1) *G* and *K* (2) *H* and *I* (3) *C* and *D* (4) *D* and *E*

Group 9

If you choose this group, be sure to answer questions 96-100.

Base your answers to questions 96 through 100 on your knowledge of earth science and on the diagram on the next page. The diagram shows an enlargement of the mid-Atlantic ridge and surrounding area in its position with respect to the continents. Magnetic polarity bands of igneous rock parallel to the ridge are illustrated according to the key.

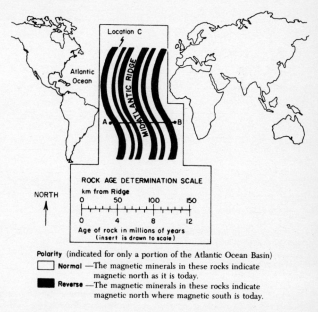

Polarity (indicated for only a portion of the Atlantic Ocean Basin)

☐ **Normal** —The magnetic minerals in these rocks indicate magnetic north as it is today.

■ **Reverse** —The magnetic minerals in these rocks indicate magnetic north where magnetic south is today.

96. Ocean floor rock found 20 kilometers west of the ocean ridge would have an approximate age of (1) 1.6 million years (2) 2.0 million years (3) 15 million years (4) 30 million years

97. What are two characteristics of ocean floor rock found at location *C*? (1) normal polarity, continental composition (2) normal polarity, oceanic composition (3) reverse polarity, continental composition (4) reverse polarity, oceanic composition

98. Along the line from position *A* to position *B*, the comparative age of the rock (1) continuously decreases from *A* to *B* (2) continuously increases from *A* to *B* (3) decreases from *A* to the mid-Atlantic ridge and then increases to *B* (4) increases from *A* to the mid-Atlantic ridge and then decreases to *B*

99. Which of the cross-sectional diagrams below best represents a model for the movement of rock material below the crust along the mid-Atlantic ridge?

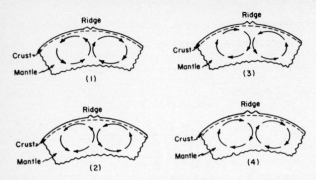

100. What is the most accurate method used by geologists to determine the age of igneous rocks on the ocean floor near the mid-Atlantic ridge? (1) walking the outcrop (2) chemical weathering rate (3) erosional rate (4) radioactive dating

Group 10

If you choose this group, be sure to answer questions 101-105.

Base your answers to questions 101 through 105 on your knowledge of earth science and the *Earth Science Reference Tables.*

101. A temperature of 80° Fahrenheit would be approximately equal to how many degrees on the Celsius scale? (1) 27 (2) 34 (3) 178 (4) 299

102. The temperature of rock located 1,000 kilometers below the Earth's surface is about (1) 200°K (2) 2,100°K (3) 2,800°K (4) 3,200°K

103. The rock type found at the location 44° north latitude and 76° west longitude was formed during which period? (1) Devonian (2) Silurian (3) Ordovician (4) Cambrian

104. A seismograph station records a difference between the arrival times of the P-wave and S-wave of 7 minutes 30 seconds. About how far away is this station from the earthquake epicenter? (1) 2,100 km (2) 4,400 km (3) 6,000 km (4) 7,200 km

105. How many calories of latent heat would have to be absorbed by 100 grams of liquid water at 100°C in order to change all of the liquid water into water vapor at 100°C? (1) 100 cal (2) 1,000 cal (3) 8,000 cal (4) 54,000 cal

EARTH SCIENCE

June 25, 1986

Part I

Answer all 55 questions in this part.   [55]

Directions (1–55): For *each* statement or question, select the word or expression that, of those given, best completes the statement or answers the question.

1. The grouping of objects or events based on similar characteristics is called
   (1) observation
   (2) interpretation
   (3) measurement
   (4) classification

2. The diagrams below represent two differently shaped blocks of ice floating in water. Which diagram most accurately shows the blocks of ice as they would actually float in water?

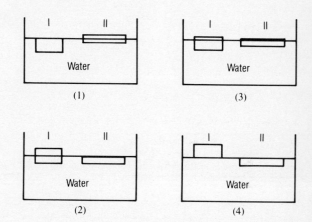

3. Which statement about a rock sample is an inference?
   (1) The rock scratches a glass plate.
   (2) The rock was formed 100 million years ago.
   (3) A balance indicates the rock's mass is 254 grams.
   (4) The rock has no visible crystals and is red.

4. Which statement provides the best evidence that the Earth has a nearly spherical shape?
   (1) The Sun has a spherical shape.
   (2) The altitude of Polaris changes in a definite pattern as an observer's latitude changes.
   (3) Star trails photographed over a period of time show a circular path.
   (4) The lengths of noontime shadows change throughout the year.

5. The rising and setting of the Sun are examples of
   (1) noncyclic events
   (2) unrelated events
   (3) predictable changes
   (4) random motion

6. A vector quantity must include both magnitude and direction. Which measurement is a vector quantity?
   (1) the highest elevation of a hill
   (2) the air temperature in a room
   (3) the rain accumulation at a weather station
   (4) the motion of water in an ocean current

7. Which statement most accurately describes the Earth's atmosphere?
   (1) The atmosphere is layered, with each layer possessing distinct characteristics.
   (2) The atmosphere is a shell of gases surrounding most of the Earth.
   (3) The atmosphere's altitude is less than the depth of the ocean.
   (4) The atmosphere is more dense than the hydrosphere but less dense than the lithosphere.

8. Based on the diagram below, what is the circumference of planet *Y*?

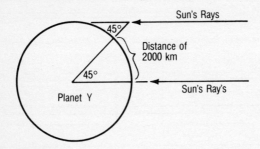

   (1) 9,000 km
   (2) 12,000 km
   (3) 16,000 km
   (4) 24,000 km

9. How would a three-hour time exposure photograph of stars in the northern sky appear if the Earth did *not* rotate?

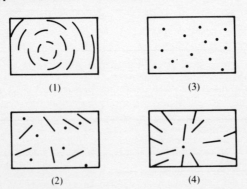

10. The Coriolis effect would be influenced most by a change in the Earth's
    (1) rate of rotation
    (2) period of revolution
    (3) angle of tilt
    (4) average surface temperature

11. Which observation can *not* be explained by a geocentric model?
    (1) Stars follow circular paths around Polaris.
    (2) The Sun's path through the sky is an arc.
    (3) A planet's apparent diameter varies.
    (4) A freely swinging pendulum appears to change direction.

12. Planet *A* has a greater mean distance from the Sun than planet *B*. On the basis of this fact, which further comparison can be correctly made between the two planets?
    (1) Planet *A* is larger.
    (2) Planet *A*'s revolution period is longer.
    (3) Planet *A*'s speed of rotation is greater.
    (4) Planet *A*'s day is longer.

13. Which part of the solar electromagnetic spectrum has the maximum intensity?
    (1) visible light radiation
    (2) infrared radiation
    (3) ultraviolet radiation
    (4) X-ray radiation

14. At which latitude would the duration of insolation be greatest on December 21?
    (1) 23½° S.
    (2) 0°
    (3) 10° N.
    (4) 23½° N.

Base your answers to questions 15 and 16 on the diagram below. The diagram illustrates equipment used to perform an *open-system* heat transfer investigation under ordinary classroom conditions.

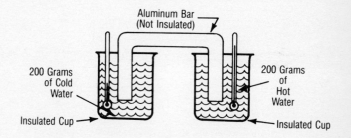

15. If the initial temperature of the cold water was 10°C and the initial temperature of the hot water was 86°C, what were the most likely temperature readings after 12 minutes?
    (1) 22°C for the cold water and 74°C for the hot water
    (2) 16°C for the cold water and 74°C for the hot water
    (3) 6°C for the cold water and 82°C for the hot water
    (4) 4°C for the cold water and 92°C for the hot water

16. The greatest amount of heat energy transferred between the hot and cold water is transferred by the process of
    (1) conduction
    (2) convection
    (3) absorption
    (4) radiation

17. The map below shows isolines of average daily insolation received in calories per square centimeter per minute at the Earth's surface. If identical solar collectors are placed at the lettered locations, which collector would receive the *least* insolation?

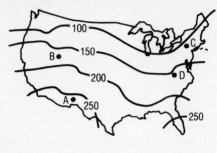

    (1) *A*
    (2) *B*
    (3) *C*
    (4) *D*

18. The diagram below represents a portion of the Earth's surface that is receiving insolation. Positions *A, B, C,* and *D* are located on the surface of the Earth.

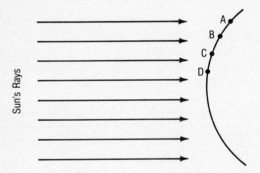

At which position would the intensity of insolation be greatest?
    (1) *A*
    (2) *B*
    (3) *C*
    (4) *D*

19. When the dry-bulb temperature reading is 10.°C and the wet-bulb temperature reading is 2.0°C, the dewpoint temperature of the air is approximately
    (1) 10.°C
    (2) 2.0°C
    (3) −8.0°C
    (4) −15°C

20. Which diagram below best represents the air circulation around a Northern Hemisphere low-pressure center?

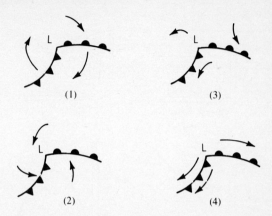

21. The diagram below represents weather station *A* in the path of an airmass approaching from the west. Which change will most likely be recorded first by weather station *A*?

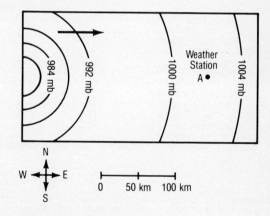

(1) an increase in air pressure
(2) an increase in wind speed
(3) a decrease in temperature
(4) a decrease in cloud cover

22. Which graph best represents the relationship between increasing distance above the water surface of a lake and the vapor pressure of the air?

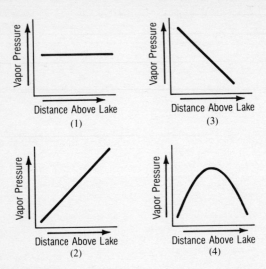

23. Which natural process removes small pollutant particles from the atmosphere?
    (1) the greenhouse effect
    (2) the Coriolis effect
    (3) transpiration
    (4) precipitation

24. According to the *Earth Science Reference Tables,* an atmospheric pressure of 978 millibars is equal to
    (1) 28.76 inches of mercury
    (2) 28.88 inches of mercury
    (3) 28.92 inches of mercury
    (4) 29.00 inches of mercury

25. Which property of loose earth materials most likely increases as particle size decreases?
    (1) capillarity
    (2) infiltration
    (3) permeability
    (4) porosity

26. Local water budget data for Buffalo, New York, is shown at the top of the next page. The numbers represent millimeters of water.

    Which statement regarding the *May* water budget data for this city must be correct?
    (1) Precipitation was equal to 0 mm for the month of May.
    (2) Actual evapotranspiration was greater than potential evapotranspiration for the month of May.
    (3) Storage was equal to 100 mm for the month of May.
    (4) There was a water deficit for the month of May.

	May	June
Precipitation, P		69
Potential Evapotranspiration, E_p	72	111
$P - E_p$	1	-42
Change in storage, ΔSt	0	-42
Storage, St		58
Actual Evapotranspiration, E_a		111
Deficit, D		0
Surplus, S		0

27. Compared to a coastal location of the same elevation and latitude, an inland location is likely to have
    (1) warmer summers and cooler winters
    (2) warmer summers and warmer winters
    (3) cooler summers and cooler winters
    (4) cooler summers and warmer winters
28. Which factor has the *least* effect on the weathering of a rock?
    (1) climatic conditions
    (2) composition of the rock
    (3) exposure of the rock to the atmosphere
    (4) the number of fossils found in the rock
29. The diagram below represents equal masses of two identical rock samples. Sample A is one large block, while sample B was cut into four smaller blocks of equal size.

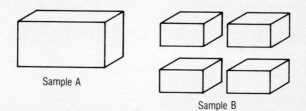

    If subjected to the same environmental conditions, sample B will weather more quickly than sample A. The best explanation for this is that the
    (1) volume of sample B is greater than that of sample A
    (2) surface area of sample B is greater than that of sample A
    (3) density of sample A is greater than that of sample B
    (4) hardness of sample A is greater than that of sample B
30. Which characteristic exists at an erosional-depositional interface in a stream where equilibrium occurs?
    (1) The downstream profile is the same as the across-stream profile.
    (2) The rate of deposition equals the rate of erosion.
    (3) The composition of the sediments deposited is the same as the composition of the sediments eroded.
    (4) The volume of streamflow equals the volume of deposition.

31. The three graphs below show information about the soil characteristics of four locations in a river valley in western New York State. Which location would probably experience the greatest rate of water infiltration at the start of the next rainstorm?

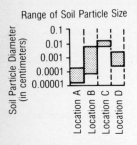 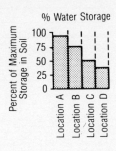 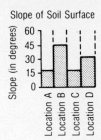

    (1) location *A*
    (2) location *B*
    (3) location *C*
    (4) location *D*

Base your answers to questions 32 and 33 on your knowledge of earth science and on the diagrams below which represent cross sections of four rock samples. Each cross section illustrates the sediments, minerals, or structural appearance of the rock sample.

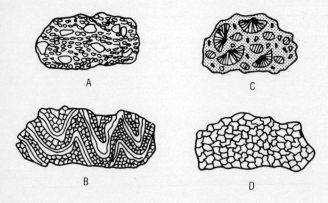

32. Which rock sample is most likely monomineralic?
    (1) *A*
    (2) *B*
    (3) *C*
    (4) *D*

Note that question 33 has only three choices.

33. Which rock sample is most likely a nonsedimentary rock?
    (1) *A*
    (2) *B*
    (3) *C*

34. Which graph best represents the relationship between a stream's velocity and the size of the largest particles it can carry downstream?

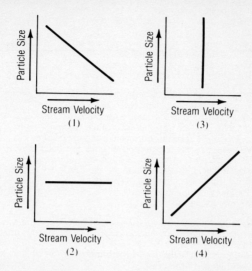

35. If all the particles below have the same mass and density, which particle will settle fastest in quiet water? [Assume settling takes place as shown by arrows.]

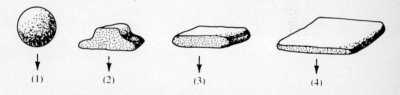

36. According to the *Earth Science Reference Tables,* which characteristic determines whether a rock is classified as a shale, a siltstone, a sandstone, or a conglomerate?
    (1) the absolute age of the sediments within the rock
    (2) the mineral composition of the sediments within the rock
    (3) the particle size of the sediments within the rock
    (4) the density of the sediments within the rock

37. Which rocks would most likely be separated by a transition zone of altered rock (metamorphic rock)?
    (1) sandstone and limestone
    (2) granite and limestone
    (3) shale and sandstone
    (4) conglomerate and siltstone

38. Large crystal grains in an igneous rock indicate that the rock was formed
    (1) near the surface
    (2) under low pressure
    (3) at a low temperature
    (4) over a long period of time

39. According to the *Earth Science Reference Tables*, what is the approximate average density of the Earth?
    (1) 2.80 g/cm³
    (2) 5.52 g/cm³
    (3) 9.55 g/cm³
    (4) 12.0 g/cm³

40. Recent volcanic activity in different parts of the world supports the inference that volcanoes are located mainly in
    (1) the centers of landscape regions
    (2) the central regions of the continents
    (3) zones of crustal activity
    (4) zones in late stages of erosion

41. Which conclusion based on the analysis of seismic data supports the inference that the Earth's outer core is liquid?
    (1) *S*-waves are *not* transmitted through the outer core.
    (2) *S*-waves are transmitted through the outer core.
    (3) *P*-waves are *not* transmitted through the outer core.
    (4) *P*-waves are transmitted through the outer core.

42. Theories about the composition of the Earth's core are supported by meteorites that are composed primarily of
    (1) oxygen and silicon
    (2) aluminum and iron
    (3) aluminum and oxygen
    (4) iron and nickel

43. The primary cause of convection currents in the Earth's mantle is believed to be the
    (1) differences in densities of earth materials
    (2) subsidence of the crust
    (3) occurrence of earthquakes
    (4) rotation of the Earth

44. The age of an igneous intrusion is 50 million years. What is the most probable age of the rock immediately surrounding the intrusion?
    (1) 10 million years
    (2) 25 million years
    (3) 40 million years
    (4) 60 million years

45. According to the *Earth Science Reference Tables*, which graph best represents the relative age of the surface bedrock along a straight line from Utica to Plattsburgh?

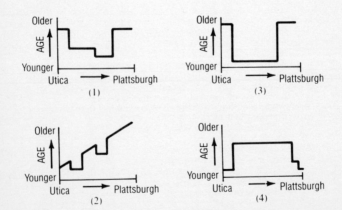

46. According to the *Earth Science Reference Tables,* which inference can be made about the fossil record?
(1) Very few life forms have become extinct.
(2) Fossils were extremely rare for most of the geologic past.
(3) A great variety of plants and animals existed during the Precambrian Era.
(4) Primitive humans have existed through most of the geologic past.

47. According to the Generalized Bedrock Geology Map of New York State, which is the youngest bedrock?

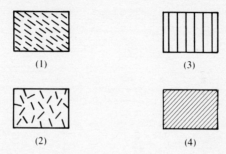

(1)   (3)

(2)   (4)

48. An unconformity between two sedimentary layers is most likely produced by
(1) the deposition of gravel followed by the deposition of sand and silt
(2) continuous sedimentation in a deep basin over a long period
(3) uplift followed by extensive erosion, submergence, and deposition
(4) a period of extrusive vulcanism followed by another period of extrusive vulcanism

49. Earth scientists studied fossils of a certain type of plant. They noted slight differences in the plant throughout geologic time. What inference is best made from this evidence?
(1) When the environment changed, this type of plant also changed, allowing it to survive.
(2) When uplifting occurred, the fossils of this type of plant were deformed.
(3) The processes which form fossils today differ from those of the past.
(4) The fossils have changed as a result of weathering and erosion.

50. Which New York State landscape region has been most extensively changed by ocean wave erosion during the last 200 years?
(1) Atlantic Coastal Lowlands
(2) Hudson-Mohawk Lowlands
(3) St. Lawrence Lowlands
(4) Triassic Lowlands

51. Which factors most directly control the development of soils?
(1) soil particle sizes and method of deposition
(2) bedrock composition and climate characteristics
(3) direction of prevailing winds and storm tracks
(4) earthquake intensity and volcanic activity

52. An area of gentle slopes and rounded mountaintops is most likely due to
(1) climatic conditions
(2) earthquakes
(3) the age of the bedrock
(4) the amount of folding

53. The landscape shown below developed in a region with an arid climate.

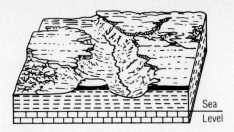

If the erosion of this plateau had taken place in a much more humid climate, which diagram below best represents how the landscape would appear?

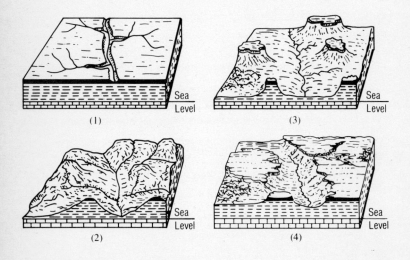

(1)

(3)

(2)

(4)

54. A landscape is characterized by much transported soil, scratched rock surfaces, and wide U-shaped valleys. The development of this landscape is probably the result of
    (1) stream action
    (2) wind erosion
    (3) uplifting
    (4) glaciation

Note that question 55 has only three choices.

55. If a radioactive material were cut into pieces, the half-life of each piece would be
    (1) less than the original specimen's half-life
    (2) greater than the original specimen's half-life
    (3) the same as the original specimen's half-life

Part II

This part consists of ten groups, each containing five questions. Choose seven of these ten groups. Be sure that you answer all five questions in each group chosen. [35]

Group 1

If you choose this group, be sure to answer questions 56–60.

Base your answers to questions 56 through 60 on your knowledge of earth science and the diagrams and graph below. The diagrams represent four solid materials, *A, B, C,* and *D*. Some of their physical properties are shown. The dimensions of the materials are recorded in centimeters. The graph indicates the relationship between the mass and volume of materials *B* and *C*.

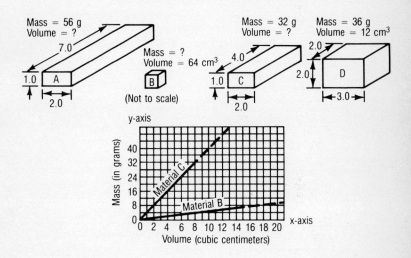

56. What is the density of sample *A?*
    (1) 0.25 g/cm³
    (2) 14 g/cm³
    (3) 56 g/cm³
    (4) 4.0 g/cm³
57. What is the mass of another sample of material *C* whose volume is 5 cubic centimeters?
    (1) 8.0 g
    (2) 20. g
    (3) 32 g
    (4) 4.0 g
58. If sample *B* is a perfect cube, what is the length of any one side?
    (1) 21 cm
    (2) 2.0 cm
    (3) 32 cm
    (4) 4.0 cm

59. If the density for material *D* were plotted on the graph, where would this line be located?
    (1) between the line for material *B* and the *x*-axis
    (2) between the lines for materials *B* and C
    (3) between the line for material *C* and the *y*-axis
    (4) on the same line as material *C*

Note that question 60 has only three choices.

60. If sample *C* were cut in half, the slope of the line for material *C* on the graph would
    (1) decrease
    (2) increase
    (3) remain the same

Group 2

If you choose this group, be sure to answer questions 61–65.

Base your answers to questions 61 through 65 on your knowledge of earth science and the *Earth Science Reference Tables*.

61. According to the Scheme for Igneous Rock Identification, compared to basalt, granite is
    (1) lighter in color
    (2) greater in density
    (3) more mafic in composition
    (4) more fine grained in texture

62. How many calories of heat energy are required to raise the temperature of 6 grams of water from 10°C to 15°C?
    (1) 5
    (2) 30
    (3) 480
    (4) 3240

63. What is the maximum size particle that can be carried by a stream having a velocity of 250 centimeters per second?
    (1) 0.0004 cm
    (2) 0.01 cm
    (3) 6.4 cm
    (4) 9.0 cm

64. The radius of the Sun is approximately how many times greater than the radius of the Moon?
    (1) 40
    (2) 400
    (3) 4,000
    (4) 40,000

65. A student determines the mass of a rock to be 196 grams, but the actual mass of the rock is 200. grams. The student's approximate percent deviation (percentage of error) is
    (1) 1.0%
    (2) 2.0%
    (3) 1.5%
    (4) 4.0%

Group 3

If you choose this group, be sure to answer questions 66–70.

Base your answers to questions 66 through 70 on your knowledge of earth science, the *Earth Science Reference Tables*, and the isoline map shown below. The map represents various temperatures taken 1 meter above the floor in a closed room. Letters *A* through *F* are various locations in the room also located 1 meter above the floor.

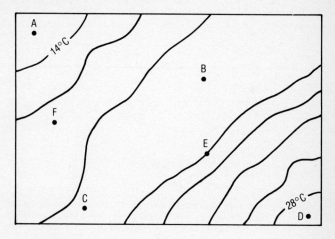

66. The approximate temperature at location *B* is
    (1) 24°C
    (2) 22°C
    (3) 19°C
    (4) 17°C
67. A heat source is most likely located at
    (1) *A*
    (2) *B*
    (3) *E*
    (4) *D*
68. By which process do air currents transfer heat energy throughout the room?
    (1) convection
    (2) absorption
    (3) radiation
    (4) conduction
69. The smallest temperature gradient exists between locations
    (1) *A* and *B*
    (2) *B* and *C*
    (3) *C* and *D*
    (4) *F* and *D*

70. Which isoline map most likely represents the temperature field at the ceiling of this room?

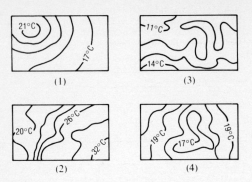

(1)   (3)

(2)   (4)

Group 4

If you choose this group, be sure to answer questions 71–75.

Base your answers to questions 71 through 75 on your knowledge of earth science and the diagram below. The diagram represents the apparent angular diameter of the Sun as measured by an observer on the Earth during one year.

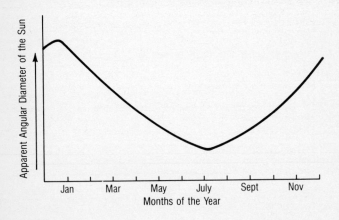

71. During which month was the apparent angular diameter of the Sun the smallest?
    (1) January
    (2) March
    (3) July
    (4) December

72. How did the apparent angular diameter of the Sun change from June to September?
    (1) It decreased steadily.
    (2) It decreased, then increased.
    (3) It increased steadily.
    (4) It remained the same.

Note that question 73 has only three choices.

73. The apparent diameter of the Sun decreases as the distance between the observer and the Sun
    (1) decreases
    (2) increases
    (3) remains the same

74. The cyclic change in the apparent angular diameter of the Sun is a result of the
    (1) Sun's daily rotational pattern
    (2) Earth's daily rotational pattern
    (3) Earth's circular orbit
    (4) Earth's slightly elliptical orbit

75. During which month was the orbital velocity of the Earth around the Sun the greatest?
    (1) January
    (2) March
    (3) June
    (4) July

Group 5

If you choose this group, be sure to answer questions 76–80.

Base your answers to questions 76 through 80 on your knowledge of earth science and on the graphs below. Graph I shows the average temperature change on the Earth between the years 1870 and 1955. Graph II shows the amount of carbon dioxide in the atmosphere between the years 1870 and 1962.

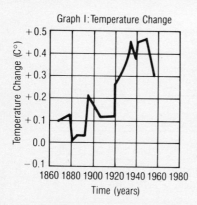

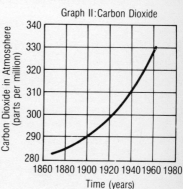

76. Which is the best interpretation that can be made from the graphs for the period between 1870 and 1955?
    (1) The amount of carbon dioxide in the atmosphere has increased steadily, and the temperature change on the Earth has shown an overall increase.

(2) The amount of carbon dioxide in the atmosphere and the temperature change on the Earth have increased at a steady rate.

(3) The amount of carbon dioxide in the atmosphere has decreased steadily, and the temperature change on the Earth has shown an overall decrease.

(4) The amount of carbon dioxide in the atmosphere has decreased at a steady rate, causing a varying change in temperature on the Earth.

Note that question 77 has only three choices.

77. As a result of the changes in temperature and amount of carbon dioxide, what probably happened to the Earth's overall rate of chemical weathering during this time?
   (1) The rate of chemical weathering decreased.
   (2) The rate of chemical weathering increased.
   (3) The rate of chemical weathering remained the same.

78. Which statement best accounts for the relationship between the carbon dioxide and temperature change data shown by the graphs?
   (1) Carbon dioxide is a good absorber of infrared radiation.
   (2) Carbon dioxide is a poor absorber of infrared radiation.
   (3) Temperature decreases usually occur when the carbon dioxide content of the atmosphere increases.
   (4) Temperature changes do *not* usually occur when the carbon dioxide content of the atmosphere increases.

79. If the trend shown in graph II continued into 1980, the amount of carbon dioxide in the atmosphere in 1980 was probably
   (1) less than 30 parts per million
   (2) between 100 and 280 parts per million
   (3) between 300 and 320 parts per million
   (4) greater than 340 parts per million

80. What was the approximate overall change in the carbon dioxide content between 1900 and 1962?
   (1) 330 parts per million
   (2) 290 parts per million
   (3) 40 parts per million
   (4) 0.4 part per million

Group 6

If you choose this group, be sure to answer questions 81–85.

Base your answers to questions 81 through 85 on your knowledge of earth science, the *Earth Science Reference Tables,* and the data table below. The table contains 9 a.m. weather readings during a four-day period for a location in New York State.

DATA TABLE

	Temperature (to nearest degree)	Air Pressure (mb)	Dewpoint (to nearest degree)	Wind Direction and Speed (knots)
9 a.m. Monday	24°C (75°F)	996.4	20°C (68°F)	NW 10
9 a.m. Tuesday	20°C (68°F)	962.4	19°C (66°F)	SSE 25
9 a.m. Wednesday	17°C (63°F)	1013.8	12°C (54°F)	W 15
9 a.m. Thursday	7°C (45°F)	1020.2	−2°C (28°F)	N 10

81. Which weather station model most likely represents the weather conditions at 9 a.m. on Monday?

(1) (2) (3) (4)

82. Which region is the most likely source of the airmass over this location on Thursday?
    (1) northern Canada
    (2) the Gulf of Mexico
    (3) the south Atlantic
    (4) southern California

83. On which day did precipitation most likely occur?
    (1) Monday (3) Wednesday
    (2) Tuesday (4) Thursday

84. According to the wind speeds shown, on which day did the highest pressure gradient most probably exist between this location and another nearby region?
    (1) Monday (3) Wednesday
    (2) Tuesday (4) Thursday

85. The relative humidity at 9 a.m. Wednesday was approximately
    (1) 8% (3) 49%
    (2) 26% (4) 72%

Group 7

If you choose this group, be sure to answer questions 86–90.

Base your answers to questions 86 through 90 on your knowledge of earth science and the block diagram below of a portion of the Earth's surface. Numbers 1 through 5 indicate layers of earth material and letters A through H indicate locations on the surface.

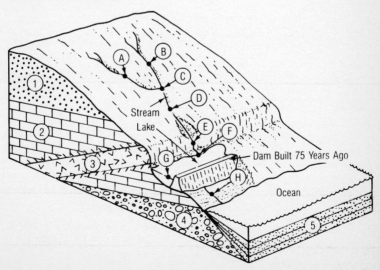

86. Which event would most likely convert the sediments in layer 5 into rock?
    (1) cementation of sediments caused by chemical processes
    (2) recrystallization due to heat from the intrusion of layer 3
    (3) rapid cooling from the contact with the ocean
    (4) heating and drying out due to rising convection currents

87. Compared to 75 years ago, why does the stream presently have less ability to downcut its channel at location *H?*
    (1) The energy of the stream is largely converted to heat from eroding the recently formed falls at location *E.*
    (2) Location *H* is now covered by a thick deposit of transported soil.
    (3) Humans have increased the discharge of water into the stream below the dam by large, sudden water releases.
    (4) Much of the sediment used as tools for downcutting is being deposited behind the dam.

88. Which earth material represented appears most resistant to weathering and erosion?
    (1) 1
    (2) 2
    (3) 3
    (4) 4

89. At which location is the stream velocity probably the greatest?
    (1) *A*
    (2) *E*
    (3) *C*
    (4) *F*

Note that question 90 has only three choices.

90. Particles from the stream are being deposited in the lake. How does the average size of the particles deposited beneath location *F* most likely compare to the average size of the particles deposited beneath location *G?*
    (1) The average size of a particle at *F* is greater.
    (2) The average size of a particle at *G* is greater.
    (3) The average size of the particles at both locations is equal.

Group 8

If you choose this group, be sure to answer questions 91–95.

Base your answers to questions 91 through 95 on your knowledge of earth science, the *Earth Science Reference Tables,* and the information and data table below.

An earthquake originated in New York State. The *P*-wave travel time for this earthquake was recorded in the data table below for four widely separated seismic stations, *A, B, C,* and *D.*

DATA TABLE

Seismic Station	*P*-wave Travel Time
A	8min 20sec
B	0min 31sec
C	12min 18sec
D	3min 20sec

91. Which of the four seismic stations is located farthest from the epicenter?
    (1) *A*
    (2) *B*
    (3) *C*
    (4) *D*

92. If the first *P*-wave arrived at seismic station *A* at 10hrs:22min:30sec, what was the origin time for the earthquake?
    (1) 02hrs:02min:30sec
    (2) 10hrs:14min:10sec
    (3) 10hrs:22min:30sec
    (4) 10hrs:30min:50sec
93. Which seismic station could be located in New York State?
    (1) *A*
    (2) *B*
    (3) *C*
    (4) *D*
94. If it takes 50 seconds for the *P*-wave to arrive at Buffalo, about how long would it take for the *S*-wave from this same earthquake to arrive at Buffalo?
    (1) 1min 40sec
    (2) 0min 50sec
    (3) 6min 40sec
    (4) 4min 00sec
95. What is the approximate distance between the earthquake's epicenter and station *A?*
    (1) 1,130 km
    (2) 2,400 km
    (3) 5,100 km
    (4) 7,500 km

Group 9

If you choose this group, be sure to answer questions 96–100.

Base your answers to questions 96 through 100 on your knowledge of earth science, the *Earth Science Reference Tables,* and the diagram below. The diagram shows three geologic columns representing widely separated rock outcrops that had a common origin. Descriptions of each sedimentary rock are indicated beside the layers. The rock layers have not been overturned.

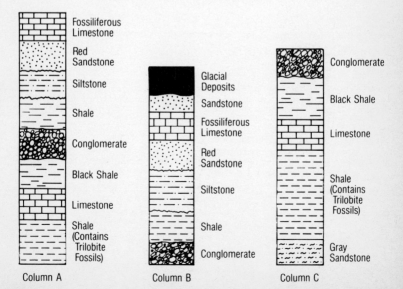

96. Which sequence of layers is present in column *A*, but is *not* shown in column *B*?
    (1) siltstone, red sandstone, and fossiliferous limestone
    (2) shale containing trilobite fossils, sandstone, and shale
    (3) shale containing trilobite fossils, limestone, and black shale
    (4) sandstone, shale, and siltstone

Note that question 97 has only three choices.

97. Which column contains the youngest rock formations?
    (1) *A*
    (2) *B*
    (3) *C*

98. Which rock layer is composed of sediments of the largest grain size?
    (1) shale
    (2) siltstone
    (3) sandstone
    (4) conglomerate

99. The shale layer containing trilobite fossils probably was deposited during which geologic time period?
    (1) Cambrian
    (2) Jurassic
    (3) Cretaceous
    (4) Tertiary

100. Which fossil might be found in the red sandstone layer if the layer was deposited during the Triassic Period?
    (1) remains of flowering plants
    (2) impressions of armored fish
    (3) mammal bones
    (4) dinosaur footprints

Group 10

If you choose this group, be sure to answer questions 101–105.

Base your answers to questions 101 through 105 on your knowledge of earth science and the *Earth Science Reference Tables.*

101. Which landscape region separates the Adirondack Mountains from the Catskills?
    (1) Taconic Mountains
    (2) Tug Hill Plateau
    (3) Hudson-Mohawk Lowlands
    (4) Champlain Lowlands

102. The primary reason that several landscape regions have formed in New York State is that the various regions of the State have different
    (1) climates
    (2) latitudes
    (3) soil characteristics
    (4) bedrock characteristics

103. In which landscape region is Ithaca, New York, located?
    (1) Appalachian Uplands
    (2) Adirondack Highlands
    (3) the Catskills
    (4) St. Lawrence Lowlands

104. The diagram below represents a cross section of a series of horizontal sedimentary rock layers.

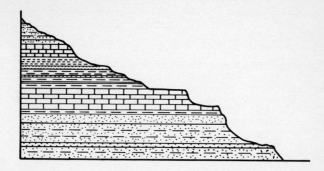

The variation in the steepness of the eroded hillslopes in the diagram is most likely due to the
(1) resistance of the rock layers
(2) thickness of the rock layers
(3) tilt of the rock layers
(4) age of the rock layers

105. The Catskills are part of which type of landscape region?
(1) plain
(2) mountain
(3) plateau
(4) coastal lowland

EARTH SCIENCE

June 18, 1987

Part I

Answer all 55 questions in this part.

Directions (1–55): For *each* statement or question, select the word or expression that, of those given, best completes the statement or answers the question.

1. A classification system is based on the use of
   (1) the human senses to observe properties of objects
   (2) instruments to observe properties of objects
   (3) observed properties to group objects with similar characteristics
   (4) inferences to make observations

2. In the classroom during a visual inspection of a rock, a student recorded four statements about the rock. Which statement about the rock is an observation?
   (1) The rock formed deep in the Earth's interior.
   (2) The rock cooled very rapidly.
   (3) The rock dates from the Precambrian Era.
   (4) The rock is black and shiny.

3. A rock's density is calculated as 2.7 g/cm³ but its accepted density is 3.0 g/cm³. Which equation, when solved, will provide the correct percent deviation from the accepted value? [Refer to the *Earth Science Reference Tables*.]

   (1) $\text{Deviation (\%)} = \dfrac{3.0 - 2.7}{3.0} \times 100$

   (2) $\text{Deviation (\%)} = \dfrac{3.0 - 2.7}{2.7} \times 100$

   (3) $\text{Deviation (\%)} = \dfrac{2.7}{3.0} \times 100$

   (4) $\text{Deviation (\%)} = \dfrac{3.0}{2.7} \times 100$

4. The average monthly discharge of a small stream in New York State is recorded over five years. This data would probably indicate that over the five years there was
   (1) a decreasing discharge each month
   (2) an increasing discharge each year
   (3) a cyclic change in the discharge during each year
   (4) a constant discharge each month

5. An observer watching a sailing ship at sea notes that the ship appears to be "sinking" as it moves away. Which statement best explains this observation?
   (1) The surface of the ocean has depressions.
   (2) The Earth has a curved surface.
   (3) The Earth is rotating.
   (4) The Earth is revolving.

6. Which line best identifies the interface between the lithosphere and the troposphere?

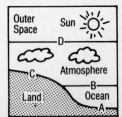

(Not To Scale)

   (1) line *A*
   (2) line *B*
   (3) line *C*
   (4) line *D*

7. An observer in New York State measures the altitude of Polaris to be 44°. According to the *Earth Science Reference Tables*, the location of the observer is nearest to
   (1) Watertown
   (2) Elmira
   (3) Buffalo
   (4) Kingston

8. The geocentric model of the solar system does *not* explain
   (1) star trails
   (2) day and night
   (3) planetary motions
   (4) Foucault's pendulum

9. The time required for one Earth rotation is about
   (1) one hour
   (2) one day
   (3) one month
   (4) one year

Base your answers to questions 10 and 11 on the diagram below which shows the Earth's orbit and the partial orbit of a comet on the same plane around the Sun.

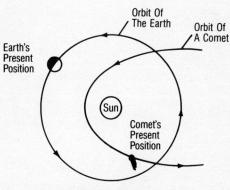

(Not Drawn To Scale)

10. Which observation is true for an observer at the Earth's Equator at midnight on a clear night for the positions shown in the diagram?
    (1) The comet is directly overhead.
    (2) The comet is rising.
    (3) The comet is setting.
    (4) The comet is *not* visible.

Note that questions 11 and 12 have only three choices.

11. Compared with the Earth's orbit, the comet's orbit has
    (1) less eccentricity
    (2) more eccentricity
    (3) the same eccentricity

12. As the ability of a substance to absorb electromagnetic energy increases, the ability of that substance to radiate electromagnetic energy will
    (1) decrease
    (2) increase
    (3) remain the same

13. The seasonal temperature changes in the climate of New York State are influenced mostly by the
    (1) rotation of the Earth on its axis
    (2) changing distance of the Earth from the Sun
    (3) changing angle at which the Sun's rays strike the Earth's surface
    (4) changing speed at which the Earth travels in its orbit around the Sun

14. Which process results in a release of latent heat energy?
    (1) melting of ice
    (2) heating of liquid water
    (3) condensation of water vapor
    (4) evaporation of water

15. Electromagnetic energy that reaches the Earth from the Sun is called
(1) insolation
(2) conduction
(3) specific heat
(4) terrestrial radiation

16. The diagrams below represent a laboratory model used to demonstrate convection currents. Each model shows a burning candle in a closed box with two open tubes at the top of the box. Which diagram correctly shows the air flow caused by the burning candle?

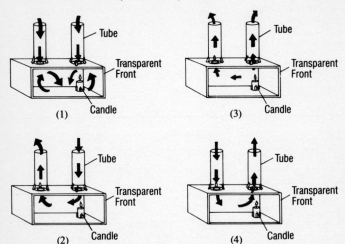

(1)   (3)

(2)   (4)

17. A greenhouse stays relatively warm on a sunny winter day. Which statement best explains this fact?
(1) The greenhouse traps long-wave infrared radiation.
(2) Sunlight is changed to shorter wavelength radiation.
(3) The plants growing in the greenhouse produce heat.
(4) Glass is an excellent absorber of sunlight.

18. The change from the vapor phase to the liquid phase is called
(1) evaporation
(2) condensation
(3) precipitation
(4) transpiration

19. In a sample of air, the saturated vapor pressure is 15.8 millibars at the dry-bulb temperature and the saturated vapor pressure is 11.4 millibars at the dewpoint temperature. Using the equation given in the *Earth Science Reference Tables,* the relative humidity would be calculated as approximately
(1) 14%
(2) 72%
(3) 85%
(4) 90%

20. The graph below represents how the rate of evaporation of water is affected by a variable, *X*. Which variable is most likely represented by *X*?

(1) temperature
(2) wind velocity
(3) exposed surface area
(4) moisture content of the air

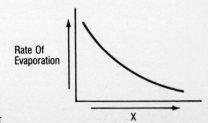

21. Which diagram correctly represents the air circulation in a Northern Hemisphere high-pressure airmass?

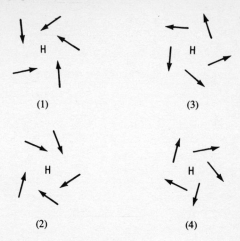

(1)

(3)

(2)

(4)

Note that question 22 has only three choices.

22. Dry soil will be recharged with moisture if potential evapotranspiration is
    (1) less than precipitation
    (2) greater than precipitation
    (3) equal to precipitation

23. The diagrams below represent two identical containers filled with nonporous uniform particles. The containers represent models of two different sizes of soil particles.

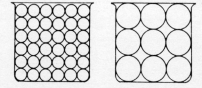

Compared to the model containing larger particles, the model containing smaller particles has
    (1) less permeability and greater porosity
    (2) greater porosity and greater capillarity
    (3) less permeability and greater capillarity
    (4) greater permeability and greater porosity

24. Which is a form of precipitation?
    (1) frost
    (2) snow
    (3) dew
    (4) fog

25. Two cities are located at the same latitude and elevation. One city, located in the center of the United States, has cooler winters and warmer summers than the other city, which is located near the coast. Which statement best explains these seasonal differences?
    (1) The air over continents is drier than the air over oceans.
    (2) Cold airmasses usually originate over continents.
    (3) A large body of water modifies coastal air temperatures.
    (4) Warm ocean currents flow along most coastlines.

26. Which type of climate causes the fastest chemical weathering?
    (1) cold and dry   (3) hot and dry
    (2) cold and humid   (4) hot and humid

27. Which erosional force acts alone to produce avalanches and landslides?
    (1) gravity   (3) running water
    (2) winds   (4) sea waves

28. In the two diagrams below, the length of the arrows represents the relative velocities of stream flow at various places in a stream. Diagram I shows the different water velocities across the surface. Diagram II shows the different water velocities at various depths.

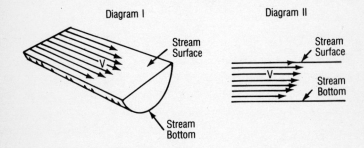

At which location in the stream is the water velocity greatest?
    (1) at the center along the bottom
    (2) at the center near the surface
    (3) at the sides along the bottom
    (4) at the sides near the surface

29. Why do the particles carried by a river settle to the bottom as the river enters the ocean?
    (1) The density of the ocean water is greater than the density of the river water.
    (2) The kinetic energy of the particles increases as the particles enter the ocean.
    (3) The velocity of the river water decreases as it enters the ocean.
    (4) The large particles have a greater surface area than the small particles.

30. Which rock particles will remain suspended in water for the longest time?
    (1) pebbles   (3) silt
    (2) sand   (4) clay

31. The grouping of rocks as igneous, sedimentary, and metamorphic is based primarily upon differences in
    (1) age   (3) size
    (2) origin   (4) hardness

32. A sediment contains particles that range in diameter from 2 to 4 centimeters. According to the *Earth Science Reference Tables,* which sedimentary rock would be formed when this sediment is compressed and cemented together?
    (1) shale   (3) sandstone
    (2) siltstone   (4) conglomerate

33. According to the *Earth Science Reference Tables,* which graph best represents the comparison of the average grain sizes in basalt, granite, and rhyolite?

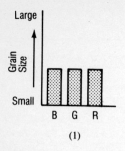

(1)

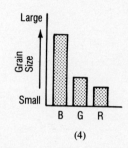

(3)

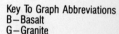

Key To Graph Abbreviations
B–Basalt
G–Granite
R–Rhyolite

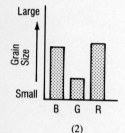

(2)

(4)

34. Metamorphic rocks result from the
    (1) erosion of rocks
    (2) recrystallization of rocks
    (3) cooling and solidification of molten magma
    (4) compression and cementation of soil particles

35. Which element combines with silicon to form the tetrahedral unit of structure of the silicate minerals?
    (1) oxygen   (3) potassium
    (2) nitrogen   (4) hydrogen

36. According to the *Earth Science Reference Tables,* in which group are the zones of the Earth's interior correctly arranged in order of increasing average density?
    (1) crust, mantle, outer core, inner core
    (2) crust, mantle, inner core, outer core
    (3) inner core, outer core, mantle, crust
    (4) outer core, inner core, mantle, crust

37. Which statement best describes the materials through which earthquake waves are transmitted?
    (1) *P*-waves are transmitted through solids, only.
    (2) *P*-waves are transmitted through liquids, only.
    (3) *S*-waves are transmitted through solids, only.
    (4) *S*-waves are transmitted through solids and liquids.

38. The difference in arrival times for *P*- and *S*-waves from an earthquake is 5.0 minutes. According to the *Earth Science Reference Tables,* how far away is the epicenter of the earthquake?
(1) 1.3×10^3 km   (3) 3.5×10^3 km
(2) 2.6×10^3 km   (4) 8.1×10^3 km

39. The thinnest section of the Earth's crust is found beneath
(1) oceans   (3) mountain regions
(2) coastal plains   (4) desert regions

40. Which observation provides the strongest evidence for the inference that convection cells exist within the Earth's mantle?
(1) Sea level has varied in the past.
(2) Marine fossils are found at elevations high above sea level.
(3) Displaced rock strata are usually accompanied by earthquakes and volcanoes.
(4) Heat-flow readings vary at different locations in the Earth's crust.

41. The diagram below represents a cross section of a portion of the Earth's crust. The rock layers shown have not been overturned. Which geologic event occurred *first*?

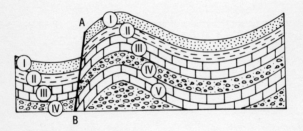

(1) faulting along line *AB*
(2) folding of the region
(3) formation of rock layer I
(4) formation of rock layer IV

Base your answers to questions 42 and 43 on the *Earth Science Reference Tables* and the diagram below which represents a cross section of an eroded fold that has *not* been overturned.

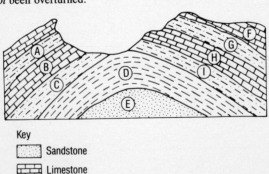

Key

▨ Sandstone

▦ Limestone

▤ Siltstone

▤ Shale

42. If rock layer *A* is of Devonian Age, rock layer *E* could be of
(1) Triassic Age   (3) Cambrian Age
(2) Carboniferous Age   (4) Tertiary Age

43. The fossils found in rock layer *G* will most closely resemble those found in rock layer
(1) *A*   (3) *C*
(2) *I*   (4) *E*

44. According to the *Earth Science Reference Tables,* the rock record preserved in New York State indicates that
(1) Jurassic rock is very abundant
(2) early Paleozoic rock is very abundant
(3) dinosaurs existed at the time of the Taconian Orogeny
(4) the Palisades Sill formed before the extinction of the trilobites

45. According to the *Earth Science Reference Tables,* which area of New York State has the youngest bedrock?
(1) the area south of the Finger Lakes
(2) the area around Mt. Marcy
(3) the area between Syracuse and Rochester
(4) the area east of Albany

Base your answer to question 46 on the diagram below which represents a cube of radioactive material (figure *A*) cut into eight identical cubes (figure *B*).

Figure A   Figure B

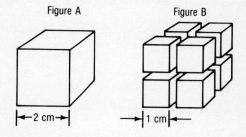

46. Compared to the half-life of the material in figure *A,* the half-life of the material in each small cube in figure *B* is
(1) ⅛ as long   (3) 8 times longer
(2) 1/64 as long   (4) the same

47. Which feature would most likely indicate the boundary between two landscape regions?
(1) deposits of unsorted sediments adjacent to polished and scratched bedrock
(2) a sharp change in elevation between two different adjoining bedrock structures
(3) a large stream flowing down a long V-shaped valley
(4) bedrock containing two distinctly different fossil types

48. According to the *Earth Science Reference Tables,* the Catskills are part of the
(1) Hudson-Mohawk Lowlands   (3) Appalachian Uplands
(2) Taconic Mountains   (4) Tug Hill Plateau

49. The Adirondack Highlands landscape region was formed primarily by
(1) changes in the water levels of the Great Lakes
(2) erosion by the Hudson and Mohawk Rivers
(3) mountain building and erosion
(4) wind erosion in an arid climate

50. A local landscape can be changed most in the shortest amount of time by
    (1) activities of humans
    (2) wind erosion
    (3) physical weathering
    (4) a changing climate

51. Which environmental factor probably would have the *least* effect on the development of a landscape region?
    (1) uplifting and leveling forces
    (2) type of climate
    (3) age of bedrock
    (4) bedrock composition and structure

52. Many elongated hills, each having a long axis with a mostly north-south direction, are found scattered across New York State. These hills contain unsorted soils, pebbles, and boulders. Which process most likely formed these hills?
    (1) stream deposition
    (2) wind deposition
    (3) wave deposition
    (4) glacial deposition

Note that questions 53 through 55 have only three choices.

53. As wind velocity decreases, the distance between isobars on a weather map will
    (1) decrease
    (2) increase
    (3) remain the same

54. Compared to the circumference of the Earth through the poles, the circumference of the Earth around the Equator is
    (1) smaller
    (2) larger
    (3) the same

55. As the temperature of the soil decreases from 10°C to −5°C, the infiltration rate of ground water through this soil will most likely
    (1) decrease
    (2) increase
    (3) remain the same

Part II

This part consists of ten groups, each containing five questions. Choose seven of these ten groups. Be sure that you answer all five questions in each group chosen. [35]

Group 1

If you choose this group, be sure to answer questions 56–60.

Base your answers to questions 56 through 60 on your knowledge of earth science, the *Earth Science Reference Tables,* and the diagram below. Object *A* is a solid cube of uniform material having a mass of 65 grams and a volume of 25 cubic centimeters. Cube *B* is a part of cube *A*.

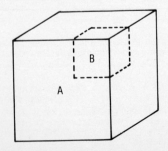

56. The density of cube A is
(1) 3.8 g/cm³   (3) 0.38 g/cm³
(2) 2.6 g/cm³   (4) 0.26 g/cm³

57. The density of the material in cube A is determined at different temperatures and phases of matter. At which temperature and in which phase of matter would the density of cube A most likely be greatest? [Assume a standard atmospheric pressure.]
(1) at 20°C and in the solid phase
(2) at 200°C and in the solid phase
(3) at 1800°C and in the liquid phase
(4) at 2700°C and in the gaseous phase

Note that questions 58 and 59 have only three choices.

58. If cube B is removed from cube A, the density of the remaining part of cube A will
(1) decrease   (3) remain the same
(2) increase

59. The mass of cube B is measured in order to calculate its density. The cube has water on it while its mass is being measured. How would the calculated value for density compare with the actual density?
(1) The calculated density value would be less than the actual density.
(2) The calculated density value would be greater than the actual density.
(3) The calculated density value would be the same as the actual density.

60. If pressure is applied to cube A until its volume is one-half of its original volume, its new density will be
(1) one-half its original density
(2) twice its original density
(3) the same as its original density
(4) one-third its original density

Group 2

If you choose this group, be sure to answer questions 61–65.

Base your answers to questions 61 through 65 on your knowledge of earth science, the *Earth Science Reference Tables*, and the diagram below. The diagram shows the Earth in its orbit. The vertical rays of the Sun are striking at 23½° South latitude. Stars X and Y are two of many which an observer would see in the nighttime sky.

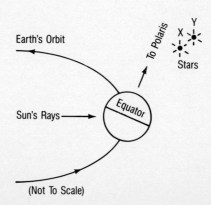

(Not To Scale)

61. Which date is represented by the diagram?
    (1) March 21   (3) September 21
    (2) June 21   (4) December 21

62. The orbiting motion of the Earth is best described as
    (1) inclination   (3) rotation
    (2) revolution   (4) declination

63. Which statement best describes the apparent motion of stars X and Y as they are observed from a location in New York State for a period of 4 hours?
    (1) Star X and star Y appear to move away from Polaris.
    (2) Star X and star Y show no apparent motion.
    (3) Star X and star Y appear to move at a constant rate.
    (4) Star X appears to move away from star Y.

64. The elliptical shape of the Earth's orbit causes
    (1) Foucault pendulums to change direction
    (2) the Earth to have an oblate spheroid shape
    (3) the Earth's axis to be inclined to its orbit
    (4) changes in the orbital velocity of the Earth

65. When will the gravitational attraction between the Earth and the Sun be greatest?
    (1) when the Earth is closest to the Sun
    (2) when the Earth is farthest from the Sun
    (3) every day at noon
    (4) every night at midnight

Group 3

If you choose this group, be sure to answer questions 66–70.

Base your answers to questions 66 through 70 on your knowledge of earth science and on the diagrams below. Diagram I represents a light source located at an equal distance from two air-filled metal cans. One can is shiny and the other is black. Diagram II represents two insulated cups, each filled with equal masses of water. One insulated cup contains cold water and the other contains warm water. A metal bar is inserted into the water of each insulated cup.

Diagram I

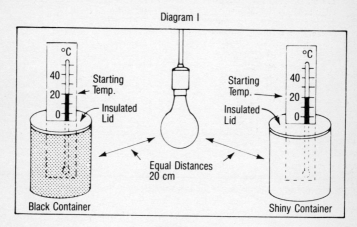

Diagram II

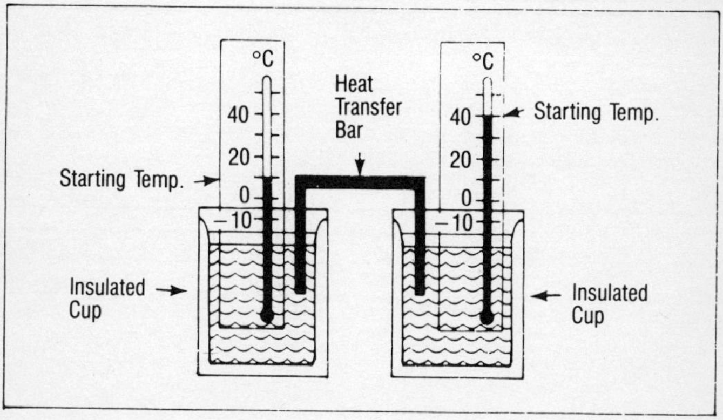

Note that question 66 has only three choices.

66. When the light source is on (diagram I), the amount of radiant energy striking the black container, as compared to the amount striking the shiny container, is
   (1) less
   (2) more
   (3) the same

67. With reference to diagram I, which graph best represents the change in temperature during the first 10 minutes after the light source is turned on?

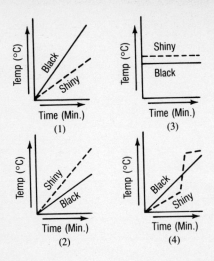

68. In the equipment shown in diagram II, heat energy will be transferred through the bar from the hot water to the cold water primarily by
    (1) density differences
    (2) flowing currents
    (3) electromagnetic rays
    (4) molecular collisions

69. In diagram II, if all the energy lost by the warm water is gained by the cold water, what will be the temperature of the water in both insulated cups following the energy transfer?
    (1) 10.°C
    (2) 25°C
    (3) 40.°C
    (4) 50.°C

70. According to the heat energy formula in the *Earth Science Reference Tables*, how many calories of heat energy must be added to 20 grams of the cold water to raise its temperature 5°C?
    (1) 120 calories
    (2) 100 calories
    (3) 20 calories
    (4) 4 calories

Group 4

If you choose this group, be sure to answer questions 71–75.

Base your answers to questions 71 through 75 on your knowledge of earth science, the *Earth Science Reference Tables,* and the diagram below. The diagram represents a section of a weather map for locations in the central United States. The letters *A* through *I* identify reporting weather stations.

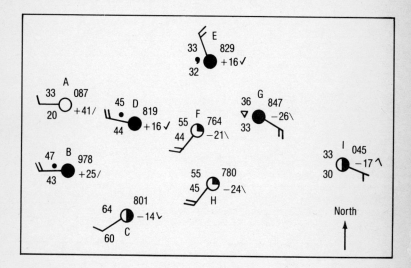

71. Which is the dewpoint at weather station *C*?
    (1) 14°F   (3) 64°F
    (2) 60°F   (4) 80°F

72. Which weather station is *least* likely to experience precipitation during the next six hours?
    (1) *A*   (3) *C*
    (2) *F*   (4) *G*

73. Which temperature field map best represents the air temperatures reported by the weather stations?

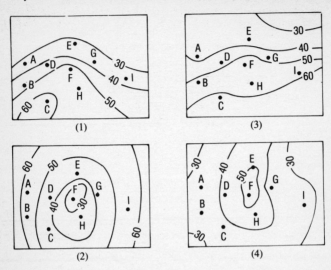

74. Which diagram best shows the fronts and their locations on the weather map?

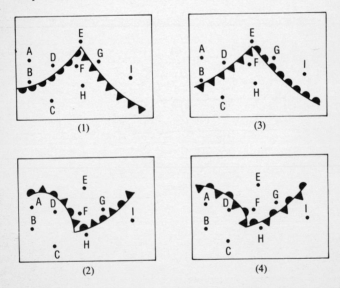

75. If the weather system follows a typical storm track, it will move toward the
(1) north
(2) south
(3) west
(4) east

Group 5

If you choose this group, be sure to answer questions 76–80.

Base your answers to questions 76 through 80 on your knowledge of earth science and on the graphs and tables below which show the water budget data for stations 1 and 2.

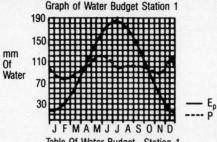

Graph of Water Budget Station 1

Table Of Water Budget—Station 1

Factors						Months							
	J	F	M	A	M	J	J	A	S	O	N	D	Yearly Total
p	88	76	84	93	118	117	97	100	102	96	88	119	1,178
E_p	17	28	62	93	140	175	182	175	135	88	41	25	1,161
∆St	0	0	0	0	−22	−58	−20	0	0	+8	+47	+45	0
St	100	100	100	100	78	20	0	0	0	8	55	100	
E_a	17	28	62	93	140	175	117	100	102	88	41	25	993
D	0	0	0	0	0	0	65	75	33	0	0	0	173
S	71	48	22	0	0	0	0	0	0	0	0	49	190

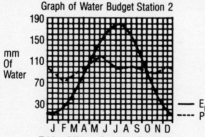

Graph of Water Budget Station 2

Table of Water Budget—Station 2

Factors						Months							
	J	F	M	A	M	J	J	A	S	O	N	D	Yearly Total
p	89	75	85	102	119	116	98	99	103	95	89	108	1,178
E_p	19	23	50	83	125	166	182	172	135	81	39	20	1,095
∆St	0	0	0	0	−6	−50	−44	0	0	+14	+50	+36	0
St	100	100	100	100	94	44	0	0	0	14	64	100	
E_a	19	23	50	83	125	166	142	99	103	81	39	20	950
D	0	0	0	0	0	0	40	73	32	0	0	0	145
S	70	52	35	19	0	0	0	0	0	0	0	52	228

E_p—Potential
P—Precipitation
∆St—Change in Moisture
St—Water Storage

E_a—Actual Evapotranspiration
D—Deficit
S—Surplus

76. The total annual precipitation (P) for station 1, as compared to that for station 2, was
(1) much greater   (3) much less
(2) slightly more   (4) the same

77. The yearly total for change in moisture storage (ΔSt) was zero for both stations because
(1) neither station had enough yearly precipitation
(2) neither station had enough vegetation
(3) both stations experienced a yearly usage ($-\Delta St$) equal to the yearly recharge ($+\Delta St$)
(4) both stations experienced a water deficit (D) for each month of the year

78. Which statement describes the water budgets at both stations from May through September?
(1) They had a continual decrease in potential evapotranspiration (E_p).
(2) They had no precipitation.
(3) They had a continual increase in actual evapotranspiration (E_a).
(4) They had no water surplus.

79. Which inference can best be made from a comparison of only the graphs for the two stations?
(1) Both stations are located in the Southern Hemisphere.
(2) Both stations have approximately the same type of climate.
(3) Station 1 is located near a large body of water and station 2 is located inland.
(4) There is a difference in the altitudes of the two stations.

80. The potential evapotranspiration (E_p) was lowest for
(1) Station 1 during the month of January
(2) Station 2 during the month of January
(3) Station 1 during the month of July
(4) Station 2 during the month of July

Group 6

If you choose this group, be sure to answer questions 81–85.

Base your answers to questions 81 through 85 on your knowledge of earth science and the data table below. The table shows the results of an investigation of four different types of rocks, weathering over a period of 30 minutes. Equal masses of similar-sized samples of rocks *A, B, C,* and *D* were placed in identical containers half-filled with water. Each container was shaken uniformly for 5 minutes and the remaining samples of rocks were removed from the water. Their masses were determined and recorded in the data table. The remaining samples of rocks were put back into the containers half-filled with water and the procedure was repeated five times. The blank graph is provided for your use.

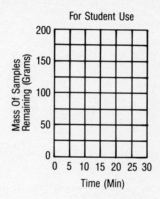

For Student Use

DATA TABLE

Mass of Rock Samples Remaining (grams)

Time (min)	A	B	C	D
0	200	200	200	200
5	160	200	120	200
10	125	200	60	195
15	100	190	20	170
20	75	180	0	150
25	55	175	0	135
30	50	175	0	125

81. Which graph best represents how the remaining mass of rock sample *A* changes with time?

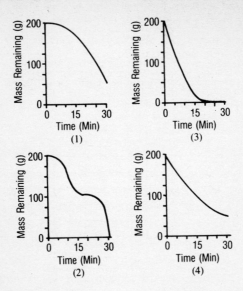

82. Which rock sample was *most* resistant to the abrasive action caused by the shaking of the containers?
(1) *A*   (3) *C*
(2) *B*   (4) *D*

83. Approximately how much of the original mass of rock sample *D* was lost after 30 minutes?
(1) 50 g   (3) 120 g
(2) 75 g   (4) 200 g

84. According to the data table, the mass of rock samples remaining at the end of 30 minutes was different for each sample. The best inference to be made is that the mass differences were the result of different
(1) containers being used for shaking
(2) rates of shaking of the containers
(3) rock sample composition
(4) masses of rock samples being used

85. After 20 minutes, the rate of abrasion decreased for all rock samples. A major factor that explains this is the
(1) smoothing of the rock samples
(2) compacting of the rock samples
(3) sharpening of the edges of the rock samples
(4) hardening of the minerals

Group 7

If you choose this group, be sure to answer questions 86–90.

Base your answers to questions 86 through 90 on your knowledge of earth science, the *Earth Science Reference Tables,* and the information below.

A group of students collected rounded, well-sorted mineral particles from a stream that flowed over only coarse-grained igneous bedrock. They sorted the particles by mineral type and then mixed equal volumes of all four minerals together and poured the mixture into a tube of water. The data table below lists the minerals. Figure *A* shows the deposit formed on the bottom of the tube as a result of the deposition of the particles.

Data Table

Mineral	Average Particle Diameter
Plagioclase feldspar	0.2 cm
Quartz	0.2 cm
Hornblende (Amphibole)	0.2 cm
Olivine	0.2 cm

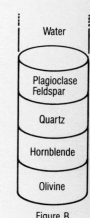

Figure A   Figure B

86. As shown in figure *A*, which mineral appears to have the fastest settling rate?
    (1) plagioclase   (3) hornblende
    (2) quartz   (4) olivine

87. When the mineral particles were collected from deposits on the stream bed, the stream velocity at the time of deposition was approximately
    (1) 50 cm/s   (3) 150 cm/s
    (2) 100 cm/s   (4) 200 cm/s

88. The pattern resulting from the deposition of the mineral particles, as shown in figure *A*, is best explained by the fact that the particles have different
    (1) volumes   (3) circumferences
    (2) densities   (4) surface areas

89. The mineral particles collected by the students were most likely weathered from
    (1) rhyolite rocks, only   (3) gabbro rocks, only
    (2) rhyolite and basalt rocks   (4) gabbro and granite rocks

90. The experiment was repeated using a second plagioclase sample with the original samples of the other minerals. What difference between the first and second samples of plagioclase would best explain the change in the pattern of deposition shown in figure *B*?
    (1) Particles from the second sample of plagioclase had greater density.
    (2) Particles from the second sample of plagioclase had greater total volume.
    (3) Particles from the second sample of plagioclase had flatter shapes.
    (4) Particles from the second sample of plagioclase were larger.

Group 8

If you choose this group, be sure to answer questions 91–95.

Base your answers to questions 91 through 95 on your knowledge of earth science, the *Earth Science Reference Tables*, and the diagram below. The diagram represents the age of the basaltic ocean crust in the Atlantic Ocean between the United States and Africa. Line *AB* is drawn for reference purposes only.

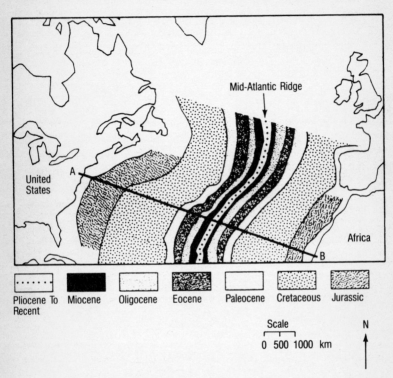

91. Which statement is best supported by the diagram?
   (1) The ocean crust is the same age along line *AB*.
   (2) The oldest ocean crust is located near the continents.
   (3) The age of the ocean crust increases from point *A* to point *B*.
   (4) Most of the ocean crust along line *AB* formed in the Paleozoic Era.

92. The age of formation of the ocean crust along line *AB* suggests that the United States and Africa are moving
   (1) eastward
   (2) westward
   (3) closer together
   (4) farther apart

93. Which diagram most closely represents the cross section of the ocean floor along line *AB*?

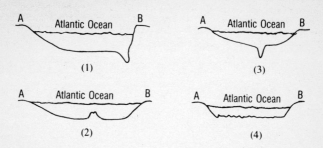

(1)   (3)

(2)   (4)

94. According to the diagram, the width of the Cretaceous rock east of the mid-Atlantic Ridge along line *AB* is approximately
(1) 1,000 km   (3) 1,600 km
(2) 1,200 km   (4) 4,000 km

95. On which map do the marks best represent the distribution of the frequency of earthquakes for this area?

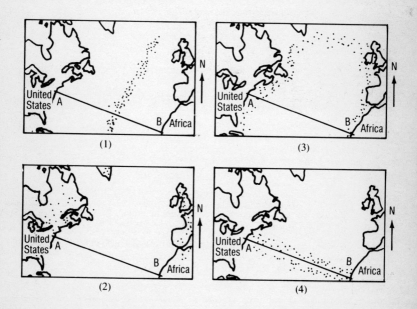

(1)   (3)

(2)   (4)

Group 9

If you choose this group, be sure to answer questions 96–100.

Base your answers to questions 96 through 100 on your knowledge of earth science, the *Earth Science Reference Tables*, and the block diagram below. The diagram represents a geologic cross section in which overturning has not occurred.

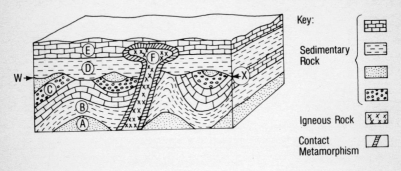

96. Which rock most likely is the oldest?
    (1) A   (3) F
    (2) B   (4) D

97. When did the folding of rock layer *B* most likely occur?
    (1) before the deposition of rock layer *A*
    (2) after the deposition of rock layer *E*
    (3) after the deposition of rock layer *C*
    (4) after the deposition of rock layer *D*

98. Which feature is represented by line *WX*?
    (1) an igneous intrusion
    (2) an area of metamorphism
    (3) a former erosional surface
    (4) a fault

99. Fossils are *least* likely to be found in which rock?
    (1) E   (3) C
    (2) F   (4) D

100. What evidence in the rock layers indicates that the formation of igneous rock *F* occurred after rock layer *E* was in place?
    (1) the presence of radioactive minerals in rock *F*
    (2) the presence of extrusive igneous rock below rock layer *E*
    (3) the unconformity between rock *F* and rock layer *E*
    (4) the zone of contact metamorphism between rock *F* and rock layer *E*

Group 10

If you choose this group, be sure to answer questions 101–105.

Base your answers to questions 101 through 105 on your knowledge of earth science and the *Earth Science Reference Tables*

101. Which graph best represents the average densities of the Sun, Moon, and Earth?

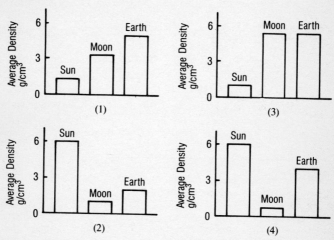

102. According to the *Earth Science Reference Tables,* what great orogeny (mountain-building episode) occurred in New York State during the Devonian time period?
(1) Taconian Orogeny
(2) Grenvillian Orogeny
(3) Alleghenyan Orogeny
(4) Acadian Orogeny

103. What is the eccentricity of an orbit having a major axis length of 100 million miles and a focal distance of 10 million miles?
(1) 1
(2) 10
(3) 0.1
(4) 0.01

104. What is the approximate dewpoint temperature if the dry-bulb temperature is 11°C and the wet-bulb temperature is 8°C?
(1) 1°C
(2) 5°C
(3) 3°C
(4) −13°C

105. According to the *Earth Science Reference Tables,* what is the approximate elevation above sea level at which atmospheric pressure is 10^{-1} atmosphere?
(1) 7.0 km
(2) 17 km
(3) 27 km
(4) 37 km

(Continued from other side)

5. HUDSON-MOHAWK LOWLANDS. The rocks of this region are distorted sedimentary rocks of Paleozoic age that have lower resistance than the surrounding rocks. They have therefore been leveled by weathering, and by the erosion of the Mohawk and Hudson Rivers, to generally low elevations. Variations in slope are associated with escarpments that have been formed by resistant layers and the valleys carved by the rivers. South of Albany the Hudson River has an elevation of sea level and may be considered an inlet of the ocean.

6. APPALACHIAN PLATEAU. This plateau is composed of horizontal sedimentary rocks, mostly of Paleozoic age. Much leveling by streams and glaciers has resulted in steep slopes and much change in elevation, so that some sections, such as the Catskills (area 6B), resemble mountains. Elevations range from about 500 meters in the west to over 1,250 meters in the Catskills. The region contains many lakes, such as the Finger Lakes, which are the result of glacial erosion and deposition.

7. ERIE-ONTARIO LOWLANDS. This region is a plain of horizontal sedimentary rocks of Paleozoic age, covered by much glacial transported sediment. The northern section is especially smooth because of deposition of sediments from glacial lakes that were the ancestors of Lakes Erie and Ontario. In some places, resistant rocks have been eroded to

escarpments up to 500 meters in elevation, but elevations and slopes are generally small throughout the region.

8. TUG HILL PLATEAU. This plateau of horizontal sedimentary rocks of Paleozoic age has a resistant surface layer that has resulted in fairly uniform elevations of about 600 to 700 meters. However, steep slopes occur where rivers have cut valleys, such as the Black River Valley that separates this region from the Adirondacks.

9. ADIRONDACK MOUNTAINS. These are mature mountains composed mostly of metamorphic rocks of Precambrian age. There are moderate elevations in the western section, but the highest elevations in the state (over 1,600 meters at mountain peaks) occur in the eastern section. The landscape is rugged, with much change in elevation and steep slopes, and with valleys related to faults and rocks of lesser resistance. Stream drainage patterns are of radial and trellis types except where glacial deposition has blocked the former drainage paths, resulting in many swamps and lakes.

10. ST. LAWRENCE-CHAMPLAIN LOWLANDS. This plain is composed generally of horizontal sedimentary rocks of lower resistance than rocks of surrounding regions, and therefore has lower elevations. The St. Lawrence section (10 A) is mostly flat, with changes in elevation usually no more than 30 meters. Some steep slopes exist in the Champlain section (10 B) as the result of uplift and subsidence caused by faults. Lake Cham-plain is the site of a subsided block.

LANDSCAPE REGIONS OF NEW YORK STATE AND THEIR CHARACTERISTICS

New York has a greater number of different landscape regions than any other state. The chief reason for this variety of landscape regions is the great variation in age, structure, and resistance of the bedrock found within the state. The present climate of the state is uniformly humid and has not been a major factor in producing variations in landscape development.

Almost all of New York was affected by the Pleistocene glaciation that ended in New York about 10,000 years ago. As a result, glacial depositional features are observed throughout the state, superimposed on the other characteristics of the different landscape regions. One of the most important features left by the glaciers is the transported soils, which are young and have small and incomplete profiles.

The landscape regions that are numbered on the facing map have the following distinguishing characteristics.

1. ATLANTIC COASTAL PLAIN. The bedrock consists of horizontal sedimentary rocks of late Mesozoic and Cenozoic age, with elevations near sea level, covered by thick glacial deposits reaching elevations of about 125 meters above sea level in some areas. The features of glacial deposition result in minor changes of slope on a generally smooth plain. Waves and ocean currents have created many typical shore features, such as bars, beaches, and lagoons.

2. TRIASSIC LOWLANDS. This region is composed of weak sedimentary rocks of early Mesozoic age, which have been leveled to lower elevations than the surrounding landscape regions. The generally smooth landscape has moderate changes in slope caused by faults. A volcanic intrusion called the Palisades Sill borders the Hudson River. Because of its greater resistance, it forms a cliff that ranges up to more than 150 meters above sea level.

3. NEW ENGLAND UPLANDS-HUDSON HIGHLANDS. These mountains in the mature and old-age stages are composed of highly distorted nonsedimentary rocks, mostly Precambrian in age, and more resistant than the rocks of surrounding regions. In the northern parts of the region there are elevations up to 500 meters with steep slopes; in the southern parts, the rocks have been eroded to low elevations and little slope typical of the plain-like topography of mountains in old age.

4. TACONIC MOUNTAINS. These greatly eroded mountains were originally uplifted in the Paleozoic Era. They consist mostly of metamorphic nonsedimentary rocks that are highly folded and faulted. Today they have moderate elevations (up to about 600 meters) and gradual changes in slope, so that the topography has the form of rolling hills.

(Continued on other side)